Information Technology Law in India

Information Technology Law in India

Talat Fatima

This book was originally published as a monograph in the International Encyclopaedia of Laws/Privacy and Technology Law.

Founding Editor: Roger Blanpain
General Editor: Frank Hendrickx
Volume Editors: Jos Dumortier, Pieter Gryffroy, Ruben Roex & Yung Shin Van Der Sype

Wolters Kluwer

Published by:
Kluwer Law International B.V.
PO Box 316
2400 AH Alphen aan den Rijn
The Netherlands
E-mail: lrs-sales@wolterskluwer.com
Website: www.wolterskluwer.com/en/solutions/kluwerlawinternational

Sold and distributed by:
Wolters Kluwer Legal & Regulatory U.S.
920 Links Avenue
Landisville, PA 17538
United States of America
E-mail: customer.service@wolterskluwer.com

ISBN 978-94-035-3516-6

e-Book: ISBN 978-94-035-3986-7
web-PDF: ISBN 978-94-035-3996-6

The Author

The author was a law teacher by profession and retired as the principal, Government Law College, Dholpur, Rajasthan in January 2016. She started her educational pursuits from Kolkata, her birthplace, and then moved to Aligarh Muslim University where she completed her Law degree with a gold medal and her LL.M. She has been working as a dedicated law teacher since. She was awarded the Ph.D. by the prestigious University of Delhi in the rare but latest subject of cybercrime in 2008. Her Ph.D. thesis has been published as a book titled *Cyber Crimes*, by the leading law publisher of the country the Eastern Book Company, the 3rd edition of which is on the stalls. *Cyber Crimes* has been translated by her in Hindi, the dominant language of India. She has a special craving for the silicon revolution vis-à-vis the legal responses.

The Author

Table of Contents

List of Abbreviations

AIR	All India Reporter
B2B	Business-to-Business
BPO	Business Process Outsourcing
BSNL	Bharat Sanchar Nigam Limited
CCC	Common Criteria Certification
CII	Critical Information Infrastructure
COAI	Cellular Operators Association of India
COD	Cash on Delivery
CP	Certificate Policy
CPS	Carrier Per Selection
CRL	Certificate Revocation List
CSC	Common Services Centres
CSR	Certificate Signing Request
DARPG	Department of Administrative Reforms & Public Grievances.
DeitY	Department of Electronics & Information Technology
DI	Digital India
DoT	Department of Telecommunications
DPIIT	Department for Promotion of Industry and Internal Trade
DSC	Digital Signature Certificate
DSL	Digital Subscriber Line
DTH	Direct to Home
EDF	Electronics Development Fund
ENISA	European Union Security Agency for Cyber Security
FRIENDS	Fast, Reliable, Instant, Efficient Network for the Disbursement of Services
GISFI	Global ICT Standardization Forum for India
GMPCS	Global Mobile Personal Communication by Satellite
GMV	Gross Merchandise Value
GSMC	Global System for Mobile Communication
GST	Goods and Services Tax

List of Abbreviations

ICANN	International Corporation for Assigned Names and Numbers
IDN	International Domain Names
IIP	International Infrastructure Providers
ILD	International Long Distance
ILDO	International Long Distance Operator
INOC	Integrated Network Operations Center
INSAIT	Indian Society of Agricultural Information Technology
IP	Internet Protocol
IPLC	International Private Leased Circuits
IPTV	International Protocol Television
ISDN	Integrated Services Digital Network
ISP	Internet Service Providers
ITU	International Telecommunications Union
IUC	Inter
KPO	Knowledge Process Outsourcing
LAN	Local Area Network
LDCC	Long Distance Charging Center
MVNO	Mobile Virtual Network Operators
MTNL	Mahanagar Telephone Nigam Limited
NABARD	National Bank for Agriculture and Rural Development
NAP	Network Access Points
NCCC	National Cyber Coordination Centre
NeSDA	National e-Governance Service Delivery Assessment
NIC	National Informatics Center
NICNET	National Informatics Centre Network
NIXI	National Internet Exchange of India
NKN	National Knowledge Network
NOC	Network Operations Center
NOFNP	Nationwide Optical Fibre Networking Project
NPE	National Policy on Electronics
ONDC	Open Network for Digital Commerce
PBX	Private Branch Exchange
PCO	Public Call Office
PIN	Personal Identification Number
PKI	Public Key Infrastructure
PMJDY	Pradhan Mantri Jan Dhan Yojana
POP	Point of Presence
PSTN	Public Switched Telecom Network
QR	Quick Response

RBI	Reserve Bank of India
RSA	Rivest, Shamir & Adelman
SAFCA	Standing Advisory Committee on Frequency
SDCA	Short Distance Charging Area
SEBI	Securities and Exchange Board of India
SIM	Subscriber Identification Module
SLDC	Short Distance Charging Center
SMART	Simple, Moral, Accountable and Responsive Government
SMI	Social Media Intermediaries
SSMI	Significant Social Media Intermediaries
STQC	Standardization Testing and Quality Certification
TBT	Technical Barriers to Trade
TCP	Transmission Connection Protocol
TDSAT	Telecom Disputes Settlement and Appellate Tribunal
TLD	Top-Level Domain
TRAI	Telecom Regulatory Authority of India
TTO	Telecommunications Tariff Order
U.K.	United Kingdom
U.S.	United States of America
UHF	Ultra High Frequency
UNESCAP	United Nations Economic and Social Commission for Asia and the Pacific
URL	Uniform Resource Locator
USO	Universal Service Obligation
USOF	Universal Service Obligation Fund
VAS	Value-Added Service
VOIP	Voice over Internet Protocol
VPN	Virtual Private Network
VSNL	Videsh Sanchar Nigam Limited
WAN	Wide Area Network
WLL	Wireless in Local Loop
WPC	Wing Wireless Planning and Coordination Wing
WTO	World Trade Organization

List of Abbreviations

Preface

Technology is the new normal. "Make in India" and "Digital India" initiatives of the government are fast pacing India's march toward a better digital tomorrow. A man sitting in a paddy field with a cell phone in his hand tells the world that India is not behind any nation in embracing technology. But technology is not just about taking great strides in making life easier and comfortable, it is also about upgrading the welfare of mankind, securing individual privacy, and preserving moral troves. Extolling the virtues of technology though is not very difficult, yet its baneful effects on legal norms have been unfortunate. India like most countries is on the cusp of a digital revolution and is giving cut-throat competition to the rest of the world in the matter of technological progress. There can be no spineless submission to the evolving technologies, and only a sensible embracing of innovations will achieve the goal of a healthy nation. The deadly Pandemic has taught the world the lesson of health, so much so that technological innovations have prioritized their use for the well-being of the nation much more than any other sector. Entry of technologies like Blockchain, Artificial Intelligence, and Internet of Things in the healthcare and clinical sectors becomes mandatory to avoid casualties in a country that spends hardly 1.5% of its GDP on healthcare. Privacy takes priority in data management though the legal position to safeguard privacy in the country is still in the doldrums. Cyber Security comes as a formidable challenge, and an appropriate Cyber Security Act looks at the regulators with great expectations. Grappling with the technological transformations with a spate of piecemeal and situation-specific notifications, rules, and sporadic amendments has become a trend with various ministries and should be replaced by long-awaited Data Protection Act, Cyber Security Act, and a meaningful legal regime in the area of e-commerce. The harsh reality is that government alone cannot succeed in ameliorating the nation from the blues of technological boom; it has to be an interplay of industry, academicians, commercial giants, and legal expertise. The country is yet to learn the rubrics of cyber law.

General Introduction

Chapter 1. General Background

§1. Geography

> India is the cradle of the human race, the birthplace of human speech, the mother of history, the grandmother of legend, and the great grandmother of tradition. Our most valuable and most instructive materials in the history of man are treasured up in India only
>
> —Mark Twain

1. Geographically too, it is a rich country having all the indications of a continent. From the snow-capped Himalayas in the north to sun-drenched coastal villages in the south, from the green basin of the Brahmaputra in the east to the sand dunes of Rajasthan in the west, the country is geographically gifted by nature. It covers an area of 3,287,260 km[1] and is the seventh largest country in the world lying entirely in the northern hemisphere. The mainland extends between latitudes 8° 4' and 37° 6' north and longitudes 68° 7' and 97° 25' east. The country spreads over the mainland having a land frontier of about 15,200 km and two sets of archipelagoes: the Andaman & Nicobar Islands and Lakshadweep Islands. It borders with Afghanistan and Pakistan in the Northwest, China, Bhutan and Nepal in the North, and Bangladesh and Myanmar in the East and the Far East. It tapers off into the Indian Ocean between the Bay of Bengal in the East and the Arabian Sea in the West. The mainland comprises four regions, namely the great mountain zone, plains of the Ganga and the Indus, the desert region, and the southern peninsula. The geological regions are grouped into three—the Great Himalayas and their associated group of mountains, the Indo-Gangetic Plain, and the Peninsular Shield. The country's climate is basically tropical type. It has rich flora and fauna being tenth in the world and fourth in Asia in plant diversity. The country has a network of great rivers: holy Ganges (Ganga), Yamuna, Brahmaputra, Indus, Tapti, Chambal, and many others providing a great source of water throughout the year.

1. United Nations Statistics Division, 2022.

§2. Demographic and Cultural Composition

2. Demography of India

Demography of India	
Population	1,579,578,923,624. (August 31, 2022)
Growth Rate	0.68 (2021)
Birth Rate	16.42 Births/1,000 Population (2021)
Death Rate	9.4 Deaths/1,000 (2021)
Life Expectancy	67.2 years (2021)
Female	68.9 years (2020)
Male	65.8 years (2021)

3. Intangible Cultural Heritage (ICH): Unity in diversity is the bottom line of Indian culture. The forefathers, the *Aryans*, the Rulers, the *Mughals,* and the mighty British left behind footprints of their own culture and ethos. Predominantly, a religious society, the country imbibes the cultural values not only of the ancient Hindu religion but also a tinge of Islamic culture, and a dash of many other local cultures, like *Punjabi, Gujarati,* and *Bengali* that make it a culturally potent society. The Indus Valley Civilization (IVC) and the Vedic Age preceding it are the flag bearers of its cultural heritage. India has one of the world's largest collections of songs, music, dance, theatre, folk traditions, performing arts, rites and rituals, and paintings and writings also known as the Intangible Cultural Heritage. In India, dancing has an unbroken tradition of 2,000 years. Its themes are derived from mythology, legends, and classical literature; two main divisions being classical and folk. *Bharatnatyam, Kathakali, Kathak, Manipuri, Kuchipudi,* and *Odissi* are the various dance forms from different states of India and have religious and ethical importance as well.

4. Tangible Cultural Heritage: The national museums, art galleries, innumerable grand edifices, like the *Taj Mahal,* and a good number of ancient temples and mausoleums reflect the majestic past of the country. The mute and majestic specimens of architecture, *Mohanjodaro*, *Ajanta Ellora,* etc., speak volumes about the tangible cultural heritage of the country. To preserve this great heritage and to save it forever the Government of India (GoI), through the Ministry of Culture and the Zonal Cultural Centers (ZCCs), takes care of it. The Ministry of Culture of the GoI is the highest body to preserve the cultural heritage of the country. The Archaeological Survey of India (ASI), established in 1861, is attached to the Department of Culture, and it maintains and conserves the centrally protected monuments and buildings apart from performing many other functions to conserve the cultural heritage of the country.

§3. POLITICAL SYSTEM

5. From a country that was for centuries under British dominion to a nation moving on the information superhighway, India has proved to be a country that truly deserves independence and self-realization. For centuries, the country longed for home rule (1600–1947), was an attraction for rulers, and an object of lust for plunderers. After the fall of the Great *Mughals*, the country fell prey to the administrative acumen of the mighty British. Dependency, slavery, and submission describe the plight of Indians under the British rule. Though during this period India got its most viable legal and educational system, yet the social, religious, economic, and cultural spirit was fully crushed. The First War of Independence in 1857 was a futile effort of a disunited India, which proved to be a miscalculation on the part of the earnest fighters regarding the might of the British. There was a bloodless fight for about 50 years thereafter when Mohan Das Karam Chand Gandhi, the *Father of the Nation,* became the flag bearer of the struggle for freedom. This fight for ideologies, philosophies, minds, and thoughts through the sacrifices of the soldiers is unforgettable. Ultimately, on August 15, 1947, India awoke to the dawn of freedom and broke the shackles of slavery and submission. A new country was born with a political structure that was unsuitable for rule by the natives. The Constitution of India, a dream house of innumerable freedom fighters, struggling natives, and hundreds of national leaders saw the light of day on November 26, 1949, and envisaged a sovereign, democratic, socialist and, secular Republic of India.

6. Political set-up: Although India became a federation under the Government of India Act 1935, yet its true spirit was yet to come. With the full enforcement of the Constitution of India on January 26, 1950, India adopted the democratic and responsible type of parliamentary system of government. India is a federal state in which the Constitution envisages that India shall be a Union of States (Article 1). As such, there is a government at the center called the GoI and also local governments at various state levels. Today, there are 29 states and 7 Union Territories.[2] While, the First Schedule shows 28 states, in the southern peninsula on June 2, 2014, *Telangana* has been added as the twenty-ninth state of the Indian Federation.[3] Following the fundamental principle of a federation, there is a division of power between the Center and the State in the legislative, administrative, and financial spheres.[4] There are three lists: the Union List with 97 subjects of national importance on which the Central Legislature or the Parliament can make laws; the State List with 66 subjects on which the State Legislatures can make laws and which are of local importance; and then there is the Concurrent List with 47 subjects on which both the Parliament and the State Legislatures can make laws regarding matters which require uniformity throughout the country.[5] The executive power of the Center rests with the President of India who is the head of the Republic and who has executive, legislative, diplomatic, military, judicial, and emergency powers to be

2. First Schedule; Part XXII, Constitution of India.
3. www.india.com.
4. Articles 245–276; Constitution of India.
5. Seventh Schedule; Part XXII, Constitution of India.

utilized by the president with the aid and advise of the Union Cabinet headed by the prime minister. Thus, the real power lies with the prime minister while the president is the de facto head of the State. At the state level, governors, as the head of the state executive, are appointed by the president who are the representatives of the president, and the duly elected state government is headed by the chief minister and other ministers.

7. Judicial System: India also adopts the federal principle of having an independent judiciary. The country has a strong judicial setup continuing from the British period although the Supreme Court of India was established on January 28, 1950. The Supreme Court is the symbol of judicial independence in the country; it is not only the last appellate court in the country but serves as the final arbitrator between the Center and the various states. There is a Chief Justice of the Supreme Court known as the Chief Justice of India. The Supreme Court Amendment Act 2019 (number of judges) raises the number of *puisne* judges from 30 to 33.[6] It is the torchbearer of the fundamental rights of the citizens and upholds the concepts of justice, liberty, equality, and fraternity so dearly cherished by the constitutional makers as well as by all Indians. At the state level, there are High Courts which are the last word in judiciary in the state though in some matters appeals can be taken to the Supreme Court of India. There are 21 High Courts in the country in all. The Constitution upholds the independence of the judiciary as the appointment and salary of the judges are kept out of political control. In every state, there is an established hierarchy of subordinate courts to dispense justice at the grass-root level though the authority of courts is established at every level. Recently, under the Legal Services Authorities Act 1987, *Lok Adalats* (People's Courts) have been the trend which are organized by the district judicial officers to dispense petty or family matters. There are also various consumer redressal forums to provide easy and fast relief to the aggrieved consumers established under the Consumer Protection Act 1986.

§4. Population and Vital Statistics

8. The last census of India was held in March 2011. The following one was due in 2019 but due to COVID-19 Pandemic, it could not be held. The next census is scheduled for 2023. Hence, as per the 2011 census, the population of India as on March 1, 2011, stood at 1,210.6 million (623 million males and 587.5 million females). Although the country covers 2.4% of the world's surface area of 135.79 million km yet it supports and sustains a whopping 6% of the world's population. The population density of India in 2011 was 382 per km^2—decadal growth 17.54%. Census 2011 was the fifteenth census of India since 1872. It was held in two phases:

6. The Gazette of India. Extraordinary. Part II—s. 1. No. 56 New Delhi, Friday, Aug. 9, 2019/ SHRAVANA 18, 1941 (SAKA).

(1) house listing and Housing Census (April to September 2010) and
(2) population Enumeration (February 9–28, 2011 with revisions round during March 1–5, 2011.

The Population: Persons 1210.6 million; Males 623 million and Females 587.4 million.

9. Vital Statistics: United Nations Estimates[7]

Period	*Average Population*	*Live Births*	*Deaths*	*Natural Change*	*Crude Birth Rate*	*Crude Death Rate*	*Natural Change*	*Total Fertility Rate*
2006	1157039	27190000	8678000	18512000	23.5	7.5	6.0	
2007	1173972	27119000	8687000	18432000	23.1	7.4	15.7	
2008	1190864	27152000	8812000	18340000	22.8	7.4	15.4	2.6
2009	1207740	27174000	8817000	18357000	22.5	7.3	15.2	2.6
2010	1224614	27064000	8817	18247000	22.1	7.2	14.9	2.5
2011	1242738	27092000	8823	18268000	21.8	7.1	14.7	2.44
2012	1261006	27237000	88270	18410	21.6	7.0	14.6	2.4

10. The 27th edition of the **World Population Prospects, 2022** was released by the **United Nations Department of Economic and Social Affairs, Population Division**. As per this Report, both China and India crossed 1.4 billion mark with India at 1.41 billion, slightly below China. As per the National Family Health Survey 5 (2021), India's Total Fertility Rate (TFR) attained 2.0 for the first time which shows a decline from 2.2. This is due to the use of family planning methods, like contraceptives, spaced pregnancies, health care improvements, and an increase in education and wealth levels as a result of which fertility and mortality rate has also declined.

11. Sex Ratio: Sex ratio defined as the number of females per thousand males is an important social indicator to measure the extent of prevailing equality between males and females in a society at a given point in time. The sex ratio in the country favors the female gender. It was 972 at the beginning of the twentieth century and thereafter showed a continuous decline until 1941. The sex ratio from 1901 to 2011 has registered a ten-point increase in census 2011 over 2001; however child sex ratio has declined to 919 females per 1,000 males.

7. World Population Prospects—2010 Revision.

12. Literacy Rate: Census 2011[8]

Literacy Rate		*Literacy Rate*
Persons	77, 84,54,120 74.04	
Males	44,42, 03, 762	82.14
Females	33, 42, 50, 358	65.46

8. Provisional Population Totals—Office of the Registrar General and Census—Ministry of Home Affairs—Government of India. New Delhi.

Chapter 2. Telecommunications Infrastructure

13. India, though an ancient country, is robust and resilient, well equipped to survive in the contemporary world. The telecommunication story started centuries ago with the introduction of the telephonic system by the British, but since then the country has come a long way in this field. Being densely populated, telecommunication is its survival plank; consequently, in the present scenario, the country has a honeycomb of legislations comprising not only of Acts but also of Rules, Guidelines, and situation-specific Policies. The Telecom and Regulatory Authority of India (TRAI) is the highest authority that regulates the entire telecommunication infrastructure. The Indian Telecommunication Network had 765.09 million subscribers in February 2021[9] and is the second largest in the world. The sector has seen a tremendous growth rate as teledensity grew from 18.23% in Financial Year (FY) 2016 to 87.26% in FY 2021.

14. History—Liberalization started in 1981 with the signing of contracts with Alcatel of France to merge with the State-owned Telecom Company (Industrial Training Institute) with the aim to set up five million lines per year. India made steady progress and in 1994, the National Telecommunications Policy (NTP) by the Indian Government changed the ownership, business management, and regulation of ITI. With the birth of TRAI in 1997, the interference of the government in the field of tariff fixing and policy making was reduced. Although the World Bank advised the Indian Government to liberalize long-distance services to minimize the monopoly of state-owned companies, the government first concentrated on the liberalization of local services. During this period, the government allowed two service providers and gave a fifteen-year license to each. Later in 1999, furthering the liberalization policy, the ministry was bifurcated into two—the policy maker and the service provider. The service provider, called the Department of Telecommunication Services (DTS), was later named *Videsh Sanchar Nigam Limited* (VSNL) which launched its first publicly available network in India on August 15, 1995. In 2002, the government reduced its stake in VSNL from 53% to 26%, and private enterprises were invited. The government's liberal attitude continued when in March 2000 the license fee was reduced for cellular service providers and a 74% stake was allowed to the foreign companies. The result was cheaper tariffs and the facility of cellular phones reaching more and more middle-class and common Indians. The liberal and technology-savvy attitude of the government as well as enthusiastic participation both by the private and public sectors have made possible the long strides in this field. Selective privatization and planned competition started as early as 1992 when private competition in value-added services was followed by the opening of cellular and basic services for the local area to private competition. As communication in the Internet age has assumed importance and usefulness as never before, India too responded to it instantly by building up an infrastructure not only of communicational hardware but also a galaxy of legislations to make such infrastructure not only viable but also safe and legal. The former state-owned VSNL

9. India Brand Equity Foundation IBEF—November 2021.

became the seventh largest telecom company in the world in terms of its number of subscribers. Companies, such as Vodafone, Bharti Airtel, Tata Indicom, Idea Cellular, Aircel, and Loop Mobile thronged the market in 2008–2009, making a big increase in rural subscribers as compared to urban subscribers.

15. In India, the tele density (defined as the number of telephone connections for every 100 individuals) stood at 87.26%, as of February 2021. The total wireless or mobile telephone subscriber base increased to 1167.71 million in February 2021, from 1160.59 million in February 2020.[10] Thus, in the area of mobile services, India has made significant progress and become one of the fastest-growing mobile markets in the world. Mobile services were launched in August 1995 and at the start the monthly subscribers' additions were around 0.05–0.1 million, and by December 2002 it stood at 10.5 million.

The telecommunication infrastructure of today is unimaginable without the Internet. To catch up with the latest communicational demands, India's response has been commendable. The total subscriber base for the Internet in India started with 13.54 million in 2009. Slowly and gradually, there is an upswing in the field and the number of broadband connections in India is on the rise since 2006; total broadband subscriptions in the country grew from 149.75 million in FY 2016 to 687.44 in FY 2020. The number of wired broadband subscriptions stood at 19.18 million in 2020. The Telecom Department has ushered in an era of unstoppable progress to keep pace with the changing global telecommunication landscape. Key companies in the market are Mahanagar Telephone Nigam Ltd. (MTNL), Bharat Sanchar Nigam Limited (BSNL) which is a 100% government company, Bharti Airtel, Vodafone Idea Limited, and Reliance Jio Infocomm.

16. Telecom Industry Scenario: The telecommunication industry in the country is divided into; Infrastructure, Equipment, Mobile Virtual Network Operators (MVNO), White Space Spectrum, 5G, Telephone service providers, and Broadband. Over the past seven years, the Indian telecom tower industry has grown significantly by 65%. The number of mobile towers increased from 400,000 in 2014 to 660,000 in 2021. Similarly, the number of Mobile Base Transceiver Stations have grown rapidly by 187% and increased from 800,000 in 2014 to 2.3 million in 2021. As per Global System for Mobile communication Association (GSMA),India is on its way to becoming the second largest smart phone market globally by 2025 with around 1 billion installed devices and is expected to have 920 million unique mobile subscribers by 2025 which will include 88 million 5G connections.

10. India Brand Equity Foundation IBEF—November 2021.

Chapter 3. The Information and Communications Technology Market

§1. General Statement

17. The dawn of the ICT sector in India has been a remarkable one and is all set to become a USD 225 billion industry by 2020. Since the adoption of the World Market Policy in 1988, India has shown great activity in the field of software development for export, telecommunications policy reform, and the privatization of telephone companies. There are a number of government policies which aim at making the ICT market in India a promising one. The IT Sector accounted for 8% of GDP in 2020, and the revenue of IT and Business Process Management (BPM) is estimated at USD 227 billion in FY 2022. The ICT sector welcomes new business technologies, like cloud, mobility, analytics, social media, and vertical-specific solutions. The SMAC (social, mobility, analytics, cloud) market stood at USD 225 billion in 2020. Quite recently, the adoption of IT in retail, healthcare, and utilities has shown an increase in uptake. The cloud market in India is expected to grow three-fold to USD 7.1 billion by 2022 with the help of the growing adoption of Big Data, Analytics, Artificial Intelligence, and Internet of Things (IoT).[11] The upswing is backed by policy makers in as much as the government has allocated INR 88,567.57 crore (USD 11.58 billion) for the IT and Telecom sectors in the Union budget of 2022–2023.

Evolution of India's Information Technology Market

18. The IT sector in India has seen steady and gradual growth. Before 1995, US-based companies outsourced work to low cost but skilled talent in the country. Soon during 1995–2000, India became a product development destination. With the starting of western companies in the country, around 2005, firms grew in size and scope of services. From 2005 to 2016, firms in the country became multinational and the IT sector moved from enterprise servicing to enterprise solutions. Ultimately, from 2017 onwards, India's USD 167 billion IT industry employs about four million people. The industry is expected to grow to USD 19.93 billion by 2025. In the Global Innovation Index (2021), India improved its position four rankings and reached 46th position.[12] The market size in the IT and BPM sectors is as follows:

Serial No.	*Segments*	*Market Size* *Details as per Electronics and Computer Software Export Council*
1.	IT Services	USD 97 billion in FY 20. Accounted for 50.50% of the IT & BPM market revenue in India in FY 20.

11. Cloud Next Wave of Growth in India Report.
12. Indian Brand Equity Foundation—March 2022 p. 7.

Serial No.	*Segments*	*Market Size Details as per Electronics and Computer Software Export Council*
2.	Business Process Management	USD 38 billion in FY 20. BPM had a 19.79% share of the IT & BPM market revenue in India in FY 20.
3.	Software Products & Engineering services	USD 34.39 billion in FY 19. It has 19% revenue share in the Indian IT space in FY 19.
4.	Hardware	USD 14.48 billion in FY 19

Source: Segments of IT & BMP Sector in India.[13]

19. The global footprint of the country is enlarging speedily The telecommunications services in India comprising fixed and mobile, and data and voice are the largest IT segments, and the growth in this area has been tremendous. As India grows and marches ahead its telecom sector plays an ever more vital role.[14] However connectivity and communication in India is mainly a wireless affair. There are though 1 billion wireless connections, 92% of which cover the urban area, on the whole, the country has 25.23 million wireline connections. The TRAI Report covers broadband statistics received from 664 service providers. Spending on information technology in India is expected to reach USD 144 billion in 2023. India's digital economy is estimated to reach USD 1 trillion by 2025. Artificial Intelligence (AI) is expected to boost India's annual growth rate by 1.3% by 2035, according to NITI *Aayog* (erstwhile Planning Commission).[15]

§2. Retail Markets

I. Fixed Communications Market

20. Market share of fixed-line telecom operators in India as on May 2022 according to the Telecom Regulatory Authority of India (TRAI)[16] is as follows:

- BSNL (28.67%)
- Jio (26.70%)
- Bharti Airtel (23.66%)
- MTNL (10.50%)

13. Indian Brand Equity Foundation—March 2022 p. 8.
14. Martyn Warwick, *As India grows and develops, so its telecom sector plays an ever more vital role,* Telecom TV https://www.telecomtv.com/content/access-evolution/as-india-grows-and-develops-so-its-telecom-sector-plays-an-ever-more-vital-role-45015/.
15. Indian Brand Equity Foundation—March 2022.
16. TRAI Report of Jul. 19, 2022, https://www.trai.gov.in/sites/default/files/PR_No.43of2022_0.pdf.

- Tata Teleservices (6.32%)
- Vi (2.32%)
- Quadrant (1.15%)
- Reliance Comm (0.68%)
- Fixed communication services in India are expected to grow at a compound annual growth rate (CAGR) of 5.8%.

II. Mobile Communications Market

21. Mobile communications in India has hit the market with a bang. It has received an ever-increasing response from the masses. India's smartphone market size was valued at USD 139 billion in 2021, and is expected to grow with a CAGR of 10.5% and reach USD 281 billion by 2028. There are a number of factors that contribute toward the growth of mobile phones, like an increase in disposable income, improved telecommunication infrastructure, availability of low-cost smart phones, and an increasing number of product launches.[17] The TRAI Report in May 2022 shows 1,017.68 million active wireless connections in the country which is a very high proportion of the 1,145.5 million registered mobile users in the country. The total number of telecom service subscribers (both mobile and fixed) hit 1,170.73 million at the end of May, up by 2.92 million over the course of the month. Overall tele density in India increased from the 84.88% reported at the end of April 2022 to 85.03% at the end of May 2022. Though urban tele density fell in April (from 134.7% to 134.66%), rural tele density increased from 58.16% to 58.37%.

III. Interactive Services

22. In India, Business Process Outsourcing (BPO), Knowledge Process Outsourcing (KPO), Domestic and International Call Centers, Network Operations Center (NOC), etc., are covered under the "Other Service Provider" category by the Department of Telecommunications (DoT). "Application Services" means providing services, like tele-banking, tele-medicine, tele-education, tele-trading, e-commerce, call center, network operation center, and other IT-enabled services by using Telecom Resources provided by authorized telecom service providers. "Telecom Resource" means telecom facilities used by the OSP including but not limited to Public Switched Telecom Network (PSTN), Public Land Mobile Network (PLMN), Integrated Services Digital Network (ISDN), and/ or the telecom bandwidth provided by authorized telecom service providers having a license under the Indian Telegraph Act 1885. The "Company" means a company registered under the Indian Companies Act 1956 including foreign companies permitted by RBI under Foreign Exchange Management Regulations, and registered under Part XI (sections 591–608) of the Companies Act 1956 for setting up a place of business in India.

17. Research And Markets-India Smartphone Market Size, Analysis, Growth, Demand, Trends, Opportunity, Forecasts (2022–2028).

Domestic OSP is the OSP providing “Applications Services” within national boundaries. International OSP is the OSP providing “Application Services” beyond national boundaries.

Chapter 4. E-commerce: Facts and Figures

§1. Introduction

23. India burdened with an approximately 1.26 billion population has only 2% population purchasing online. This is a meagre proportion as the e-commerce potential in the country is crippled by low urbanization, limited computer literacy, and low internet penetration (19%) covering 243 million people. However, smart phone penetration is growing by 150% annually. The cursed Pandemic has accelerated the online buying trend and the government push in this field has enlarged the area of e-commerce in the country. The buying interest is inculcated basically in non-essential items, such as clothes and electronics yet quite recently essential goods, like groceries, green groceries, and medicines are also witnessing a sharp increase. The government's Digital India initiative, Foreign Direct Investment (FDI) and a lawful agenda on cross-border data flow, benefits of internet, domestic investment and support from key industrial players are all proving to be a driving force in the area of e-commerce growth. Resultantly, India's e-commerce transactions increased by 77% in 2020–2021.

§2. The Future of E-commerce

24. In 2021, the number of internet connections in India significantly increased to 830 million, driven by the "Digital India" drive by the government. The total volume of wireless internet data usage has surged 7 times over since 2018. Internet penetration stands at 4% in 2007 to 45% in 2021. According to Payoneer Report, India's cross-border e-commerce is expected to grow 17.3% by 2022. India's consumer digital economy is expected to become a USD 1 trillion market by 2030, growing from USD 85–USD 90 billion in 2020, driven by strong adoption of online services such as e-commerce and *edtech*; hence the country's e-commerce market is expected to reach USD 99 billion by 2024 and USD 300 billion by 2030 (India Brand Equity Foundation (IBEF) February 2022). Moreover, in the commercial world, there has been a constant effort to expand the area of e-commerce marketing. Both the government and the businesses are making a joint effort in this direction. In March 2021, the Confederation of All India Traders (CAIT) comprising 80 million traders and 40,000 Traders Associations launched "Bharat E-market" Traders portal thereby giving small traders an easier opportunity to participate in e-commerce.

Chapter 5. E-government Initiatives

§1. The Concept

25. E-government means a citizen-friendly, fast, accountable, transparent, and interactive government. Modern-day government along with the internet and information technology gets new hands and limbs, to outreach the people and dispense their services in an easier and faster way with the aid of electronics, hence the term E-governance. With the onslaught of information and communication technologies (ICT) the old archaic manual systems, though not done away totally, have however taken a back seat. The fundamental motivation for the implementation of e-governance in India was to provide SMART government (Simple, Moral, Accountable, and Responsive). The focus of e-government is not only computerization of government offices but also transformation of government with the aid of ICTs. The National e-Governance Plan (NeGP) takes a holistic view of the various e-governance plans in the country. The e-governance plan 2.0 is to follow on the key decisions taken earlier in the Apex Committee of Digital India program held in 2014. *E-Kranti* (meaning electronic revolution) aims at delivering all government services electronically to the citizens. It is the primary pillar of Digital India and its vision is "Transforming e-Governance for Transforming Governance." However, the extent of e-governance is still far beyond its goal as 70% of India lives in villages and the penetration of ICT is just scanty in these areas. The personal identification document, namely the *AADHAR* card a 12-digit number which gives a unique identity to every citizen of the country has been started to expedite the mission. Thus with the aid of *AADHAR*, NeGP, and State Wide Area Network (SWAN) e-governance is expected to reach the remotest living citizen and will take to him the fruits of democracy and good governance. The Government of India has launched the NeGP which aims at creating an atmosphere where there can be successful implementation of G2G, G2B, G2E, and G2C services. The reality is that many development schemes of the government are done in isolation and there is no single agency to integrate all of these under one platform. There is an attempt to unite them through e-governance.

§2. The History

26. The Government of India established the Department of Electronics in 1970. The first major step toward e-Governance in India was the establishment of the National Informatics Centre (NIC) in 1977. The movement became active in 1987 with the launch of NICNET—National Informatics Centre Network, which is the National Satellite-based computer network. NICNET reached all district headquarters in 1990. That was the starting point of governments both the Union and states embracing the fruits of ICT for connecting with the people and for dispensing their services as per the ongoing technological changes in the world. By 1990, NICNET was prevalent in all district headquarters via the state capitals. There are various facets of e-governance which are as follows.

§3. FACETS OF E-GOVERNANCE

27. The government approved the National e-Governance Plan (NeGP), comprising 27 Mission Mode Projects (MMPs) and 8 components, on May 18, 2006. In the year 2011, 4 projects—Health, Education, Public Distribution System (PDS), and Posts were introduced to make the list of MMPs from 27 to 31. The entire project is launched by the Ministry of Electronics and Information Technology (MeitY). It is an umbrella program to cover all the aspects of government activity and also make it pan India. The various facets of e-governance are as given below.

1G2C

28. This is government-to-citizen initiative: It encompasses the following services of government departments:

- Computerization of land records—In collaboration with NIC, it ensures that landowners get computerized copies of ownership, crop, and tenancy and updated copies of Records of Rights (RoRs) on demand.
- *Bhoomi* Project—In the State of Karnataka the project includes the computerized delivery of 20 million rural land records to 6.7 million farmers through 177 government-owned kiosks.
- *Gyandoot*—Launched in 2000 in the Dhar District of Madhya Pradesh to provide relevant information to the general public.
- *Lokvani* project in Uttar Pradesh is a public-private partnership project in Sitapur District in Uttar Pradesh which was initiated in November 2004. Its objective is to provide a single window, self-sustainable-governance for handling public grievances, etc.
- Project FRIENDS was launched in the District of Kerala which entails, (Fast, Reliable, Instant, Efficient Network for the Disbursement of Services) a single-door facility for citizens for payment of taxes and other dues to the State.
- *E-Mitra* Project in Rajasthan—It is to help urban and rural masses to make payments of certain bills, etc., through kiosks.
- *E-Seva*in Andhra Pradesh state is designed to provide “Government to Citizen” and “e-business to citizens” services.
- Admission to Professional Colleges—Through Common Entrance Test (CET) the process of admission tests in professional courses was started in the early 1990s to make it transparent and objective.

G2B

29. Government-to-Business projects include the following:

- E-procurement project in Gujarat and Andhra Pradesh was introduced to reduce time and cost both for the people and for the government.

- MCA 21—The Ministry of Corporate Affairs provides easy and secure online access to all registry relating to companies under the Companies Act 1956 and New Companies Act 2013.
- E- procurement project in Gujarat and Andhra Pradesh was introduced to reduce the time and cost both for the people and for the government.
- Central Government initiatives such as Mission Mode Project (MMP).

G2G

30. Government-to-Government initiatives include the following.

I. Central Government Projects

31. E-office—The entire working desks were modernized on ICT lines making the increase of workflow, rule-based file routing, quick search and retrieval of files and office orders, digital signatures for authentication, forms and reporting components, etc., easier to access.

Immigration, Visa and Foreigner's Registration & Tracking (IVFRT)—This is to facilitate the entry of tourists and foreigners at Immigration.

UID—The unique identification project recognizes each resident of the country making it easier for them to receive the fruits of all governmental welfare schemes.

Pensions—The Pensions MMP is mainly to benefit the needy pensioners thereby also bridging the gap between the government and the pensioners.

Banking—The Banking MMP aims at streamlining various e-services initiatives taken by various banks.

Posts—All the Postal Departments in the country are interconnected, and there is a central server-based system with Computerized Registration Centres (CRCs).

II. State Mission Mode Projects

32. State Government Projects

E-governance in Municipalities—This unique initiative by the Central Government aims at bringing operational efficiencies in all the urban local bodies and bringing them under the umbrella of National Governance Plan (NeGP) and the Jawaharlal Nehru National Urban Renewal Mission (JNNURM).

Public Distribution System (PDS)—It includes areas of storage, utilization and distribution of food grains, grievance redress and transparency portal, digitization of beneficiary database, Fair Price Shop automation, etc.

Health—Ministry of Health & Family Welfare in the Mother and Child Tracking System (MCTS) program entails comprehensive use of ICT in these areas. It also provides ICT tools to women workers called ASHA and ANM workers, and National Rural Health Mission is also implemented through this.

The country has a grass root level administrative unit called *Panchayati Raj* Institutions (PRI). Due to scant financial resources, lesser qualified personnel, etc., the fruits of ICT have not reached places in full measure. The government thus takes over the computerization of PRIs so that the grass root level is benefitted from the welfare schemes. It aims at the electronic delivery of high-volume, citizen-centric government services so that the three infrastructure pillars of State Wide Area Networks (SWAN), State Data Centers (SDC), and Common Service Centers (CSCs) will deliver welfare services to the citizens at their doorstep.

National Land Records Modernization Programme (NLRMP)—Effort has been to replace the old and faulty manual system with the computerization of land records which started in 1988–1989. Since then there has been a constant attempt to introduce the IT system in the area of land records to make the system more efficient and people-friendly.

III. Integrated Mission Mode Projects

33. E-procurement—Ministry of Commerce & Industry (Department of Commerce) has been nominated as the Nodal Ministry for implementation of e-Government Procurement (e-GP) Mission Mode Projects (MMP). The vision of e-procurement is to make public procurement more transparent and efficient through the use of e-Government Procurement.

e-Court—There has been an attempt to overhaul the Indian judicial system along the ICT program. The e-Committee under the Supreme Court of India submitted a report on the basis of which there has been a clear effort to re-engineer processes to make the justice delivery system affordable, accessible, cost-effective, transparent, and accountable.

e-Biz—The e-Biz Mission Mode Project, being executed by the Department of Industrial Policy and Promotion (DIPP), Ministry of Commerce and Industry, Government of India, has the vision to transform the entire business services area with efficient, convenient, and transparent and integrated electronic services.

Common Services Centres (CSCs)—The CSCs would provide high-quality and cost-effective video, voice, and data content and services, in the areas of e-governance, education, health, telemedicine, entertainment as well as other private services. It mainly aims at web-enabled e-governance services in rural areas.

IV. E-governance in the Aftermath of COVID-19

34. E-governance in 2022–Though the country moved gradually toward utilizing the fruits of ICT and taking it to the remotest echelon of society yet the movement is constant and untiring. Apart from many health lessons, the Pandemic has taught us to make better use of technology even during bad times. Digital technology proved to be a key enabler. The App *Arogya Setu* of the Government of India became a successful contact tracing, syndrome mapping, and self-assessment digital service. During the pandemic, the e-Pass service provided movement during the period. The country made maximum use of ICT services through e-governance in matters, like information on accommodation in hospitals, symptoms and initial treatment of COVID patients, etc. E-governance has also helped in matters of economic growth. The government aimed at boosting domestic demand by about USD 9.94 billion. The Government of Delhi created an employment exchange in which employers could hire and employees could get themselves registered. It proved to be a great success as, by August 8, 2020, there were about 1 million employees benefitting from it.[18]

The National Conference on E-governance

35. The Department of Administrative Reforms & Public Grievances (DARPG) and Ministry of Electronics & Information Technology (MeitY), Government of India, in association with the State Government of Telangana organized the 24th Conference on e-Governance (NceG) 2021 on February 7–8, 2022 at Hyderabad, Telangana. The theme of the Conference was *"India's Techade: Digital Governance in a Post-Pandemic World."* The Conference was attended by all the dignitaries of the Government of India and governments of various states. After a two-day-long deliberations, the Conference ended with adopting *Hyderabad Declaration*[19] to be followed by all the governments in the area of E-governance. The highlights of the Declaration are as follows:

- Bringing citizens and governments on one digital platform.
- Transforming the citizen services through artifacts, like *Aadhar*, UPI, DigiLocker, *UMANG*, e-Sign, and consent framework.
- Fast-tracking the implementation, at national level, of public digital platforms in the areas of health, education, and agriculture by adopting open interoperable architecture for joined-up connected services.
- Enable data sharing among government entities and data protocols for data collection, data harvesting, data privacy, data anonymization, data security, and data preservation which will be helpful in building a data economy.
- To use upcoming technologies, like Artificial Intelligence, Machine Learning, Blockchain, 5G, Augmented Reality, and Virtual Reality for social empowerment.
- NeSDA 21 (National e-Governance Service Delivery Assessment)[20] to be adopted in collaboration with the Ministry of Electronics and Information Technology for improving the e-governance landscape.
- Integration of all state and district portals with CPGRAMS for redressal of grievances.
- Adoption of e-office version 7.0 in all ministries and departments.

18. 2022—The Year of E-Governance. By Elets News Network, https://egov.eletsonline.com/2022/01/2022-the-year-of-e-governance/.
19. 24th. National Conference on e-Governance 2021. Concluded at Hyderabad city on Jan. 7, 2022. Ministry of Personnel, Public Grievances & Pensions, https://pib.gov.in/PressReleaseIframePage.aspx?PRID=1788564.
20. The portal was launched on Jun. 9, 2021 by the Secretary DARPG. (Department of Administrative Reforms and Public Grievances).

Resultantly, the Hyderabad Declaration goes a long way in achieving the goal of Digital India, for making all government activities digital and making the common man digitally literate and savvy.

Part I. Digital Market Regulation

§1. Introduction

36. The rise of the digital sector in India has thrown a big challenge for Indian regulatory authorities, particularly for the Competition Commission of India (CCI). A chorus has been raised globally to bring online platforms into the legal mesh and hold them responsible for any adverse impact caused by them. There is an attempt to define the term "relevant market" within which platforms, like Google, WhatsApp, Apple, Zomato, and Swiggy work. The Competition Act 2002 requires the CCI to define "relevant market." So far, until 2016 there has been the approach of CCI to regard e-commerce companies and marketplaces, like Snapdeal, e-Bay, etc. as two different channels of distribution and not two different marketplaces. However, in 2018 when examining a complaint against an e-commerce company regarding discrimination in the matter of pricing, the CCI drifted away from its earlier view and held that there is a distinction between the online and offline segments. There is no exclusive law in India that deals with digital markets. Consumer Protection Rules are however in place to deal with e-commerce industries and data protection of individuals. Parties can have pre-filing consultations with CCI which was introduced in 2020.

Chapter 1. Legal Status of Standards and Technical Specifications (Non-binding Self-Regulation)

§1. General Statement

37. 1947 can be marked as the starting point of India's entry into the world of standardization of services and products. The Indian Standards Institution (ISI) was established as a society under the societies Registration Act 1860 to promote adoption of national standards. In 1952, ISI was given the responsibility of operating a certification marking scheme under an Act of Parliament.[21] In 1986, the Government of India felt the need to give a new thrust to standardization and quality control activities, to evolve a national strategy for giving appropriate recognition and importance to standards, and for integrating them with the growth and development of production and exports in different sectors. As a result of these activities of the government, the Bureau of Indian Standards Act 1986 was passed and by virtue of which the Bureau of Indian Standards (BIS) was established on April 1, 1987. It has now been given the status of a National Standards Body of India under the Department of Consumer Affairs, Ministry of Consumer Affairs, Food and Public Distribution, Government of India. It is established by the Bureau of Indian Standards Act 2016 which came into effect on October 12, 2017. The new BIS Act makes it easier for the government to notify or declare products, systems, and services for which compliance with specified standards is mandatory. "Quality Control Orders" means notifications for technical regulations by the government. According to Article 16(1) of the BIS Act 2016, the Central Government can do so "in public interest or for the protection of human, animal or plant health, safety of the environment, or prevention of unfair trade practices, or national security."

Make In India: A State Initiative

38. Launched in 2014, "Make in India" is a Government of India policy that encourages companies to develop, manufacture, and assemble products in India. It is based on four pillars, namely New Mindset, New Sectors, New Infrastructure, and New Processes. It aims to give a boost to entrepreneurship in India and to make the country a global manufacturing hub. Under it, the obsolete and orthodox frameworks have been dismantled and replaced by a transparent, user-friendly system that invites investment, encourages innovation, protects Intellectual property, and builds in-class manufacturing infrastructure. To make the "Make in India" drive a reality there has been an overhauling not only of the system but also the laws that have been made suitable for the goals. Like amendments in Labor Law, rationalizing of licensing rules and online filing of returns are giving the industry a relaxed environment to work, opening the doors of investment and empowering the country on the economic front.

21. Resolution No. 1 Std. (4)/45 dated Sep. 3, 1946.

Technical Regulations in India

39. India has gone a long way in the emergence of the country's mandatory certification schemes and data from the Technical Barriers to Trade (TBT) Committee of the World Trade Organization (WTO).[22] Standards are helpful for the consumer to make the right decision as they inform him about the worth and utility of a product, and are also helpful in facilitating international trade. As per Article 2.2 of the TBT Agreement, legitimate objectives of maintaining standards are national security, prevention of deceptive practices, human health or safety, and protection of plant life and the environment. The standardization in India is done by the Bureau of Indian Standards, a government body. The Act of 2016 through its "Quality Control Orders" (QCO) notifies technical regulations to manufacturers and companies. The regulations include QCO and also Compulsory Registration Orders (CRO) based on various Conformity Assessment Schemes. The International Relations& Technical Information Services Department of BIS is the nodal department that provides technical information services to interested parties. The Government of India was party to the Agreement on Technical Barriers to Trade (WTO-TBT Agreement) of the World Trade Organization (WTO). In this regard the Ministry of Commerce has designated two WTO—TBT Entry Points to answer all the inquiries which may come from foreign nations regarding standards and technical regulations conformity assessment procedures. These are:

(1) BIS—For all inquiries.
(2) Telecommunication Engineering Centre (TEC)—For inquires relating to the telecom sector.

These Entry Points also give an opportunity to individuals and organizations to review and express their opinions on notifications of other members. The TBT notifications of other countries are disseminated electronically to the national stakeholders in India. BIS being the National Standards Body of India and a member of the International Organization for Standardization, acts as the WMI (manufacturers of vehicles globally are identified by World Manufacturer Identifier) coordinator in India and issues WMI to vehicle manufacturers in India. BIS, as the National Standards Body, is responsible for issuing Issuer Identification Numbers (IIN) to various card issuers to operate within the country.[23]

§2. Indian Standard Organizations

40. BIS being the National Standards Body is responsible for the development and formulation of standards and promotes activities related to standardization, marking, and quality certification for imported and exported goods. India has always tried to harmonize its national standards with international norms and most

22. Philip Grinsted, Alok kesari & Khushwant Singh, *Quality Rules in India: Trade, Technical Regulations and Consumer Protection.* Issue Briefs and Special Reports, Jun. 29, 2018.
23. Indian Standards, https://www.bis.gov.in/index.php/standards/technical-information-services/.

of these are harmonized with the International Standards Organization (ISO). BIS also lays down the policy for India's participation in ISO and the International Electro-Technical Commission. However, Food, Safety and Standards Authority of India serves as the statutory body for implementing and regulating food standards.

§3. Testing, Inspection and Certification

41. Government agencies and Non-Governmental Organizations (NGOs) in harmony with BIS carry out an inspection under mandatory compliance. The product standards are voluntary in nature and after the removal of quantitative restrictions on imports in India in 2000, the import goods were made subject to certain mandatory compliance after getting registered with BIS. BIS also has a system for foreign goods to give them automatic certification provided for the products which have the "standard mark" on them. The certification of products was also done by making visits to the country of origin but this witnessed a drawback during the COVID-19 Pandemic. Suppliers and manufacturers of products under the Foreign Manufacturers Certification Scheme are required to maintain a presence in India.

42. The National Accreditation Board for Testing and Calibration Laboratories (NABL) provides accreditation for testing and calibration laboratories for the Indian Government, industry associations, and the private sector. To date (September 8, 2022), NABL has accredited more than 6,920 testing and calibration laboratories. NABL is a member of the International Laboratory Accreditation Co-operation and the Asia Pacific Laboratory Accreditation Co-operation (APLAC). NABL is a signatory to the International Laboratory Accreditation Co-operation as well as APLAC Mutual Recognition Arrangements, which are based on mutual evaluation and acceptance of other Mutual Recognition Arrangements Partner laboratory accreditation systems. India has gradually taken the path of progress in this field and with a few plants under ISO 9000 and ISO 14000 accreditations in the early 1990s it has moved to thousands of plants in the country today.

§4. Powers and Duties of the Bureau (Section 8 of the BIS Act)

43. The BIS is a body under the direct control of the Government of India which constitutes the Governing Council comprising the relevant Minister, Secretary to the Ministry, Director General as ex officio, and other members. The Executive Committee of the Bureau comprises the Director General who is the chief executive of the Bureau and some other members. The Governing Council frames the powers of the Bureau. These will include the following powers and functions:

(a) Establishment of branches, offices, and agencies within and outside India.
(b) Recognize and reciprocate with international bodies regarding specifications and grants of marks, goods, articles, and services, and seek recognition of the bureau at the national and international levels.

(c) Inspection and search of premises and vehicles and having the power to seize them.
(d) Providing services to manufacturers and consumers of goods for compliance with standards so as to meet the specifications as agreed upon.
(e) Providing training for quality management, standards, conformity assessment, laboratory testing, and calibration.
(f) Publish Indian Standards, and sell such publications and publications of international bodies.
(g) Authorize agencies both within and outside India to carry out the activities of the Bureau.
(h) Obtain membership in regional, international and foreign bodies having objects similar to that of the Bureau and participate in the international standards-setting process.
(i) Undertake to test samples.
(j) Undertake activities relating to legal metrology.

§5. Legal Status

44. The entire standards and technical specification system in the country is governed by a number of legislations, the relevant provisions of which mainly aim at consumer protection making the consumer well-informed and helping him in making the right decision. The Consumer Protection law forms the pivot which is laced with a number of short acts all of which protect the consumer from unethical market tactics, false advertisements, and overpricing. The Department of Consumer Affairs under the Ministry of Consumer Affairs, Food& Public Distribution has the responsibility of implementing these laws and issuing notifications to various industries whenever required. These laws are as under.

45. The Consumer Protection Act 2019—The new Act replaces the old Consumer Protection Act 1986 with more stringent provisions to protect the rights and interests of the consumer. It provides punishment for adopting "unfair trade practices" by the manufacturer of goods, provider of services, seller of goods, etc. The unfair trade practice shall include false representation regarding particular standards, quality, quantity, grade, composition, or style or model of any article. Actual misleading about the price and other specifications about the goods which are required by a competent authority (BIS) will invite punishment if such misleading statement is given on the outer label, wrapper, or is contained in any other informative document regarding the said article. (Section 2(47) Explanation (A) to (C)). The manufacturer, seller, or the product service provider as the case may be shall entail product liability under Chapter VI of the Act of 2019. (Sections 82–87). The punishment may extend to imprisonment up to six months or a fine of INR 10 lakhs (1 million), or both (Chapter VII, section 88).

46. Implementation of Standards of Weights and Measures Act 1976—It is an Act to establish weights and measures to regulate inter-state trade or commerce in weights, measures and other goods which are sold and distributed by weights and measures. Its ultimate objective is to protect the interest of the consumer and to encourage fair practice in the market. Its violation invites a fine of rupees 500–1000 and imprisonment of up to seven years. The violations are subject to punishment as prescribed under Part VI (sections 50–75). To implement its provisions the Standards of Weights and Measures (Enforcement) Act 1985 was passed.

47. The Legal Metrology Act 2009. The Act establishes and enforces standards of weights and measures, and regulates trade and commerce in weights, measures, and other goods which are sold or distributed by weight, measure, or number.

48. The Legal Metrology (Packaged Commodities) Rules, 2011. This was made on March 8, 2022, and is named Legal Metrology (Packaged Commodities), (Second Amendment) Rules 2022 which would be enforced in October 2022. It allowed electronic products to declare certain mandatory declarations through the Quick Response (QR) Code for a period of one year, if not declared in the package itself. By virtue of this Amendment, the Department of Consumer Affairs notification is issued. The Notification[24] says that in case of an electronic product that is manufactured, packed or imported after July 15, 2022, the package of such product shall, for a period of one year from such date, declare the name of the manufacturer, packer or importer, as the case may be, on the package itself and such declaration shall also inform the consumers to scan the QR code for the address and other related information, in case such information is declared through the QR Code and not declared on the package itself. The QR Code must inform the consumer of the common or generic name of the commodity and its size and dimension. It must also contain the telephone number and email address and inform the consumer that such information is contained in the QR code. The BIS requires the compulsory use of a standard mark in all goods and articles as per the Electronics and Information Technology Goods (Requirement of Compulsory Registration) Order, 2021.[25] Goods include the ones specified in Column 2 of the Schedule of the Order after getting a license from BIS for the same. This will not apply to those goods which are meant for export and which should be as per the specifications required by a foreign buyer and which are exempted by an order of the Government of India for this purpose.

49. On August 22, 2022, Legal Metrology (Packaged Commodities), (Third Amendment) Rules 2022 were passed to insert a new clause in Rule 26 of Rules 2011 granting exemption to certain packaged commodities. This will come into force on January 1, 2023. By virtue of this Amendment, a Notification[26] is issued which contains rules regarding garments hosiery and requires that when the garment hosiery is sold in loose or open at the point of sale then the consumer should be given the opportunity to inspect the same and the product should bear the name

24. G.S.R. 577(E)—Ministry of Consumer Affairs, Food& Public Distribution, Government of India. (Department of Consumer Affairs), Dated Jul. 14, 2022.
25. The Gazette of India—Part II—s. 3-Sub-s. (ii). No 1156. New Delhi, Thursday Mar. 18, 2021.
26. G.S.R. 648I—Ministry of Consumer Affairs, Food& Public Distribution, Government of India. (Department of Consumer Affairs)—New Delhi, Dated Aug. 22, 2022.

and address of the manufacturer, the brand, country of origin, etc., the consumer care email id and phone number, size of the garment indicated by S, M, L, XL, etc.

50. The Guidelines for Prevention of Misleading Advertisements and Endorsements for Misleading Advertisements, 2022.[27] These guidelines are applied to all sorts of advertisements irrespective of any medium or format and to all sorts of services, products, or goods. This is another step toward protecting the consumer from false advertisements and preserving his rights. Its aim is to see that the consumers are not fooled by unsubstantiated claims, and puffed and fake promises. If an advertisement violates the right of the consumer to free choice and the right to be informed correctly about the product or service then such misleading advertisements are termed as "bait advertisements" and "surrogate advertisements." The provisions also protect children and young minds from exaggerated and unrealistic claims. The Central Consumer Protection Authority (CCPA) can impose a penalty of up to 10 lakh INR (1 million) upon manufacturers, advertisers, and endorsers for any misleading advertisement.[28]

Non-binding Self-regulation

51. Self-Regulation in a number of industries, like healthcare, higher education, fashion, professional sports, and nuclear power govern industry practices.[29] The private sector mainly relies on self-regulation to address a number of issues, like establishing industry standards, developing codes of conduct, and achieving consumer trust; it has become an important part of global economy. Self-regulation can be defined as "a regulatory process whereby an industry-level organization (such as a trade association or a professional society), as opposed to a governmental or firm level organization, sets and enforces rules and standards relating to the conduct of firms in the industry."[30] Regulation may be non-state or governmental or it can also be co-regulation where both the industry and the state jointly venture on certain rules and regulations. Consumer protection and privacy take center stage in regulatory regimes whether it is by the government or it is by Self-Regulating Organizations (SROs). Thus industries resort to self-regulation to inculcate consumer confidence, gain public trust, and also achieve goodwill. But self-regulation does not work in isolation and hence, monitoring and self-policing are adopted to ensure compliance.

Self-Regulation in India

52. The regulators in the country do not discourage self-regulation in a bid to impose strict governmental rules. This gives an opportunity for industries to grow and adopt innovations. The advertising Standards Council of India (ASCI) devises

27. Gazette of India-Extraordinary—Part III—s. 4. New Delhi, Thursday, Jun. 9, 2022.
28. Press Information Bureau—Ministry of Consumer Affairs and, Food and Public Distribution, Jun. 10, 2022, https://pib.gov.in/PressReleasePage.aspx?PRID=1832906.
29. Neil Gunningham &Joseph Rees, *Industry Self-Regulation: An Institutional Perspective*, Law & Policy 19(4) (October 1997).
30. Anil K. Gupta &Lawrence J. Lad, *Industry Self-Regulation: An Economic, Organizational, and Political Analysis*, The Academy of Management Review 8(3) (1983), 417.

guidelines for the industry. However, the self-regulation mechanism in the country is not very promising, and it has so far been ineffective and difficult to implement. The government is in favor of a "layered regulatory structure"[31] for industries. The Ministry of Consumer Affairs looks over the compliance of self-regulatory rules and issues guidelines from time to time. These guidelines are legally binding and invite penalties.

53. In May this year, the Federation of Indian Chambers of Commerce and Industry (FICCI) unveiled a self-regulatory code of conduct for online diagnostic platforms in India. The diagnostic industry so far has been unregulated and as the deadly Pandemic has underlined the importance of diagnostics, the regulatory code is a welcome move and the results are yet to be disclosed. The industry associations must pressurize their members to resort to self-regulation honestly so that the legal noose is kept at bay. Pharma companies have a self-regulatory "Uniform Code of Pharmaceutical Marketing Practices" (UCPMP) since 2015 to control unethical practices although in spite of this these have become under the lens of the Central Bureau of investigation. In March 2022, a plea was filed in the Supreme Court which said that "No enforceable law exists which regulates the promotion of drugs by pharmaceutical companies *visa vis* healthcare professionals and therefore unethical practices continue unfettered." The plea mentioned that pharmaceutical companies are bribing doctors to adopt unethical practices. The Court has asked the Central Government to frame the "Uniform Code of Pharmaceutical Marketing Practices" (UCPMP) on a statutory basis and to make it effective, and devise a monitoring mechanism for transparency, accountability as well as consequences of violations.[32]

Need to Legislate

54. The Indian pharmaceutical industry is replete with unethical marketing tactics. Though the pharmaceutical industry tries on self-regulation but that proves to be weak and ineffective. Stories are abundant about how exorbitantly healthcare professionals are being lured and bribed to prescribe medicines that are unnecessarily high-rated and most of the time not required. Poorly designed clinical trials in medical colleges with munificent honorariums[33] as an enticement are just the tip of the ice berg. Distribution of freebies to doctors is rampant. In a bid to curb this, the Finance Bill 2022 in its memorandum says "any expense incurred in providing various benefits in violation of the provisions of Indian Medical Council (Professional Conduct, Etiquette and Ethics) Regulations, 2002 shall be inadmissible under section 37(1) for being prohibited by the law." Though the Indian Medical Council forbids doctors from taking gifts, etc., but that does not complete the purpose as the

31. KK Somvanshi, *View: Is Self Regulation Defeating Its Purpose*? Dated July 2022, https://economictimes.indiatimes.com/opinion/et-commentary/view-is-self-regulation-defeating-its-purpose/articleshow/92651012.cms.
32. Medical Dialogues, https://medicaldialogues.in/news/industry/pharma/unethical-marketing-practices-of-pharma-companies-sc-to-examine-ucpmp-code-implementation-89841?infinitescroll=1.
33. T. Sri Krishna & S. Srinivasan, *Why Do Unethical Pharma Practices Thrive?*, The Hindu Business Line, Aug. 30, 2022.

regulations do not apply to pharmaceutical companies. The price of medicines ranges arbitrarily and propaganda run by the companies brand these medicines more effective. The drugs in the National List of Essential Medicines (NLEM) 2015 are under price control but that covers only 18% of the entire drug market. These irregularities led to Public Interest Litigation (PIL) in the Supreme Court urging the Court to intervene and direct regulation. The "Uniform Code of Pharmaceutical Marketing Practices" (UCPMP) since 2015, has remained "toothless and voluntary and not mandatory." Legislation for ethical pharmaceutical marketing is the need of the hour and looks up to the legislators to act promptly.

Chapter 2. Legal Status of Standard Terms and Conditions

§1. General Statement

55. The terms and conditions in digital marketing differ slightly from the traditional market in the sense that the traditional market is a one-way communication while digital marketing is a two-way communication between a business and the actual or prospective customer. Every day new technologies are entering the market arena thereby rendering the traditional market outdated and obsolete. Digital contracts have become common and the relationship with consumers becomes shady due to the intangible environment in which they are made. The terms and conditions used by them are lengthy and less comprehensible to a common mind. Consequently, legal issues are also intertwined with the trending changes. These can be enumerated below.

§2. IPR Issues

56. The advertisements used by digital marketers often swipe copyrighted materials, like photographs, artwork, music, video footage, etc. This practice is unmindful of the copyright holders of such materials and thus this entails legal answerability unless the consent of the holder is taken. The Copyright Act 1957 is often invoked and the wrongdoer is made liable under it.

§3. Consumer-Related Issues

57. Consumer is the king of the market whether traditional or digital. In India, the Consumer Protection Act 2019 is a robust act that closely protects the rights and interests of consumers. It applies to all digital market entities including product manufacturers, product sellers, traders, advertising agencies, endorsers, and digital market players, like e-commerce entities, etc. The Act requires that all digital market practices be compliant with the provisions of the CPA 2019. The act guards against misleading advertisements and requires the players to give accurate messages regarding their products. The aim of the Act is to curb unfair trade practices which have become rampant due to technological changes.

§4. Privacy Issues

58. As per the Supreme Court ruling, the status of the right to privacy has been upgraded from a mere legal right to a constitutional right. Marketing emails and messages swipe the personal profile of the consumers. To escape the liability regarding violation of this right the sellers and manufacturers enter certain "disclaimers" and/or "exemptions" over their products or service clauses thereby asking the consumer to "agree" or "accept" their terms and conditions through a clickwrap method. Such terms and conditions usually include the scope of the work, market strategies, deliverable timelines, payment methods, the confidentiality of information shared, and dispute resolution processes. This practice often gives the sellers a ground of defense.

The E-Contracts in India like most countries include a browse wrap agreement which intends to be binding on the user and anyone who uses the website is understood to agree to the terms and conditions of the website. Then there is the shrink wrap agreement which is a license agreement in which the terms and conditions of the agreement are enforced upon the consumer as soon as he opens the package. The license agreement indemnifies the user for any copyright or IPR violations of the manufacturer as soon as the package is accepted.

Then there is click wrap agreement in which the consumer or user agrees to the terms and conditions by clicking on the "I accept" icon as discussed above. In India, there is no judicial precedent on the validity of shrinkwrap or clickwrap contracts though the provisions regarding standard terms and conditions come indirectly under the purview of the Indian Contract Act 1872 though no specific provision deals with them. The contract which has the term and conditions before the acceptance of the contract, exists from before under the name Standard Form Contracts (SFC) and which are now used profusely in the digital market area also. However, there is no specific rule regarding these conditions in the Indian Contract Act 1872 though they are governed by the provisions of the Railways Act, public transportation control by the government, or in various areas of services. There is a need to formulate laws to deal directly with the clickwrap or shrinkwrap types of contracts.

Chapter 3. International Private Law Applied to the Online Environment

§1. GENERALLY

59. The fast-paced digital technology has not left anything untouched. The world has become borderless and everything has become global. But that does not solve the legal puzzle so easily. Meaning and implications of a good number of legal concepts have suffered a jolt, and consequently have undergone a formidable change; jurisdiction, evidence, investigation, and freedom of expression to name a few. Earlier the situation was bilateral in nature where the laws of the two parties involved were possibly applied to a particular case. Formerly, when two parties in litigation were of different countries the "choice of law" and private international law came as a solution. Today, in the internet environment there is an overlapping of laws of a number of countries may be of all countries where the effect of a particular action or posting is rippled. The present human society has been international in character and with the advent of science; it has become closer and closer, forgetting the different hues of culture, philosophies, legal criteria, and judicial preferences. The interaction among the various corners of the globe, though slow, has always played an important role in political, social, commercial, and legal considerations. Private international law or conflict of laws is the body of law that seeks to resolve certain issues that result from the presence of a foreign component in legal relationships.[34]

The information society today is more international and more global than ever as the technological revolution has reduced the distances of days and hours into nanoseconds. The result is the intermingling of laws and philosophies, and beliefs and conventions giving birth to a confused cyber society. So to say, the online environment has undermined the public and private international law regime. Both public and private international law present a case of "hyper regulation."[35] Private international law has a long tradition in legal systems[36] but today the online environment has changed the picture totally where one action sends repercussions globally, with the wrongdoer in one jurisdiction, the aggrieved in another jurisdiction and a wrong or a hate speech will entail all the countries where the obnoxious content is "seen", "read," or "downloaded." This only subjects the wrongdoer to a number of jurisdictions. In traditional private international law whenever there is some dispute regarding the multiplicity of laws in a certain area involving some private dispute, the conflict is resolved by resorting to the established rules of private international law. As cyberspace is shared by all the nations of the world, private international

34. Raman Mittal, Chapter 10 "Dispute Resolution in Cyberspace: Determining Jurisdiction and Applicable Law" in S.K. Verma & Raman Mittal (eds.), *Legal Dimensions of Cyberspace* (Indian Law Institute, 2004) 269.
35. Prof Dr Dan Jerker B. Svantesson, *Private International Law for a Digitised World: Collision Co-existence or Combination?* The European Association of Private International Law, November 24, 2020.
36. *Supra* note 34.

law issues could arise in areas such as contracts, crimes, torts, consumer protection, taxation, marriage, intellectual property, etc. The following issues arise in the context of private international law:[37]

(1) Jurisdiction to adjudicate a dispute at a particular location (i.e., the forum or situs).
(2) Applicable law to the dispute.
(3) Enforcement of judgments in courts in foreign jurisdictions.

Today, the global internet scenario presents a crisscross of various laws and hence, various jurisdictions. Moreover, the nature and implications of crimes committed in the internet environment have undergone a drastic change giving birth to almost a new generation of crimes, like hacking, cyber fraud, identity theft, cyber defamation, and hate speech. Private international law helps in resolving these problems.[38] But the online environment challenges the proper functioning of private international law which was already an intersection of the laws of various states.

In India, private international law is not codified and it is dispersed over a number of legislations namely; the Civil Procedure Code 1907, the Indian Contract Act 1872, the Indian Succession Act 1925, the Indian Divorce Act 1869, and the Special Marriages Act 1954. However, the lack of codification of private international law in India gives birth to unpredictability and uncertainty.

37. *Ibid.*

38. A very broad principle on which private international law is based is that the place which has the closest connection with that transaction should have the jurisdiction. When two or more laws apply to a particular situation, simply because two or more countries are involved, the seller in one country and the buyer in another country, then the law will look to that country which has the closest nexus or connection to the transaction at hand. For example, in case of a contract, it may be looked at where the contract was formed. If the contract was formed in country *B*, then there is a better chance of claiming jurisdiction in country *B*. Similarly, if it can be proved that the goods were defective when they left the seller, and therefore, the performance was affected in the seller's country itself, and then there might be a good reason for claiming that jurisdiction is in that country.

Chapter 4. Competition Law Applied to the Digital Market

§1. GENERALLY

60. Digitization has opened a new world for competition. The archaic laws are insufficient to tackle the upcoming situations in the area of competition in digital markets. Many times the players get an easy escape with respect to predatory prices, abuse of dominance and exclusionary conduct. The Big Five in tech namely, Google, Amazon, Apple, Facebook, and Microsoft conquer more than half of the global digital market. Their empowerment has given them an opportunity to engage in anti-competitive activities. To bring them under regulation is a challenging task even for mature jurisdictions, like the U.S., U.K., etc., while India is still in its infancy regarding the regulation of competition. Also, though India rates high in the internet user scales yet its low literacy and very low computer literacy make the population a plaything in the hands of digital tycoons, and hence the consumer is being specifically protected since 1986 when its first consumer protection act was passed and which now in the digital environ has been refurbished in the form of 2019 act. The Competition Act 2002 is the fountain of legal provisions to regulate competition and unfair trade practices in digital markets.

§2. COMPETITION ACT 2002

61. The benefits of a competitive communications market are public interest and social good. With India becoming a telecommunication hub and a contestable market for IT products and ITES, the Competition Act 2002[39] was formulated right at the time when ICTs were gaining momentum in the country. The Competition Act 2002 seeks to ensure fair competition by combating anti-competitive malpractices. The Act establishes the Competition Commission of India (CCI) which is at the apex of the entire anti-competition drive and which is responsible for looking into the complaints, grievances, and practices having an adverse effect on competition, and also has the power to punish the defaulters. For determining whether a market constitutes a "relevant market" for the purposes of the Act, the Commission shall have due regard to the "relevant geographic market" and "relevant product market." For the "relevant geographic market" the Competition Commission of India shall have regard to the following factors:[40]

(a) Regulatory trade barrier.
(b) Local specification requirements.
(c) National procurement policies.
(d) Adequate distribution facilities.
(e) Transport costs.
(f) Language.

---

39. It is successor of the Monopoly and Restrictive Trade Practices Act 1969 which has now been repealed.
40. Section 19(6) the Competition Act 2002.

(g) Consumer preferences.
(h) Need for secure or regular supplies or rapid after-sales service.

While determining the "relevant product market," the CCI shall have regard to all or any of the following factors:[41]

(a) Physical characteristics or end use of goods.
(b) Price of goods or services.
(c) Consumer preferences.
(d) Exclusion of in-house production.
(e) Existence of specialized producers; classifications of industrial products.

§3. Competition Commission of India

62. The Competition Commission of India 2002 for the purpose of determining whether a combination would have or is likely to have an appreciable adverse effect on competition in the relevant market, has to have regard to the following[42] factors:

(1) actual and potential level of competition through importers in the market;
(2) extent of barriers to entry into the market;
(3) level of combination in the market;
(4) degree of countervailing power in the market;
(5) likelihood that the combination would result in the parties to the combination being able to significantly and sustainably increase prices or profit margins;
(6) extent of effective competition likely to sustain in the market;
(7) extent to which substitutes are available \or are likely to be available in the market;
(8) market share, in the relevant market, of the persons or enterprise in a combination individually and as a combination;
(9) likelihood that the combination would result in the removal of a vigorous and effective competitor or competitors in the market;
(10) nature and extent of vertical integration in the market;
(11) possibility of falling business;
(12) nature and extent of innovation;
(13) relative advantage of any combination by way of its contribution to economic development;
(14) whether the benefits of the combination outweigh the adverse impact of the combination if any.

41. Section 19(7) the Competition Act 2002.
42. Section 20(4) the Competition Act 2002.

§4. Definition of Relevant Market

63. The digital market boom has thrown many challenges before the regulatory mechanism of India like any other country. As the businesses in these online platforms expand to formidable limits, their interaction with the consumers also increases abundantly. Disputes are bound to arise and there is a global feel to fix the responsibility of players in these markets and to make them accountable. For this, there comes a question of their identity and to define them clearly. It is required by the Competition Act 2002 that the Competition Commission of India must define "relevant market." Such definition will take into consideration the physical characteristics or end use of the goods, price of goods or services, consumer preferences, regulatory trade barriers, and local specification requirements. Until 2016, while defining a "relevant market" for e-commerce companies and marketplaces (such as Snapdeal, Ebay, Yepme, Cloudtail, etc.), the CCI viewed online and offline segments as different channels of distribution and not different relevant markets.[43] This was necessitated by the view of the CCI that the two segments are different and a buyer before purchasing compares the two and adapts to the one in which he gains more. In 2018, the view of the CCI changed when it was scrutinizing a complaint against e-commerce companies that alleged "abuse of dominance" by way of predatory prices and discrimination among sellers. The CCI realized that there is a difference between online and offline segments. It redefined the relevant market by limiting it only to online market segments. In *All India Online Vendors Association v. Flipkart India Private Limited & Anr.*[44] CCI defined "relevant market" as "services provided by online marketplace platforms for selling goods in India." In another case in 2019,[45] CCI defined "relevant market" as the market for "online intermediation services for booking of hotels in India." Following this, the CCI has considered "relevant market" for certain online-only players in several cases related to digital markets.[46] For instance, it has defined the relevant market for; (a) Google as "the market for Online General Web Search Services in India and the market for Online Search Advertising Services in India,"[47](b) WhatsApp as "the market for

43. CCI's order in *Deepak Verma v. Clues Network Pvt. Ltd. & Ors.,* Case No. 34 of 2016, dated Jul. 26, 2016; as available at, https://www.cci.gov.in/sites/default/files/342016.
44. *See*, the CCI's order in *All India Online Vendors Association v. Flipkart India Private Limited & Anr.*, Case No. 20 of 2018, dated Nov. 6, 2018; as available at, https://www.cci.gov.in/sites/default/files/20-of-2018.pdf; this order was subsequently reversed by the appellate tribunal. As on date, the Supreme Court of India has stayed the appellate tribunal's order.
45. *Federation of Hotel & Restaurant Associations of India v. MakeMyTrip India Pvt. Ltd. & Ors.,* Case No. 14 of 2019, dated Oct. 28, 2019; as available at, https://www.cci.gov.in/sites/default/files/14of2019_0.pdf.
46. Simran Dhir & Others; *India: Relevant Markets Must Be Defined Well for Competition Regulation,* May 2022, https://www.mondaq.com/india/antitrust-eu-competition-/1194564/digital-markets-must-be-defined-well-for-competition-regulation.
47. *Digital News Publishers Association v. Google LLC,* Case No. 41 of 2021, dated Jan. 7, 2022; as available at, https://www.cci.gov.in/sites/default/files/order_41_2021.pdf.

Over-The-Top (OTT) messaging apps through smartphones in India,"[48] and (c) Apple as "the market for app stores for iOS in India."[49]

The CCI has been meticulous about the definition of "relevant market"" and even though in an investigation against Amazon and Flipkart it agreed that "online intermediation services are "key enablers of entrepreneurship" but they are still short of the definition of "relevant market." In an Urban Clap case in 2021, the CCI opined that the "Relevant Market Test" should be applied on a case-by-case basis. Ultimately, the CCI should define "relevant market" in the digital sector by taking into consideration all substitutable and interchangeable products or services for each industry, including what's available offline.[50] CCI's approach toward the digital market must be co-extensive, careful, and considerate so that the growth of the market is not hampered by overriding rules and regulations.

Privacy Issues in Digital Market

64. The online players in the digital market have the potential to intrude into the privacy of consumers. It has become a competition law concern in India. In digital markets, "unreasonable data collection and sharing may grant competitive advantage to dominant players leading to exploitation and exclusion."[51] Though earlier the CCI refused to look into privacy issues due to jurisdictional issues later it took up the matter in a *suo motu* case which involved WhatsApp's recent privacy policy update allowing data-sharing with Facebook. Thus consumer privacy can be an abuse of dominance which would lower consumer welfare.[52] The "take-it-or-leave-it" privacy policy was considered a weak type of consent by the CCI and regarded that building user profiles through cross-linking of data collected across services (like the one between WhatsApp and Facebook) amounts to abusive dominance and is a worrisome factor in the digital market *vis-a-vis* the consumer's privacy. The CCI regarded the denial of privacy-sharing choice by consumers considered by the German Supreme Court[53] as problematic. The CCI acknowledged privacy as a non-price parameter of competition.[54] The CCI while dealing with privacy issues in the digital market may face jurisdictional hindrances with the regulator, once the Data Protection Law is implemented, or with other sectoral regulators.

---

48. *Re: Updated Terms of Service and Privacy Policy for WhatsApp Users, Suo Moto* Case No. 1 of 2021, dated Mar. 24, 2021; as available at, https://www.cci.gov.in/sites/default/files/SM01of2021_0.pdf.
49. *Together We Fight Society v. Apple Inc.,* Case No. 24 of 2021, dated Dec. 31, 2021; as available at, https://www.cci.gov.in/sites/default/files/24-of-2021.pdf.
50. Simran Dhir & Ors.
51. Paragraph 13 I In Re: Updated Terms of Service and Privacy Policy for WhatsApp Users, CCI Suo Moto Case No. 01 of 2021, https://www.cci.gov.in/sites/default/files/SM01of2021_0.pdf.
52. CCI, Market Study on the Telecom Sector in India (Jan. 22, 2021), https://www.cci.gov.in/sites/default/files/whats_newdocument/Market-Study-on-the-TelecomSector-In-India.pdf.
53. Klaus Wiedemann (2020) *A Matter of Choice: The German Federal Supreme Court's Interim Decision in the Abuse-of-Dominance Proceedings* Bundeskartellamt *v.* Facebook (Case KVR 69/19), IIC 51:1168–1181, https://doi.org/10.1007/s40319–020–00990–3.
54. Shilpi Bhattacharya & Pankhudi Khandelwal, *Indian Competition Law in the Digital Markets: An Overview of National Case Law—e-Competitions,* Antitrust Case Laws e-Bulletin. Concurrences Anti-Trust Publications & Events, July 2021.

This was adjudicated by the Supreme Court in *CCI v. Bharti Airtel*[55] in which the Court left it upon the sectoral regulator to decide if there was a competition issue that necessitated the intervention of CCI. The CCI's other observation relating to abuse by leveraging of data is in line with the proposed EU Digital Markets Act which also prohibits the combination of personal data collected across services.[56] Entry of CCI in the field of consumer privacy and its jurisprudence regarding it needs more clarification.

65. The Competition (Amendment) Bill, 2022 (*Bill No. 185 of 2022*) (the "**Bill**") was introduced in the Lok Sabha (Lower House of the Parliament) on August 5, 2022. It seeks to, "*carry out certain essential structural changes in the governing structure of the Competition Commission of India and changes to substantive provisions to address the needs for new age markets,*" and amend the Competition Act, 2002.

55. Civil Appeal No(s).11843 of 2018 (Supreme Court), https://main.sci.gov.in/supremecourt/2017/40072/40072_2017_Judgement_05-Dec-2018.pdf.

56. Article 5(a), Proposal for a Regulation of the European Parliament and of the Council on contestable and fair markets in the digital sector (Digital Markets Act), SEC(2020) 437 final.

Chapter 5. Regulation of the Electronic Communications Market ("Telecommunications Law")

§1. BACKGROUND

66. To start with, the Indian Telegraph Act 1885 was the first attempt by the British to broaden the horizon of telegraphic activities in the simpler and less-developed India at that time. The Act gives more power to the government and the licensed companies to conveniently use private and public land for placing telegraphic lines. The path was open for moving ahead in this field without hurdles. A number of policy reforms, legislations,[57] and rules since have formed the legal framework of the country in this field. Regulation on telegraph is a Central Government mandate which is empowered by the Constitution of India (Union List-Entry 31) to the exclusion of State or local governments. There is a plethora of legislations, rules, policies, guidelines, and orders which go together to regulate the entire telecommunication world in India.

§2. THE LEGAL WEB

67. Under the term "telecommunications" and due to the wide definitions of certain terms under the TRAI Act 1997 the Indian legal framework takes into its scope certain services, like the internet, radio paging, voice mail, V-Sat communications, e-commerce, broadcasting services, etc. As telecommunications falls under List I or the Union list of the GOI, the Central Government has an upper hand in this field and has greater legislative competence. Thus, the entire legal framework in the telecommunication sector consists of: the Indian Telegraph Act 1885 and the rules made there under; the Wireless Telegraphy Act 1933 and rules made there under; the Telegraph Wires (Unlawful Possession) Act 1950 and the rules made there under; the Cable Television Network (Regulation) Act 1996 and the rules made there under; the TRAI Act 1997 and rules made there under. This legal framework,, however, deals with a specialized form of telecommunication services under one single law

57. Indian Telegraphs (Presidency Towns) Act, 1888 (11 of 1888).

- Indian Telegraph (Amendment) Act 1914 (7 of 1914).
- Indian Post Office and Telegraph (Amendment) Act 1914 (14 of 1914.
- Indian Telegraph (Amendment) Act 1930 (27 of 1930).
- The Government of India (Adaptation of Indian Laws) Orders 1937.
- Indian Telegraph (Amendment) Act 1948 (45 of 1948).
- The Adaptation of Laws Order 1950.
- The Part B States (Laws) Act 1951 (3 of 1951).
- The Indian Telegraph (Amendment) Act 1957 (47 of 1957) (w.e.f. 1–7–1957).
- The Telegraph Laws (Amendment Act 1961 (15 of 1961) (w.e.f. 2–5–1961).
- The Indian Telegraph (Amendment) 1971 (33 of 1971) (w.e.f. 10–8–1971).
- The Indian Telegraph (Amendment) Act 1972 (38 of 1972) (w.e.f. 21–8–1972).
- The Indian Telegraph (Amendment) Act 1974(48 of 1974) (w.e.f. 1–6–75). The Indian telegraph (Amendment) Act 2003 (8 of 2004) w.e.f. 1–4–2002.)CHECK.
- The Indian Telegraph (Amendment) Act 2006 (57 of 2006) (w.e.f. 3–10–2006).

like the Telegraph Act of 1885, and hence often financial and other legal issues result from it. The Information Technology Act 2000(Amended 2008) though basically deals with facets of IT, like electronic signatures, etc., it also covers the telecommunication service providers. In the Amendment, telecommunication devices like cell phones are classified as "communication devices" and telecommunication services such as services provided through the wired, satellite, wireless or terrestrial line, or other communication media are classified as "computer networks" which fall under the IT Act. Furthermore, the telecom and internet service providers are classified as "intermediaries" and the IT Act along with the Information Technology (Intermediary Guidelines and Digital Media Ethics Code) Rules 2021 establish conditions within which the intermediary can claim safe harbor under the IT Act.[58]

§3. The Archaic Law: Government's Privilege

68. The Indian Telegraph Act 1885 gives exclusive privileges to the government for establishing, maintaining, and working telegraphs within India (section 4(1)). The Telegraph Act stands as the time-tested pillar not only from the view point of its age but also from the viewpoint of its applicability in the modern communication world. This owes to the import of the term "telegraph" which means any appliance, instrument, material, or apparatus used or capable of use for transmission or reception of signs, signals, writing, images, and sounds, or intelligence of any nature by wire, visual, or other electromagnetic emissions, radio waves or Hertzian waves, galvanic, electric, or magnetic waves.[59] The government may part with its privilege by issuing a license on certain terms and conditions. The government by issuing a license to the service provider (the licensee) authorizes him to offer the services as agreed under the license. Thus, telecom and broadcast services are illegal if they are offered without a telegraph license.[60] The TRAI Act enlarges the legal concept of a telegraph, although somewhat indirectly. As a textual matter, the TRAI does not actually define a telegraph instead it defines the term "telecommunication service" to include service of any description (including electronic mail, voice mail, data services, audio text services, radio paging, and cellular mobile services) which is transmitted though signs, signals, writing images, and sounds or intelligence of any nature by wire, radio, visual, or other electromagnetic means and also includes broadcasting and cable services (section 2(1)(k) as expanded in January 2004).

58. Namita Vishwanath & Two Others, *In Brief, Telecoms Regulation in India*. Jun. 24, 2022. Lexology, https://www.lexology.com/library/detail.aspx?g=d626eaef-f300-4dbf-85a7-34a015300226.
59. An explanation to this section states that "radio waves" or "Hertzian waves" mean electromagnetic waves of frequencies lower than 3,000 giga-cycles per second propagated in space without artificial guide s. 3(IAA)/The Telegraph Act.
60. It is an offense to establish, maintain or work a telegraph in contravention of the Telegraph Act and makes it a crime for any person, with knowledge or belief about an illegally operated telegraph, to use that telegraph for messaging. (Sections 20, 21 of the Telegraph Act 1988).

§4. Key Ministries & Departments

69. (1) The Ministry of Communications which is empowered to manage, license, and regulate all matters relating to telecommunications and networks; and (2) the Ministry of Electronics and Information Technology (MeitY) which is responsible for information technology policy, strategy, and development of the electronics industry.

Departments

70. As mentioned earlier the entire telecommunication network in the country is under the control and surveillance of a number of acts, notifications, regulations, circulars, etc. These are issued from time to time to keep pace with technological changes. A number of Government Departments under the Ministries are responsible for updating the entire infrastructure as mentioned below:

- The Department of Telecommunications (DoT). The Indian communications law consists primarily of regulations issued by the DoT under the aforesaid statutes. DoT is empowered under the Telegraph Act and the Wireless Telegraphy Act to grant licenses for telecommunications services and telecommunications infrastructure.
- The Telecom Regulatory Authority of India (TRAI). This regulator of the telecommunications sector in India was set up under the Telecom Regulatory Authority of India Act 1997 (the TRAI Act). TRAI is empowered to hold consultations and make recommendations to DoT in certain areas, issue regulations or guidelines, and regulate certain other areas of communications law.
- The Telecommunications Commission. This is a high-level body represented by various union ministers and high-ranking bureaucrats. This body is responsible for policy formulation, implementation of government policy in all matters concerning telecommunications, and working with foreign governments toward better cooperation.
- The Telecom Dispute Settlement Appellate Tribunal (TDSAT). TDSAT is a quasi-judicial body created under the TRAI Act and is the authority responsible for adjudicating telecommunications-related disputes. The TRAI Act 1997 as amended in 2000 has a new segment,—the Telecom Disputes Settlement and Appellate Tribunal (TDSAT). While on the one hand, the TRAI takes care of recommendatory and regulatory functions, the Tribunal, on other hand, takes care of dispute settlement. Under the term "telecommunications" and due to the wide definitions of certain terms under the TRAI Act 1997 the Indian legal framework takes into its scope certain services, like the internet, radio paging, voice mail, V-Sat communications, e-commerce, broadcasting services, etc. As telecommunications falls under List I or the Union list of the GoI, the Central Government has an upper hand in this field and has greater legislative competence. Thus, the entire legal framework in the telecommunication sector consists of: the Indian Telegraph Act 1885 and the rules made there under; the Wireless Telegraphy Act 1933 and rules made there under; the Telegraph Wires (Unlawful Possession) Act 1950 and the rules made there under; the Cable Television Network (Regulation)

Act 1996 and the rules made there under; the TRAI Act 1997 and rules made there under. This legal framework,, however, deals with a specialized form of telecommunication services under one single law like the Telegraph Act of 1885, and hence often financial and other legal issues result from it.

§5. Communications Market

71. The Telecom sector in the country is subject to ex-ante regulations. The TRAI through its regulations ensures uniformity between telecom service providers and users. The Prohibition of Discriminatory Tariffs Regulations 2016 prohibits service providers from charging discriminatory tariffs from their users. It regulates discriminatory, arbitrary, and anti-competitive pricing from its users. Recently, the government allowed hundred percent foreign investments in the Telecom sector under the automatic route but in certain cases, it also orders government approval.

§6. The Code of Ethics for Intermediaries Etc.

72. The Meity in 2021, introduced the intermediary guidelines. It has the following areas of regulation:

(1) It regulates intermediaries, like telecom service providers, network service providers, internet service providers, web hosting service providers, search engines, online payment sites, online auction sites, online market places, cyber cafes, etc.
(2) Publishers of news and current affairs content, like online papers, news portals, news aggregators, news agencies, etc., who publish news and current affairs content, etc.
(3) Publishers of online curated content like publishers who make available to their users a curated catalog of audiovisual content through subscription over the internet or computer networks and includes films, audiovisual programs, documentaries, television programs, serials, podcasts, and other such content, etc.

Chapter 6. Regulation of Broadcasting Activities (Audio-Visual Services)

§1. HISTORY

73. Television broadcasting was introduced in India in 1959 from New Delhi on an experimental basis but the regular broadcasting service started in 1965 as part of All India Radio (AIR). The commercial aspect of the broadcasting service started in 1967 under the name *Vividh Bharti*. After a journey of all sorts of political hurdles, TV and radio became India's Public Service Broadcasters having the household name of All India Radio and *Doordarshan* (TV). This was the time when cable TV services and satellite TV channels had started making inroads.

§2. PUBLIC BROADCASTING

74. Broadcasting both audio and visual was exclusively under the government's control until 1990. The regulating acts were the Indian Telegraph act 1885, and the Indian Wireless Telegraphy Act 1933. With the advent of time, foreign content broadcasting through satellite TV marked a turning point in the history of broadcasting in the country. The consumers could now have access to them on payment of a fee. In 1993, a ruling of the High Court made license compulsory for cable operators saying that they are governed by the Telegraph Act 1885 and the Indian Wireless Telegraphy Act 1933.[61] From 1993, following the Cable Television Network (Regulation) Act 1995, cable operators were required to be accountable and registration was made mandatory. Resultantly, the newly entered technologies: (Direct to Home) DTH, HITS, and Internet Protocol Television (IPTV) were required to be licensed under the said acts. The Supreme Court ruled in *Secretary, Ministry of Information and Broadcasting v. Cricket Association of Bengal* (1995) that airways/frequencies are public property and should be regulated by a public authority.[62] The GoI was directed to have an independent and autonomous body for the purpose of mentioning that the two acts are inadequate to govern media, like radio and television. Consequently, in 2004 the government reclassified broadcasting and cable services as "telecommunication service," and the TRAI was entrusted with their regulation.

§3. PRIVATE BROADCASTING

75. Private satellite broadcasting as it uses the airwaves would be regulated like any other public property.[63] The consumers could now have access to them on payment of a fee. In 1993, a ruling of the High Court made license compulsory for cable

61. *Shiv Cable TV System v. State of Rajasthan*, AIR 1993 Raj. 1997.
62. *Secretary, Ministry of Information and Broadcasting v. Cricket Association of Bengal*, 1995 (2) SCC (161).
63. *Ibid.*, para. 24.

operators saying that they are governed by the Telegraph Act 1885 and the Indian Wireless Telegraphy Act 1933.[64] From 1993, following the Cable Television Network (Regulation) Act 1995 (CTN), cable operators were required to be accountable and registration was made mandatory. Resultantly, the newly entered technologies: (Direct to Home) DTH, HITS, and Internet Protocol Television (IPTV) were required to be licensed under the said acts. The Supreme Court ruled in *Secretary, Ministry of Information and Broadcasting v. Cricket Association of Bengal* (1995) that airways/frequencies are public property and should be regulated by a public authority.[65] The GoI was directed to have an independent and autonomous body for the purpose of mentioning that the two acts are inadequate to govern media like radio and television. Consequently, in 2004 the government reclassified broadcasting and cable services as "telecommunication service" and the TRAI was entrusted with their regulation.

§4. The Incomplete Journey of Bills

76. The Government of India made a number of attempts to regulate the only unregulated industry of its size anywhere in the world.[66] These are enumerated below:

- The first proposal was to establish an independent authority to control broadcasting services in the country. This was named Broadcasting Bill 1997. An attempt was made to establish a Broadcasting Authority of India equipped with wide powers to regulate. There was a proposal to impose limitations on foreign participation which was frowned upon by the media industry saying that it lacked harmony with the Copyright Act.
- The Communications Convergence Bill 2001—The Draft Committee also came up with recommendations to repeal the Telegraph Act 1885 and the Indian Telegraphy Act 1933 among others. The Statement on object and Reasons stated "to promote, facilitate and develop in an orderly manner the carriage and content of communications (including broadcasting, telecommunications and multimedia), for the establishment of an autonomous Commission to regulate carriage of all forms of communications, and for establishment of an Appellate Tribunal … " It was a stillborn law.
- Broadcasting Services Regulation Bill 2006—The Bill proposed to establish a Broadcasting Regulatory Authority of India (BRAI). The Bill was destined to be vested with powers ranging from licensing, registration, and quality of service to adjudicating disputes and certifying content. The Bill received strong resistance from industry stakeholders due to its content censorship provisions and the Editors Guild of India totally rejected the Bill. Ultimately, the Bill was lost amid such controversies and for a lack of political will.

64. *Shiv Cable TV System v. State of Rajasthan*, AIR 1993 Raj. 1997.
65. *Secretary, Ministry of Information and Broadcasting v. Cricket Association of Bengal*, 1995 (2) SCC (161).
66. Namita Bhandare, *Pulling the Plug*, India Today, Jul. 28, 1997.

Presently, the regulatory functions are being performed by the Ministry of Information & Broadcasting in respect of the broadcasters under several guidelines issued from time to time. On the other hand, the cable operators only need to register themselves with the local post office. The root of regulatory challenges in broadcasting in India is the lack of regulatory distinction between broadcast content and distribution.[67] The broadcasting regulating hand of the government is strong and it has "led to a steady attrition of the Indian broadcasting market, with 26 million consumers."[68]

67. Varun Ramdas, *History of TV Broadcasting Regulation in India,* Special Issue, 204, October 2020.
68. FICCI-EY (2020), *The Era of Consumer A.R.T.:* Media and Entertainment Sector Report 2019.

Chapter 7. Regulation of Online Interactive Services (Electronic Commerce, Online Platforms, B2B Platforms)

§1. Generally

77. As per data published by the Statistics in February 2022, global retail e-commerce sales have increased from USD 1,336 billion in 2014 to USD 4,938 billion in 2021. The e-commerce market is thriving in India. The Indian e-commerce market is expected to grow from USD 46.2 billion in 2020 to USD 111.40 billion by 2025 and is further projected to attain a value of USD 200 billion by 2026.[69] This was made possible by the rapid growth of the digital economy which received a boost during the COVID-19 Pandemic. There is a tremendous upswing in mobile usage all through India though in the rural area it is still not very popular due to lesser internet penetration. Further, India's social commerce Gross Merchandise Value (GMV) stood at USD 2 billion in 2020 and is expected to reach USD 20 billion by 2025, with a potentially monumental jump to USD 70 billion by 2030.[70] All this is further accelerated by the attractive benefits and luring tactics, like wider choice, heavy discounts, ease of cash on delivery (COD) and easy returns, and faster doorstep deliveries by online platforms which impress the common buyer as well as the seller. The e-commerce industry also offers the power to create an innovative, sustainable, consistent, and seamless shopping experience across all channels. All this has adversely affected the traditional market of brick and mortar. Quick Commerce is another new upcoming model which is expected to touch about USD 5.5 billion market size by 2025.

Standing Committee's Report

78. The number of registered e-commerce operators as per the Report of the Department for Promotion of Industry and Internal Trade (DPIIT) as per mandatory Tax Collected at Source (TCS) registration under the GST system is 15,638 as on March 31, 2022. However, the comfortable shopping experience has given rise to a number of allegations against the platform industry. The e-commerce market giants have overtaken the entire market and charges like anti-competitive and unfair trade practices have become frequent. Many trade organizations and unions in India have repeatedly approached the Competition Commission of India (CCI), the Ministry of Commerce and Industry, and the Enforcement Directorate to take action against this. The first step was taken by the Department Related Parliamentary Standing Committee on Commerce on the subject, "Promotion and Regulation of E-Commerce in India" for examination. The Report analyses the entire market situation with the objective of ensuring that the benefits of e-commerce are shared by all stakeholders, namely platforms, buyers, sellers, and consumers. The Committee also addressed the challenges in the e-commerce marketplace, like the digital exclusion of MSMEs, IPR infringement, loopholes in the regulatory mechanism, issues regarding logistics and courier services, GST (Goods and Services Tax) regime, and

69. Indian Brand Equity Foundation (IBEF) Report—November 2021.
70. Bain & Company Report.

exports. Another flaw is that the e-commerce companies are not registered with the parent department, namely the Department for Promotion of Industry and Internal Trade (DPIIT) which results in weaker regulation of these platforms.

§2. CHARACTERISTICS OF E-COMMERCE PLATFORMS

79. The functionality of e-commerce platforms depicts a number of features that have become their typical characteristics. These can be enumerated below:[71]

(1) Data as an Economic Resource

Every transaction done by a consumer leaves behind a trove of personal information which is recorded automatically and without the knowledge of the consumer. This reveals a great deal about the choices, preferences, inclinations, and personal uses of the consumer thereby accumulating a huge veritable goldmine for e-market places. The data so collected benefits the owners and becomes a subject of privacy issues.

(2) Network Effects

It refers to the increased utility that a user derives from a service when the number of users utilizing the service increases. It creates an effect when not only the product but the network of its users bears utility to the user. The increased popularity of a digital platform makes it difficult to have an equally competent competitor.

(3) Economies of Scale

It refers to a situation where the cost of production of goods or services decreases with the increase in the number of goods or services produced. This phenomenon though true about all markets is all the more true in the case of digital platforms. The pre-existing dominant players enjoy an advantage over new entrants in the matter of the price of service offered by such platforms. Thus in order to extend their business with the goal of reaping the benefits of economies of scale the large platforms even prefer to forego their profits.

Fragmented Regulatory Regime in E-Commerce

80. The digital platforms being innovative entities like any other phenomenon of the internet era are peculiar and special in nature and have distinct characteristics. This poses a challenge for the legal administration. So long in India, there is no e-commerce-specific legislation and resultantly there is a mosaic of laws that partake of various aspects of digital platforms. The platforms reap a rich harvest and by extending their arms day by day have made serious inroads into the physical

71. *Promotion and Regulation of E-commerce in India.* 172nd. Report. Presented before the Parliament in June 2022. Rajya Sabha Secretariat, New Delhi June 2022/Jyaishtha, 1944 (Saka).

market and ultimately their regulation and control become a challenge for the regulators. It is a little bit of many laws which is applied to these platforms in a piecemeal manner. These are: FDI Policy on E-Commerce and Foreign Exchange Management Act 1999, Consumer Protection Act 2019, Competition Act 2002, Central Goods and Services Tax (CGST) Act 2017, Finance Act 2016, Equalization Levy under Income Tax Act 1961, TDS on E-Commerce transaction, etc. Furthermore, there are more upcoming models of e-commerce, like social commerce, open-commerce, etc. Quick Commerce is another model which is coming up rapidly in India and is expected to touch about USD 5.5 billion by the year 2025.[72] All this is widely unregulated and calls for more legislation. Some of the important legislations are as follows.

FDI Policy on E-Commerce and Foreign Exchange Management Act, 1999.

81. The Foreign Direct Investment (FDI) Policy in India permits FDI-backed e-commerce entities to operate as marketplaces and prohibits them from operating as inventory-based model. Foreign Exchange Management Act 1999(FEMA) also regulates e-commerce in the country. Certain codes of conduct are enjoined upon these e-marketplaces like maintaining a level playing field by refraining from directly influencing the price of the products sold on their platform, offers like cash back to be made available to all sellers indiscriminately, and prohibiting the platforms to sell any product exclusively on their platforms. These platforms are required to maintain an auditor report by September 30, every year. Any violations of these mandates would entail an investigation by the Enforcement Directorate (ED). The FDI Policy is limited in scope because it is applicable only to foreign-funded e-commerce entities while domestic entities escape the obligations.

§3. The Consumer Protection Act 2019 & Consumer Protection (E-Commerce) (Amendment) Rules, 2021

82. The Consumer Protection Act 2019 stands for the protection of consumers in the market be it the physical market or online platforms. The Consumer Protection Rules 2020 are devised by the Ministry of Consumer Affairs, Food and Public Distribution. The Rules spell out the duties and liabilities of the sellers and the entities. The Rules were further amended and named Consumer Protection (E-Commerce) (Amendment) Rules, 2021.[73] The Rules 2021 require that the entity which is an e-commerce company registered under the Companies Act 2013 or it is a foreign company under it or it is an agency or office in some foreign country owned or controlled by a resident of India then it should appoint a nodal officer or any senior designated functionary to ensure compliance with the provisions of the Act. This rule was added with a view to further consumer welfare and induce transparency and accountability. Moreover, Information Technology (Intermediary Guidelines and Digital Media Ethics Code) Rules, 2021 (IT Rules) has adopted a

72. *Ibid.*

73. The Gazette of India—Extraordinary, Part II—s. 3 Sub s. (i). No. 262. New Delhi, Monday, May 17, 2021/VAISAKHA 27, 1943.

calibrated approach to digital regulation whereas the social media intermediaries have been classified on the basis of the number of registered users.

§4. COMPETITION ACT 2002

83. The Competition Act 2002(CA 2002) aims at preventing anti-competitive practices, protecting the interest of consumers, and ensuring freedom of trade. The Competition Commission of India while acting under section 3 of the CA 2002 is made to consider factors under section 19(3) of the Act which are insufficient to cover the digital platforms. The Act of 2002 was passed when in India e-commerce was at the initial stage and hence many provisions of the act cannot adequately be applied to digital platforms. Hence, the Competition Law Review Committee (CLRC) Report recommended widening the scope of delineation of relevant markets under sections 19(6) and 19(7) of the Competition Act to accommodate for factors that may apply to new-age digital markets. The regulation of combinations (Acquisitions /mergers) becomes quite necessary as, in digital markets acquisitions often derive value from some business innovation or acquiring data of target companies which often do not have a large asset base. The earlier provisions of the Competition Act 2002 are incapable of capturing the significance of combinations in the digital sector for competition. This gap in regulation helps the entities in escaping scrutiny under the said act, for instance, acquisitions, like Myntra by Flipkart, Taxiforsure by Ola, WhatsApp by Facebook, and Freecharge by Snapdeal.[74]

84. Pending Bill—Competition Law (Amendment) Bill 2022 was introduced in the Lower House (Lok Sabha) which aims at overhauling the extant competition regime in India and implement the recommendations of the CLRC. The Bill seeks to implement the practices followed by the U.K., Europe, and Singapore in India thereby empowering the Competition Commission of India to settle certain cases under the Act through settlement and commitment mechanisms.

85. B2B Platforms—Foreign Direct Investment Policy and the Foreign Exchange Management Act 1999 are the regulatory regime for business-to-business (b2b) platforms in India apart from a number of other legislations which guarantee consumer protection. The FDI lays down rules for the ownership by a foreign individual or entity, the nature of business, and the quantum of investment that can be made for acquiring business in the country. Hundred percent direct investment is permissible for companies engaged in cash and carry wholesale trading and b2b e-commerce businesses without the approval of the Government of India. Cash and carry wholesale trading includes sales through b2b e-commerce including the sale of goods or merchandise to retail, industrial, commercial, institutional, or other

74. Rahul Bajaj, *Towards a Framework for Scrutinizing Combinations in the Digital Market: A Roadmap for Reform,* VIDHI, Centre for Legal Policy, January 2022,https://vidhilegalpolicy.in/research/towards-a-framework-for-scrutinizing-combinations-in-the-digital-market-a-roadmap-for-reform/.

business users.[75] The conditions which apply to companies with FDI and b2b e-commerce include first, customers to whom goods can be sold include entities holding applicable tax registration, entities that hold trade licenses, persons who undertake retail trade, registered institutions, or public trust. Second, companies engaged in b2b e-commerce should maintain a day-to-day record of customers, their legal status, their registration or license numbers, and the value of the sale. Third, the sale of goods to one's own group companies should not exceed 25% of the total turnover of the company engaged in wholesale trading. Lastly, they should obtain the necessary registrations and licenses as required by local laws. Apart from this the Consumer Protection Act 2019 & Consumer Protection (E-Commerce) (Amendment) Rules, 2021 also apply to b2b e-commerce entities.

75. Isha Mohanty & Two Others, *Digital Business Laws Regulations India 2022*.ICLG.com, https://iclg.com/practice-areas/digital-business-laws-and-regulations/india.

Chapter 8. Regulation of Cryptography and Dual-Use Goods

§1. General Statement

86. Cryptography is an ancient art, but in the digital context, it has undergone a revolution to match the internet environment. The computer revolution even revolutionized the cryptographic means, and the most genius quality of computers to calculate monstrous numbers with lightning speed and comfort gives a new definition to the art of cryptography.[76] Classical cryptography mainly resting on language and words is supplanted by computers using cipher design and cryptanalysis and is characterized by their operation on binary bit sequences. The 1970s saw an increase in the use of computers in the West, and encryption of computer data to give secrecy and confidentiality to it progressed further but together with it the means and methods to challenge cryptography grew with the defaulters and the vandals. Thus, the mathematical approach, the computer processing power, and the cryptographic algorithm led to countering the problem of code breaking in an effective manner. Thus, the U.S.'s Data Encryption Standard (DES) designed by the International Business Machines; the key agreement algorithm published by Whitfield Diffie and Martin Hellman, and the Rivest, Shamir & Adelman (RSA) algorithm published in Martin Gardner's Scientific American column unleashed an era of modern cryptography.[77]

87. Need to Regulate: The proliferation of computers and the widening horizons of telecommunication systems expanded the use of high-quality cryptography. The users, the criminals, and the law enforcers were equally attracted by it, and concepts, like privacy, civil rights, and authentication problems raised their heads. Although the encoded message promised reliability of the data yet after being transmitted it "cannot itself provide conclusive evidence that it did originate from the alleged sender."[78] Consequently, to make cryptography more reliable and less vulnerable there originated the idea of "Trusted Third Parties" (TTP). This system soon became popular with governments as it allowed the State to play a role in online dealings but to regulate them. In the U.S., the Escrowed Encryption Standard (EES) also known as "clipper chip" was approved though it was criticized by the liberals. The security of the cryptographic approach became a crucial problem both with the parties and the State. The aim of the crypto analysis is to find some weakness or insecurity in a cryptographic scheme. State efforts to regulate cryptography were speeded up and in March 1997, the Council of the OECD adopted guidelines for Cryptography Policy including directions to enable countries to include it in their national laws. These are:

76. Fatima Talat, *Chapter 9: Electronic Signatures and Crime*; *Cyber Crimes*, 2021.
77. *Ibid.*
78. Ian Lloyd, *Chapter 8: Legal Barriers to Electronic Contracts: Formal Requirements and Digital Signatures* in Lilian Edwards & Charlotte Waelde (eds.), *Law and the Internet: Regulating Cyberspace* (Hart Publishing, Oxford 1997) 144.

- Cryptography methods must be such that they inculcate trust and confidence in the prolific use of modern communication systems.
- Cryptographic methods must give the "right to choose" to countries to meet suitability to their national laws.
- Cryptographic methods must equally suit the needs of governments, businesses, and individuals.
- There must be technical criteria to suit national and international needs.
- The right to privacy must be respected.
- Parties must have a well-defined policy regarding lawful access to plaintext or cryptographic keys of encrypted data.
- Organizations and individuals must have fixed liabilities under the law. There must be coordination among governments to have a unified policy on cryptography.

Not only from the viewpoint of national security but also from the viewpoint of criminal and law enforcer cryptography cannot be left unregulated. Regulation started in the U.K. in 1999. In France, the use of cryptography was restricted. In countries like Belarus, Kazakhstan, Mongolia, Pakistan, Russia, Singapore, Tunisia, and Vietnam restrictions were imposed.

88. Case of India: In India, there are few companies involved in the development of cryptography. For quite a long time cryptography remained a defense subject, and it was in 1995 that India introduced a list of items that required licensing before export. Encryption software for telemetry systems specifically was on the list and it did not relate to encryption in general.[79] In 1997, the Council of OECD issued guidelines for Cryptography Policy urging nations to adopt methods to inculcate trust and confidence in online communication systems. India was a signatory to the United Nations Commission on International Trade Law (UNCITRAL) which adopted the Model Law on Electronic Commerce in 1996. Thus, in conformity with the said Model Law 2001, India came up with its first cyber—legislation, namely the Information Technology Act 2000 (21 of 2000) which recognized digital signatures based on asymmetric cryptosystems bringing them at par with manual signatures. For regulating cryptography India adopted the PKI system.[80]

---

79. "Cryptography and Liberty 1999; an International survey of Encryption Policy," at, http://www.gilc.org/crypto-survey-99.html.
80. The PKI-Infrastructure There arose a need to keep an intermediary which could act as an agency between contracting parties so as to avoid doubts regarding the authenticity of electronic signatures. The public-key cryptography is highly mathematical hence, "all users must have confidence in the skill, knowledge and security arrangements of the parties issuing the public and private keys." If the users themselves issue such public and private key there may be lack of trust in the certifiers of the public keys." (Chapter 1: Introduction to the Model Law: Purpose and Origin of the Model Law: Purpose in UNCITRAL *Model Law on Electronic Signatures with Guide to Enactment* 2001, 25. Thus though the certification of the public key could be given by involvement of third party who could act as a reliable mediator "to associate an identified signatory or the signatory's name with a specific public key" became a practical and legal necessity. In the Model Law 2001 the terms "Certifying Authority," "Certification Authority" and "supplier of certification services" are used for such third party.

89. PKI Scenario in India—The IT (Amendment) Act 2008 has now substituted the term "electronic signature" for the term "digital signature." The Act provides for the Controller of Certifying Authorities (CCA) who is entrusted with the responsibility of regulating the working of certification authorities who in turn are given the responsibility to issue the Digital Signature Certificates (DSCs) for electronic authentication of users. The CCA certifies the public keys of Certifying Authorities using its own private key, which enables users in cyberspace to verify that a given certificate is issued by a licensed Certifying Authority. For this, it operates the Root Certifying Authority of India (RCAI). The CCA by virtue of section 20 of the IT Act 2000 maintained repositories that have now been deleted under the Amendment Act of 2008.[81] The RCAI is operated using the SmartTrust software. The Certification Practice statement of the RCAI guides the CCA personnel to perform Root Certifying Authority functions. The Term "root" signifies the entire Certifying Authority matrix including the software and its operations. The National Root Certifying Authority uses a 2048-bit RSA key pair, and the Certifying Authority entity uses a 1024-bit RSA key pair.[82]

90. Regulatory Provisions—The main regulatory provisions are limited and the earlier law[83] has been replaced by a new one. Under the new section 69 of the IT (Amendment) Act 2008 violation of the directions to intercept, monitor, or decrypt information is made a punishable offense with imprisonment of up to seven years with fine.

I. Regulation of Dual Use Goods

91. India's recent non-proliferation policies have impacted companies that trade in goods and technologies with potential applications to weapons of mass destruction (WMD), missiles, and conventional arms collectively called "strategic items." To facilitate greater access to advanced technology products (ATP), India is currently seeking membership in the four main multilateral export control regimes (MECRs)): the Nuclear Suppliers Groups (NSG), Australia Group (AG), Missile Technology Control Regime (MTCR), and Wassenaar Arrangement (WA). Thus, India is following the guidelines and practices of these regimes.

92. Dual-use goods and technologies are those items, goods, software, or technology which are beneficial both for defense and civilians. It is the prerogative of

81. Formerly under the IT act 2000, the Controller had the job maintaining a repository of all the Certifying Authorities in the country. The National repository of Digital Certificates (NRDC) maintained it under s. 20.
82. Sandeep Oberoi, *India PKI Forum,* Presentation made at PKI Consortium Seminar, Nov. 8, 2007.
83. Section 69—IT Act 2000 (21 of 2000). *Directions of Controller to subscriber to extend facilities to decrypt information*-Such directions could be issued on the grounds of: (1) interest of the sovereignty and integrity of India; (2) the security of the state; (3) for friendly relations with foreign states; (4) public order or for (5) preventing incitement to the commission of any cognizable offense. Such subscriber or in charge of the computer is kept under obligation to provide technical assistance to decrypt the information failing which a punishment of imprisonment up to seven years is provided.

the state to control the goods and investments which are used by the defense department from being misused by the general public. This is not only in the interest of the defense department but also in the interest of the country. The internet, infrared, and many other technologies exist today because of the increasing technology dependence in war. A greater part of these restrictions takes the form of "end user" licenses and laws that prevent export to certain "end users" or nations. The Foreign Trade Development and Regulation Act No. 22 of 1992 (FTDR) (amended 2010)[84] is the principal legal document for India's strategic control system which empowers the GoI to "make provisions for prohibiting, restricting, or otherwise regulating" all or specified classes of exports or imports upon public notification in the Official Gazette. It also authorizes the GoI to formulate and amend India's foreign trade policy which the GoI issues in five-year increments and updates annually. In India, the export and import of dual-use items are regulated by the Directorate General of Foreign Trade (DGFT) situated within the Department of Commerce and Industry (DCI). The DGFT regularly issues the "Exim Policy" which regulates and governs the terms and conditions of the export and import of such dual-use items. Such dual-use items are classified as Special Chemicals, Organisms, Materials, Equipment and Technologies (SCOMET). The DGFT is empowered to license the export and import of items on the India Tariff Classification (Harmonized System (HS)) or the ITC (HS) list.

93. The Exim Policy: As per the present policy, it is mandatory for all entities, whether public or private, to obtain permission from the DGFT before entering into any arrangement regarding the export or import of any SCOMET items when such arrangements involve an obligation to facilitate or undertake site visits, on-site verification, or access to records/documents of the foreign states, or foreign third parties, The DGFT before granting such permission must take into consideration the bilateral or multilateral agreements to which India is also a party. The regulation of the export or import of such dual-use items depends on the prohibition or permission of such items under a license. Grant of a license depends on many factors like the end use of the item. The export or import of such items must be in conformity with Indian Laws but export from a country outside India also requires compliance with the laws of that country. Thus, where such items are not allowed under the laws of a foreign country then it will be considered an offense in India. The GoI has the power to make rules to prohibit the export of certain goods, technologies, and equipment and prohibit unlawful activities in respect of Weapons of Mass Destruction (WMD) delivery systems under the Prohibition of Unlawful Activities Act 2005.

II. The List of Dual-Use Items and Technology

94. The Government of India has made changes to its national export lists that could have impacted companies that trade in dual-use and munitions goods and technologies from India. Thus, India follows the path set by other countries in this

84. *The Foreign Trade Development and Regulation Act No. 22 of 1992 (FTDR)*,Ch. II, s. 3(2) available at Director General of Foreign Trade homepage, http://dgft.delchi.nic.in/.

matter.[85] The WMD Act authorizes the GoI to regulate the export, re-transfer, re-export, transit, and transshipment of any items related to the development, production, handling, operation, maintenance, storage, or dissemination of a WMD or missile delivery device. The DGFT, as empowered,[86] announces the Indian Trade Classification (Harmonized System) of Export and Import Items 2012.[87] The list harmonizes with both HS 2012 of the World Customs Organization and the Tariff Schedule of Customs. The ITC (HS) 2012 contains "Schedule 1 Import Policy" and "Schedule 2 Export Policy."

95. Imports—New ITC (HS) Import Schedule 1. Import Policy 2012. The import licensing system is substantially less developed than its controls on exports items found on ITC (HS); Schedule I:

- Section I—Live Animals and Animal Products.
- Section II—Vegetable Products.
- Section III—Animals or Vegetable Fats and Oils and their Cleavage Products. Prepared Edible Fats: Animal or Vegetable Waxes.
- Section IV—Prepared foodstuffs: Beverages, Spirits, and Vinegar. Tobacco, Manufactured Tobacco and Substitutes.
- Section V—Mineral Products.
- Section VI—Products of the Chemical and Allied Industries.
- Section VII—Plastics and Articles thereof; Rubber and Articles thereof.
- Section VIII—Raw Hides and Skins, Leather, Fur Skins and Articles thereof; Saddlery and Harness; Travel Goods, and Handbags and Similar Containers. Articles of Animal Guts (other than Silkworm Guts).
- Section IX—Wood and Articles of Wood, Wood Charcoal Cork, and Articles of Cork; Manufacturers of Straw of Esparto or other Plaiting Materials, Basket ware and Wicker ware.
- Section X—Pulp of Wood or of other Fibrous Cellulosic Material; Waste or Scrap of Paper or Paperboard; Paper and Paperboard and Articles thereof.
- Section XI—Textile and Textile Articles.
- Section XII—Footwear, Headgear, Umbrellas, Sun umbrellas, Walking Sticks, Seat-Sticks, Whips, Riding-Crops and Parts thereof; Prepared feathers and Articles made thereof; Artificial Flowers; Articles of Human Hair.
- Section XIII—Articles of Stone, Plaster, Cement, Asbestos, Mica or Similar Materials; Ceramic Products; Glass and Glassware.

---

85. January 2012—Canada's Foreign Affairs International Trade's Export Controls Division (ECD) announced a number of changes in the Canadian Export Control List which included dual-use items; in February 2012 at the 6th European Forum on Export Controls there was much discussion on Art. 22 of the European Control Regulations which focuses on dual-use goods and the US Bureau of Industry and Security (BIS) also implemented changes to the Export Administration Regulations which focuses in the dual-use goods.
86. In exercise of powers conferred by s. 5 of the Foreign Trade (Development & Regulation) Act 1992 (22 of 1992) read with para. 2.1 of the Foreign Trade Policy of the Government of India.
87. Notification No. 111/RE (2010) /2009–2014 dated Apr. 18, 2012. File No. 01/89/180/66/AM-12/ PC.2A.: *Government of India, Ministry of Commerce and Industry, New Delhi.*

- Section XIV—Natural or Colored Pearls, Precious or Semi-Precious Stones, Precious Metals, Metals Clad with Precious Metal and articles thereof; Imitation Jewelry Coin.
- Section XV—Base Metals and Articles of Base Metals.
- Section XVI—Machinery and Mechanical Appliances; Electrical Equipment; Parts thereof; Sound Recorders and Reproducers, Television Image and Sound Recorders and Reproducers, and Parts and Accessories of such Articles.
- Section XVII—Vehicles, Aircraft, Vessels, and Associated Transport Equipment.
- Section XVIII—Optical, Photographic, Cinematographic, Measuring, Checking, Precision, Medical or Surgical Instruments and Apparatus; Clocks and Watches; Musical instruments; Parts and accessories thereof.
- Section XIX—Arms and Ammunitions; Parts and Accessories thereof.
- Section XX—Miscellaneous Manufacturers.
- Section XXI—Works of Art, Collectors' Pieces and Antiques.

96. Exports: Export of dual-use items and technology under India's Foreign Trade Policy is regulated. The FTDR defines an export as "taking out of India any goods, technologies or services by land, sea or air." Goods and technologies and services subject to export licensing requirements are listed in India's national export product control list known as the Special Chemicals, Organisms, Materials Equipment and Technologies (SCOMET) list. The list is periodically amended by the GoI.[88] The SCOMET list is located in Appendix 3 of Schedule 2 of the ITC (HS) divided into eight distinct categories (Categories 0–7). The DGFT is the primary licensing agency for most items on the SCOMET list (Categories 1—7)[89] while the DAE issues licenses for all the nuclear and nuclear dual-use commodities found in SCOMET Category 0.[90] These categories are as follows:

- Category 0—Nuclear materials, nuclear-related other materials, equipment, and technology.
- Category 1—Toxic chemical agents and other agents.
- Category 2—Microorganisms, toxins.
- Category 3—Materials, Materials Processing Equipment, and related technologies.
- Category 4—Nuclear-related other equipment, assemblies and components; test and production equipment; and related technology not controlled under Category-0.
- Category 5—Aerospace systems, equipment including production and test equipment, related technology, and specially designed components and accessories thereof.
- Category 6—(Reserved).

88. FTDR, s. 5 and Foreign Trade Policy (2009–2014) para. 2.1.
89. The export of items in Category 2 of the SCOMET list (microorganisms, toxins, pathogens, etc.) may also be controlled by other applicable guidelines. Foreign Trade Handbook of Procedures. Vol. 1 (2010–2011 supplement), para. 2.48, Note 3.
90. India's System of Controls over Exports of Strategic Goods and Technologies," Ministry of External Affairs website.

- Category 7—Electronics, computers, and information technology including information security. Each category contains an exhaustive listing of items covered under that category. Special conditions applicable to items under different categories are mentioned under each category.

III. Transfer of Dual-Use Goods from the EU

97. Common Rules for Export—The Regulation lays down the rules that the export of items from the European Union (EU) to non-EU countries are free from non-quantitative restrictions.[91] The Regulation lays down important protective measures and procedures for unusual developments in the market. Consultation with other EU countries within an Advisory Committee chaired by a member of the Commission and having other representatives from the EU countries must take place, where the trends and export conditions are discussed and the countries are asked to send the statistical data for assessing the economic and commercial conditions. The Commission may also ask the countries to exercise surveillance over the products according to their national legislations.

98. Protective Measures—The EU in its own interest may require the adoption of appropriate measures to prevent or control a critical situation as follows:

- The Commission may also make the export of a product subject to export authorization as per rules set by the Commission.
- These protective measures may be confined to exports to specific countries or exports from certain regions of the EU.
- The Commission may also implement certain measures for immediate action.
- There may also be a consultation regarding the effects of these measures and the necessity for their continuation or revocation in certain areas.
- The Regulation does not prevent the EU countries from applying quantitative restrictions on exports on the ground of public morality, the welfare of people at large, animal welfare, in the interest of historical or things of artistic value, commercial importance, etc.

IV. Intracommunity Transfers

99. The Weapons of Mass Destruction and their delivery systems (Prohibition of Unlawful Activities) Act (No. 21 of 2005). WMD Act authorizes the GoI to regulate the export, re-transfer, re-export, transit, and transhipment of any items related to the development, production, handling, operation, maintenance, storage, or dissemination of a WMD or missile delivery device. It also established a catch-all control that restricts exports of non-listed items destined for a WMD end use and it provided a rudimentary legal basis to regulate technology transfers.

---

91. Council Regulation (EC) No. 1061/2009 of Oct. 19, 2009 establishing common rules for exports.

100. Technology Transfer: The DGFT is authorized to license and regulate electronic transmissions of strategic technologies designated on the SCOMET list. The WMD Act and the FTDR (as amended) define "technology" as "any information (including information embodied in software), other than information in the public domain, that is capable of being used in the development, production, or use of any goods or software; or the development of, or the carrying out of an industrial or commercial activity, or the provision of a service of any kind."[92]

101. Transfer of Sensitive Technologies: Such technologies listed or restricted under India's catch-all provision are subject to control in India under the following circumstances:

- A person located within India seeks to transfer restricted technologies to a person or place outside India.[93]
- An Indian located outside India wishes to transfer restricted technologies to a person who too is outside India.[94]
- An item is exhibited, sold, supplied, or transferred to a foreign entity or foreigner who is resident, operating, visiting, studying, or conducting research or business within Indian territory, airspace, or an Exclusive Economic Zone (EEZ).[95]

"Catch-All" Control: Restrictions are imposed on trade in non-listed items that appear to be for a WMD-relevant end use by the WMD Act and FTDR. Thus, if a trader "knows" that the item is "intended to be used in the design or manufacture of a biological weapon, chemical weapon, nuclear weapon, other nuclear explosive devices, or in their delivery systems"[96] but it does not appear on the national control list, even then he will have to apply for the export license from the DGFT. The Indian catch-all control extends to individuals or entities facilitating the execution of a transaction (brokers and intermediaries) if they are aware that the transaction in question is related to a prohibited activity.[97]

End User Controls: India prohibits transfers to non-state actors or terrorists of any material, equipment, or technology that could contribute to the development of a WMD. India abides by UN Security Council (UNSC) Resolutions and has enacted export prohibitions against several sanctioned countries, entities, and terrorists. India prohibits the "direct and indirect" import or export of designated arms and WMD-related goods and technologies to or from Iran, North Korea, and Iraq.

India also maintains an Exporter Black List known as the Denied Entities List (DEL), which consists of parties who are previously refused or denied an export license; though the DEL is not in the public domain. GoI denies export licenses not

92. When technology is described wholly or partly by reference to the uses to which it (or the goods to which it relates) may be put, it shall include services which are provided or used, or which are capable of being used, in the development, production or use of such technology or goods. FTDR Amendment Act 2010, s. 2(m). Also *see*, WMD Act, s. 4(I).
93. WMD Act, s. 13(3)(a).
94. WMD Act, s. 13(3)(b).
95. WMD Act, s. 13(4).
96. WMD Act, s. 11 and FTDR Amendment Act 2010, Art. 14C.
97. WMD Act, ss. 11 and 12, FTDR Amendment Act 2010, Art. 14C.

only to the listed entities on the DEL but also to anyone who controls such entities on the DEL (are reportedly those who also appear on the list maintained by the U.S. Government (USG), the UN, and other countries), and also entities who are listed on Indian inputs. If a company submits an inquiry to DGFT concerning a particular end user, DGFT will provide a "yes" or "no" answer regarding the entity's status on the DEL. The exporters are bound to procure an End User Certificate (EUC) and assurances that the recipient will not re-export or re-transfer the item to anyone other than the end user of record.[98] For some items in Category 0 of the SCOMET list, the DAE may also require formal assurances from the recipient state to certify that adequate physical protection and International Atomic Energy Agency (IAEA) safeguards will mitigate the risk of diversion and ensure that the items will not be used in a nuclear explosive device.

98. *Chapter 2: Handbook of Procedures* (Vol. 1). Also available on the Government of India website, http://dgftcnic.in/exim/2000/procedures/ftphbconnects0910.pdf.

Part II. Online Public Services

Chapter 1. E-government Legal Framework

§1. Digital India

102. Digital India (DI) is a flagship program of the Government of India with a vision to transform India into a digitally empowered society and knowledge economy. The vision of Digital India has three objectives: a digital infrastructure for maximum benefit of citizens, secondly governmental services on demand, and lastly digital empowerment of citizens. The most important initiative taken under it is the Unified Payments interface (UPI) which was launched in 2016 by the National Payments Corporation of India. In July 2022, UPI managed 6.28 billion transactions which are the highest ever since its launch. All this is contributing toward "financial inclusivity"[99] in the country. According to the latest Report of the Mobile Association of India, due to increasing mobile penetration and inexpensive data, the digital boom has reached even the remotest part of rural India so much so that there are 692 million internet users in India. The latest mission of the government is the Open Network for Digital Commerce (ONDC) which aims at promoting open networks for the exchange of goods and services. Digital India also focuses on the manufacturing of electronics in the country so much so that from just two units of mobile phone manufacturing in the country in 2014 it has touched two hundred in 2022.

Nine Pillars of Digital India

103. To achieve the goal of Digital India there are Nine Pillars on which the edifice of Digital India stands. These are:

Pillar 1

> Broadband Highways—It is the first pillar which denotes "Broadband highways on the lines of Road highways." The program was launched by the Government of India on July 1, 2015. It visualizes connectivity of the internet to be taken to every district, city, and village of the country and providing Wi-Fi facility to all. The Nationwide Optical Fiber Networking Project

99. Anand Kumr Bajaj, MD, CEO. Nachiket Kelkar: *Digital India Has Nudged Indians into Adopting New Technology,* Aug. 21, 2022, https://www.theweek.in/theweek/specials/2022/08/13/digital-india-has-nudged-indians-into-adopting-new-technology.html.

(NOFN) is used to meet the target of Broadband Highway. Thus, the Broadband aims to fast track the growth of digital communications infrastructure and to bridge the digital divide under the Strategy 2021 which includes the following:

- Broadband facilities will be taken up to establish BPO centers to the North-Eastern and other inaccessible parts of the country.
- The Electronics Development Fund (EDF) aims at the creation of resource bridges of IP in the country.
- The national center for Flexible Electronics will be created to encourage research and innovation.
- The Center of Excellence for Internet of Things (IoT) is a joint initiative of the Department of Electronics and Information Technology (DeitY), India Education& Research Network (ERNET), and NASSOKEM for systematic implementation of Broadband Highway facilities.

Pillar 2

Universal Access to Mobile connectivity—This aims at outreaching even the backward and inaccessible areas of the country and bringing people within mobile connectivity.

Pillar 3

Public Internet Access Program—It has two facets: Common Service Centers and post offices. There is a plan to increase the CSCs and make them multifunctional. About 150 post offices are being turned into multi-service centers.

Pillar 4

E-Governance Reforming through Technology—The aim is to overhaul and reengineer all government offices on IT lines making government schemes and services fast, efficient, and sure delivery to the people at large. This will include electronic databases, workflow computerization, and making ways for Pubic Grievance Redressal platforms.

Pillar 5

E-Kranti—The term "*Kranti*" means revolution and hence the term *E-Kranti* aims at bringing a revolution in all the spheres of public life. There are already a number of e-Government Mission Mode projects while there is the addition of implementing technology in the fields of education, health, planning, farming, financial security, financial inclusivity, justice, and cyber security.

Pillar 6

Target NETZERO imports: Electronics Manufacturing—This aims at making India electronically independent by producing indigenous electronic products, like set-top boxes, VSATs, mobiles, consumer and medical electronics, smart energy meters, smart cards, micro ATMs, incubators, clusters, etc.

Pillar 7

IT for Jobs—This entails training the youth and preparing them for taking up jobs in the IT sector and in IT-enabled services (ITES)

Pillar 8

Early Harvest Programs—This entails those projects which will be implemented within a short time. These include: IT platforms for messages, government greetings to be E-Greetings, biometric attendance, Wi-Fi in all universities, secure e-mail within government, standardize government e-mail design, public Wi-Fi hotspots, school books to be e-books, SMS-based weather information, disaster alerts, and national portal for lost and found children.[100]

Pillar 9

Information for All—As we live in the information age it is very necessary that the more people are well informed the better will be their progress toward achieving the goal of Digital India. Communication with the government, easy access to all its schemes and reports, and access to a huge amount of informative data will keep them abreast of the activities of the government.

§2. The Digital Identity

104. November 8, 2016, can be called the threshold moment in the digital transformation of the country when 86% of the country's currency notes were removed from circulation. Demonetization and later Goods and Services Tax (GST) can be termed as formidable steps toward building a digital infrastructure. This is slowly and gradually leading India to a digital-first economy.[101] The "India Stack" lies at the bottom of the digital infrastructure comprising layers of multiple services and at

100. Digital India, https://ambermishra99.wixsite.com/digiindia/early-harvest-programme.
101. Arvind Gupta &Philip. E. Auerswald, *How India Is Moving Towards a Digital-First Economy*, Harvard Business Review, Nov. 8, 2017.

the bottom of "India Stack" lies the digital identity of every resident Indian, the UI or unique identification number commonly known as *Aadhar*. *Aadhar* meaning "basis" denotes the digital identity of every Indian and is proven to have the fastest one billion users. It is a biometric authenticated 12-digit number launched in 2009. *Aadhar* accelerated and expanded the banking system and was quite helpful in making the *Pradhan Mantri Jan Dhan Yojana* (PMJDY). On the very first day that the scheme was launched, the government created 300 million no-frills bank accounts with great incentives for the common man to get attracted toward the banking system. To this bank account opening through digital identity (*Aadhar*) another layer was added to the service stack, namely mobile payments. This ultimately led to a trinity known as "JAM" or *Jan Dhan, Aadhar,* and Mobile Numbers (JAM). Thus the "India Stack" could now have four layers: an identity layer, a documents layer, a payments layer, and a transactions layer.[102]

Previously the government grants had a long and tedious journey to reach the beneficiary sitting at the corner of a paddy field in a village. Often the grant or scheme to the rural have-nots went stray or even died out, it being a still less literate and socially handicapped section of the country. But now the JAM project and the India Stack have changed the world for the poor. The mobile-linked bank account number gives speed and security to governmental schemes. But India Stack is a technical scheme not only for dispensing government services but it can also be seen as a "new social infrastructure" giving traditional India strength to change and embrace the revolution of digitization.

The National Government Service Portal (https://services.india.gov.in) offers a good number of services covering the areas of education, health, tax payment, agriculture, public grievances, jobs, justice, law and grievances, travel and tourism, businesses, births, deaths, marriages and child care, and pensions and other benefits. Moreover, the mobile app *UMANG* is a single platform to access a number of government services. Though the poor internet penetration especially in the remote rural areas pulls back the spirit to resort to online services but government's effort to reduce digital divide and user interface will take the country toward a better digital tomorrow.

102. *Ibid.*

Chapter 2. Legal Framework for E-Health

§1. General Statement

105. As per the World Health Organization (WHO) e-health is the use of ICTs for health.[103] Though India is progressing fast to achieve the cherished goal of Digital India yet due to the lack of certain resources, the remote areas of the country still look up for better facilities whether it be transportation, education, or even health. Health is the most neglected aspect of rural India though manual and physical Primary Health Centres (PHC) and clinics are constantly on the rise to cope with this drawback. Resultantly, the Ministry of Health and Family Welfare has taken a number of e-Government initiatives in this regard. The Ministry has a separate division that strives to deliver better health services in matters of access, quality, affordability, lowering disease burden, and efficient monitoring of health entitlements to citizens.[104] The advantages of e-Health are several which can be enumerated as follows:

§2. Advantages

106.

- It is cost-efficient.
- The quality of health care services is improved.
- The consumers can easily access the knowledge based medicines and personal electronic records. E-Health opens a new method for patient-centered medicines and enables evidence-based patient choice.
- As all the knowledgeable data is available on the net hence patient-doctor trusted partnership is established.
- Both the physicians and patients are benefitted from the medical education, health education, and preventive information available online.
- There is information exchange in a standardized way between health care establishments.
- E-Health provides Health care and medical advice globally.

Thus not only in other facets of life the internet has entered the most important facet, namely health and life thereby not only making it cheap but also making it easily available. This is a golden chance for the citizens living in the remotest and most disconnected areas, like deserts, hilly areas, and villages. However, the fruits of this great change will yield slow results as the country still grapples with low internet connectivity, especially in those areas where it is required the most.

103. https://www.who.int/ehealth/about/en/.
104. E-Health Laws and Regulations—Samisti Legal—Advocates & Legal Advisers-Apr. 11, 2020, https://samistilegal.in/e-health-laws-and-regulations/.

§3. HEALTH CARE OUTLINE IN INDIA

107. The country still has multiple approaches to health and treatment comprising allopathic, *ayurvedic*, homeopathic, and *Unani* systems. The country being predominantly traditional with religion as its main plank, a portion of the population still believes in sole treatment by *ayurvedic* and non-scientific methods. Allopathy comes as a last resort for some though modern medicine covers the major part of medical aid. The other branches of medicine being ancient however are not regarded outdated, and hence in 2014 the Government of India established a new Ministry named *Ayush* thereby encouraging and further developing sciences, like *Ayurveda, Yoga* and Naturopathy, *Unani, Siddha,* and Homeopathy (*Ayush*).

The services in the medical field are catered by both public and private institutions, general physicians, and specialists. Healthcare services can be classified into primary, secondary, tertiary, and quaternary. Rural India is mainly having PHCs which are good enough only for initial illness, and they lack first aid facilities too. They ultimately become the referral centers for more qualified aid available in secondary, tertiary, and quaternary levels of special care. With this fragmented background, e-Health becomes a challenge though not an impossibility.

§4. BASIC STRUCTURE REQUIRED FOR E-HEALTH ACHIEVEMENT

108. The entire e-Health framework presupposes a structure on which it can work. It is Electronic Medical Record, Electronic Health Record, and Personal Health Record. The following chart[105] will explain the introduction of each:

Electronic Medical Records (EMR)	*Electronic Health Records (EHR)*	*Personal Health Records (PHR)*
Clinical data by a single physician	It is an e-Data of health spreading over a number of institutions	E-Data of health records by multiple institutions accessible by patients
Linear Records Within one institute	Longitudinal Records to follow patients across institutes	Longitudinal Records to follow patients across institutes and beyond
Controlled by a single physician. Does not require interoperability standards.	Followed by a number of physicians. Requires interoperability standards.	Controlled by patients Requires interoperability standards

Source: Chart Showing various Types of Electronic Records.[106]

105. Courtesy: Harleen Kaur—Electronic Health records in India—Legal framework and Regulatory Issues—Email id: harleen2707@gmail.com.
106. *Ibid.*, p. 6.

109. India works toward evolving an EHR framework that will ensure medical administrative ease, achievement of economical expenses, and collection of records of people from birth to death and will be helpful in the collection of epidemiological data. There is a difficulty in collecting data as the medical service scattered over the country is governed by the Government of India, by the various states, and by private practitioners. The Health Management Information System (HMIS) is a database that has taken up the mammoth task of streamlining data from across the country. Data is collected through surveys and censuses carried out by the Government of India which includes National Sample Survey Organization (NSSO) reports, etc. However, the healthcare data in the private sector is unregulated and unorganized, and hence the entire picture still remains incomplete. Amidst all this, the Government has set standards for her in India.

§5. EHR Scene in India

110. An EHR is the real-time digital version of patient records. It is a comprehensive report of an individual's health. "An Electronic Health Record (EHR) is defined as a collection of various medical records that get generated during any clinical encounter or events (Vikaspedia 2019)." The Ministry of Health and Family Welfare for the first time came out with the EGR standards in 2013. The recommendations were made by the Committee meant for the purpose and it contained the creation of a uniform system for EHRs and maintenance by healthcare providers. Benefits of her include; easy accessibility of a patient's health records, requires less time for storage, has a lesser chance of loss, the quality of patient records is cost-effective, possible to track a patient's clinical record, and provides a summary report of the various clinical encounters in a patient's life, helps to improve quality of diagnosis, it is easily transferable through all the health facilities, can be easily updated, facilitates improved health care decisions, and the records can be used for research purposes.[107]

§6. The Initiatives and Policies by the Government of India

111. Policymakers have recently focussed on unleashing the e-Health benefits to the common man in the country. India is faced with communicable and non-communicable diseases.[108] The Government of India has come up with a number of health benefit schemes, like *Rashtriya Swasthya Bima Yojana* (RSBY) and the *Pradahan Mantri Jan Aarogya Yojana* (PMJAY) among others. The schemes include free medical aid, tests, and hospitalization for an identified lot of the population based on their income levels, etc. The data on digital health care records is not well-defined in the country. The main reason is the lack of interoperability as

107. Manisha Wadhwa, *Electronic Health Records in India*—ITC India Working Paper Mar. 25, 2020.
108. India: Health of the Nation's states, The State level Disease Burden Initiative—Department of Health Research. Ministry of Health and Family Welfare, Government of India.

the data remains within the institutions.[109] Government hospitals are being brought under the digital health network through e-Hospital which is a Hospital Management Information System (HMIS) by the government. This step will help secure health records from all over the country and help improve public health and research.

The country is yet to see a robust legal framework for e-Health but there are a number of steps taken by the government in the form of Policies that aim at creating an environment of e-Health in the country. These are enumerated below:

- National e-Health Authority of India (NeHA) was proposed to be set up in 2015, the aim of which is to establish an e-Health ecosystem in the country. Other aim includes "laying down data management, privacy and security policies, guidelines, and health records of patients in accordance with statutory provisions."
- The Ministry of Health and Family Welfare has come up with the draft (2018) of an Act called the Digital Information Security in Health Act (DISHA) as a statutory body for the promotion and adoption of e-Health standards. It mainly aims to establish e-Health Authorities "to regulate processes related to collection, storing, transmission and use of digital health data; and to ensure reliability, data privacy, confidentiality and security of digital health data and such other matters related and incidental thereto." The draft was submitted before the Ministry of Electronics and Information Technology (Meity) for its opinion and comments. Meity was in the process of enacting "Data Protection Framework on Digital Information Privacy, Security& Confidentiality" Act, with the objective of providing a framework for the Ministry to utilize patient data in programs in a secure manner and it will be applicable to all domains including health. Thus, it is planned that the DISHA will be subsumed into the Data Protection Act to avoid any duplicity of provisions.[110]

National Digital Health Blue Print

112. Another Policy Document, namely National Digital Health Blue Print was open for public comments in 2019. The final blueprint proposes a federated architecture with building blocks defined, Unique Health Identifier (UHID), registries for patients, Privacy and Consent management, National Portability, EHR Standards, and provisioning of health services across multiple access channels. All this will be a great contributor to building a futuristic health system in the country.

National Digital Health Mission (NDHM)

113. National Digital Health Mission (2020) seeks to "provide the necessary support for integration of digital health infrastructure in the country" The NDHM has been launched on a pilot basis in six Union Territories including—Chandigarh,

109. *Reimagining Health Data Exchange: An application programming interface Enabled Roadmap for India* (2018).

110. Press Information Bureau—Ministry of Health and Family Welfare—Government of India. Jul. 16, 2019, https://pib.gov.in/Pressreleaseshare.aspx?PRID=1578929.

Ladakh, Dadra & Nagar Haveli and Daman & Diu, Puducherry, Andaman & Nicobar Islands, and Lakshadweep. The process of health services in these areas has already gained momentum. In pursuance of the NDHM, the Ministry of Health and Family Welfare released the draft Health Data Management Policy which elaborates upon the rights of data principals, data fiduciaries, and the voluntary nature of Health ID, etc.

National Health Stack

114. The NDHM presupposes the National Health Stack (NHS) to be the building block on which the digital edifice will be erected and on which the NDHM will work. It is a visionary digital framework proposed by the National Institution for Transforming India (NITI Commission) to create digital health records for all citizens by 2022. It has the potential of putting under one document the health records of 1.3 billion citizens of India, hopefully, the largest in the world, and will bring India on the digital health care map of the world digitizing the entire health information of the country and facilitating medical research. The NDHM aims to provide every citizen with a 14-digit Health ID which will contain the holder's entire medical history including tests, diagnosis, treatment, etc. The Health ID will be accessible to the entire healthcare industry including hospitals, laboratories, insurance companies, etc.

§7. LEGAL FRAMEWORK

115. EHR and e-Health regulation implementation is at the initial stages in the country. So far the policies by the government can be termed as mere baby steps in this direction. The main law, namely the Data Protection law is yet to see the light of day and is still in the pipeline in the parliament:[111]

- The Telemedicine Guidelines (2020)—Issued by the Ministry of Health and Family Welfare, these Guidelines enable registered medical practitioners to provide health care using telemedicine. The term "telemedicine" denotes the delivery of healthcare services from a distance where the healthcare professionals on information provided by the patients move to deliver advice using ICTs.[112]
- The Information Technology (Intermediaries Guidelines) Rules, 2011 ("Intermediary Guidelines"). It is the most crucial document so far regarding the preservation of the medical privacy of patients. Whenever the medical record of a patient comes to any intermediary the Rules 2011 make it incumbent upon them to secure and preserve them. The intermediaries include telecom service providers, network service providers, internet service providers, web-hosting service

111. Personal Data Protection Bill, 2019(India).
112. Telemedicine.pdf (mohfw.gov.in).

providers, search engines, online payment sites, online-auction sites, online-market places, and cyber cafes.[113] It has been made mandatory for the intermediaries to follow certain directions regarding notifying and publicizing their rules, regulations, and policies that the users will be subjected to termination of access in case of default. They are directed to preserve the information for 180 days. In case any intermediary exceeds users beyond five million then they must be incorporated under the Companies Act 2013 (Rules 3–7).
- The draft Digital Information Security Healthcare Act 2018 (DISHA) was released by the Ministry of Health and Family Welfare for public consultation.

113. Section 2(w) of the Information Technology Act, 2000.

Chapter 3. Online Voting

§1. General Statement

116. India has come a long way on the path of democracy and proudly gets the status of being the largest democracy in the world. From the manual ballot papers, with indelible marks on the index finger to the Electronic Voting Machines (EVM) of today, there are tremendous changes in the voting system. The country goes to elections every five years to constitute the Lower House of the parliament. 912 million voters participated in the General Elections in 2019. However, the digital infrastructure and the embracing of ICTs have urged the government to opt for online voting as well. The Online Voting System allows the voter to scan his or her fingerprints which are to match with an already stored image in the government database. The main log in mechanism is through the *Aadhar* Card, the unique 12-digit identification number for each citizen of India. The EVM has an advantage over the traditional voting system with respect to accuracy, convenience, flexibility, privacy, verifiability, and mobility. Nevertheless, the system has revealed many drawbacks, like the sudden failure of the machinery, time-consuming uploading, exclusion of higher officials, consumption of paperwork, etc.[114] Such drawbacks are done away with the Online Voting System. With the use of wireless and web technologies, the online voting system ensures a secure and safe way to capture and count votes. *Aadhar* is the key authentication system but often it falls short of reliability as the biometric system is not used here. Although the system presents non traceability and integrity of votes, the proposed Smart Card used in voting is not very reliable as the Card is prone to damage or any other misuse.

§2. Online Voting System

117. Online voting System is still not a reality in India—India has been exploring the possibility of implementing a remote system of voting using blockchain technology. The system promises a transparent and accountable record of data. The Election Commission of India is working with IIT-Madras for using blockchain technology to enable app-based e-voting to make the process more convenient. However, remote voting may be a reality in 2024 when the country goes for the five-yearly General Elections. The decentralized blockchain system is immutable which means date once entered will become irreversible and any tampering will be traced easily. Though the country is yet to implement it, the State of Telangana in South India aims at implementing an experiment with an e-voting proposal[115] and aims at building voters' trust toward impeccable elections.

114. Rajesh M. Ghadi & Priyanka S. Shelar, *Online Voting System,* International Research Journal of Engineering and Technology (IRJET) 4 (Dec. 12, 2017).

115. Mustafa Rajkotwala, *E-voting to Become Reality Soon? Here's What Election Commission Should Do Before Going for Blockchain Polls,* Oct. 9, 2021, https://www.firstpost.com/india/e-voting-to-become-reality-soon-heres-what-election-commission-should-do-before-going-for-blockchain-polls-10038021.html.

Proposed Method—The Online Voting System will require the profile of the voter as entered in the *Aadhar* Card. A database stored by the Election Commission of India contains all details of the voter. Thus, *Aadhar* ID is the main tool through which the vote of the voter can be authenticated or he may also be asked to get registered with personal details. A system that gives a list of the candidates to be voted along with his ward or area will be more correct and reliable. The proposed system will diminish the hazard of defilement. It will work under two authorities, namely the National Database and Registration Authority of India (NADRA) and the Election Commission of India. The Online Voting platform offers the least demanding and most helpful technique both for directors and voters alike.[116] It will also avoid invalid voting.

116. Ramya G. Kumarean Perumal, *Online Voting System Using Cloud*—International Conference on Emerging Trends in Information Technology and Engineering. Conference Paper—February 2020.

Chapter 4. Other E-government Services

§1. General Statement

118. The traditional government office with sick staff, outdated settings, and belated services is being replaced by smart digital systems. The motto of the government "minimum government, maximum governance" is giving a boost to the e-government services where ICT benefits are being untapped to milk maximum mileage to achieve the goal of an effective, robust, and resilient government. The future in the country is foreseeing digital transformation of governance, new-age technology for government services, mobility solutions for last-mile governance, the transformation of cities to smart cities, innovations for Digital Education in the country, and global good governance. Department of Administrative Reforms & Public Grievances (DARPG) had constituted the National e-Governance Service Delivery Assessment (NeSDA) in 2019. The Study undertakes biennial research and makes an assessment of the states and Union Territories and aids the ministries in achieving effectiveness in e-Governance service delivery. NeSDA 21 covers several services across various sectors, like Finance, Labor & Employment, Education, Local Governance and Utility Services, Social Welfare, Environment, and Tourism.[117] The NeSDA 21 Portal was launched in June 2021 which gives a single window access to information and service links. Apart from this, there are individual Portals of all the states and union territories. The Portal of the Ministry of Home Affairs has the highest compliance score while the Central Public Procurement Portal, Digital Police Portal, and *Bhavishya* (Future) Portal also have about 85% compliance score. The NeSDA has been a great success which accelerates the vision of Digital India. Consequently, the DARPG plans to conduct the next version of NeSDA in 2023.

117. NeSDA 21 Report-Ministry of Personnel, Public Grievances and Pensions, Press Information Bureau, Delhi, June 2022.

Part III. Online Transactions

Chapter 1. Electronic Contracting (Incl. Smart Contracts and Blockchain)

§1. General Introduction

119. The formation of a contract in the physical world requires competent parties, offer and acceptance, free consent, consideration, and a lawful object. The word "smart contract" was first introduced by computer scientist and cryptographer Nick Szabo at the University of Washington, who says that the digital revolution has given birth to new relationships. He says:

> I call these new contracts "smart," because they are far more functional than their inanimate paper-based ancestors. No use of artificial intelligence is implied. A smart contract is a set of promises, specified in digital form, including protocols within which the parties perform on these promises.[118]

The world of the internet has recently seen a novel contract, a contract which is purely an automatic exercise, moves on computer code, and is concluded on a blockchain platform. Such code is either the sole manifestation of an agreement between the parties or it may support a traditional type of contract and execute certain provisions like transferring funds from Party A to Party B.[119] Self-performing quality is the hallmark of a smart contract. The decentralized nature of blockchain technology, the main plank of a smart contract, facilitates its execution. As human intervention is absent here, hence there is also no chance of human error in the performance of the contract. Smart contracts are unalterable once they—are finally codified. They are also cost-effective and time-saving. Blockchain is a distributed database of records or a public ledger of all transactions or events recorded with the consent of participants. Bitcoin, the digital currency uses blockchain technology the most. Once entered, the information can never be erased. The structure can be explained by the example of a cookie being easily stolen from a cookie jar kept in

118. Nick Szabo, *Smart Contracts: Building Blocks for Digital Market*, 1996.
119. Stuart De Levi &Others: *An Introduction to Smart Contracts and Their Potential and Inherent Limitations,* Harvard Law School Forum and Corporate Governance, May 2018.

a known place but it is difficult to steal it from a jar kept in the marketplace as thousands of eyes are watching. Michael Crosby et.al, *Blockchain Technology: Beyond Bitcoin,* Applied Innovation Review (AIR). Cryptocurrency is still not recognized in the country.

§2. Smart Contracts in India: Legal Position

120. The legal scene *vis-a-vis* smart contracts in India is an amalgamation of various provisions, traditional orders by the TRAI, and ruling of the Supreme Court of India. So far, there is no separate and specific Smart Contract legislation in the country. Even though as per the traditional Indian Contract Act 1872, the basic features of a contract, namely competent parties, free consent, consideration, and a lawful object are found in Smart Contracts yet these Contracts being drastically different in nature from the traditional type of contracts do not easily fit into the legal requirement. The scattered law provisions which aid each other in legalizing the Smart Contract in the country can be enumerated as under:

(a) The Indian Contract Act 1872, section 10 of the Act enumerating the essentials of a valid contract requires two parties competent to contract, free consent of parties to have a legal relation, and a lawful object of the contract. Thus the basic moving point is section 10 which signals the recognition of a Smart Contract as a valid contract in the country as all these features are found in smart contracts though it moves in a digital environment.
(b) Sections 5 & 10 of the Information Technology Act 2000—section 5 of the "IT Act permits digital signatures and holds a contract to be legitimate and enforceable." The provision legalizes the use of digital signatures in a contract and thus it recognizes this part of the smart contract which has a digital signature for its authentication.
(c) The Telecom Regulatory Authority of India in 2018 in its notification briefly defines the term "smart contract." It says that "they work on a programmable code which can implement predetermined tasks or rules so as to check regulatory compliance in advance, in the absence of human intervention." It also declared that it is suitable for Distributed Ledger Technology (DLT).[120]
(d) Cryptocurrency which forms "consideration" in a smart contract still lacks legal recognition in India. However, the Supreme Court in March 2020, lifted the ban on cryptocurrency imposed by the Reserve Bank of India (RBI). Earlier the RBI had issued directions to the banks to stop providing bank services to those who were engaged in cryptocurrency dealings. The trading formerly was from crypto to crypto and not from crypto to Indian National Rupee (INR, the currency of India).

---

120. Telecom Regulatory Authority of India, "The Telecom Commercial Communications Customer Preference Regulations, 2018," Gazette of India (Jul. 19, 2018).

§3. Cryptocurrency: The Ban

121. The Reserve Bank of India in 2018 banned the use and trading of cryptocurrencies in the country. It prohibited all banks in the country to refrain from meting out services to those individuals who were indulging in cryptocurrency trading. However, the ban continued until the Supreme Court lifted it as discussed *supra.* Recently, the finance minister opined that the RBI supports the ban but she laid stress on an international collaboration to make crypto prohibition law effective in the country as cryptocurrency is borderless. Thus, there is stress on legislation to make the ban effective, and international cooperation in this field is a must.[121]

§4. The Future of Cryptocurrency in India

122. In December 2021, in the Lower House of the parliament a bill called The Cryptocurrency and Regulation of Official Digital Currency Bill, 2021 was listed to be introduced.[122] The Bill plans to create a facilitative framework for the creation of the official digital currency to be issued by the Reserve Bank of India. The Bill also seeks to prohibit all private cryptocurrencies in India, however, it allows for certain exceptions to promote the underlying technology of cryptocurrency and its uses. The finance minister declared that bitcoin[123] is not money and warned the investors that soon cryptocurrency legislation will be introduced.[124] She also urged the International Monetary Fund (IMF) to take a lead role in regulating crypto assets and to have a globally coordinated and synchronized approach to the issue. Though Bill 2021 intends to impose a ban on crypto but as more and more investors are embracing it, it looks that the policy will undergo a change and it is difficult to put a blanket ban on it. The RBI regards it as a threat to the economy in the future. However, it plans to introduce a new digital currency instead.[125] Thus, all the information indicates that the future of cryptocurrency is not very promising though there is an indication that these will be regulated and will be treated as an asset. As trading in crypto involves cross-border transactions hence a statutory body is required to regulate it, and the interest of investors takes center stage hence the entire crypto environment will be an interplay of a number of laws, like the Consumer Protection Act, FEMA, Indian Contract Act, Information Technology Act, Prevention of Money Laundering Act, Payments and Settlement Systems Act, Deposits related laws, Securities laws, Taxation laws, etc.

---

121. Finance Minister Ms. Nirmala Sitharaman.
122. Lok Sabha—BULLETIN Part II-(General Information Relating to Parliamentary and other matters). Nos. 3293–3304. Tuesday November 2021.
123. Was introduced in 2008 by a persona named Satoshi Nakamoto as flexible payment system to be used internationally.
124. At Economic Cell Event. Aug. 17, 2022, https://www.dnaindia.com/personal-finance/report-finance-minister-nirmala-sitharaman-issues-warning-against-cryptocurrencies-new-regulations-to-be-announced-2977295.
125. Jui Kadam, *Key Features of an official Digital Currency Bill 2021*, https://blog.ipleaders.in/key-features-official-digital-currency-bill-2021/.

§5. BLOCKCHAIN

123. It can be defined as a digital ledger of transactions that is maintained by a network of computers. It does not require any government, banks, or other intermediaries and is supposed to be the most impeccable and secure system of transactions. In Blockchain, the growing list of records called blocks is linked to each other with the help of cryptography. Each transaction is verified by a peer-to-peer computer network added to a growing chain of data that is ultimately unalterable. The use of Bitcoin, Ethereum, etc., provides us with a promising application for legal contracts and for a number of medical or other records. So far there is no Indian law that defines blockchain technology.[126]

126. The term blockchain first appeared in 1982 during which it was discussed as "the design of a distributed computer system which can be established, maintained and most importantly trusted by mutually suspicious groups."

Chapter 2. Electronic Signatures

§1. Introduction

124. Electronic signatures are the new generation of signatures. In the new medium of information society originally nothing existed to match a human hand which lends originality, authenticity, and legality to a document. On June 30, 2000, President Clinton became the first person to use electronic signatures when he signed the Electronic Signatures in Global and National Commerce Act (ESIGN)[127] using his electronic signature ID adducing validity and legal recognition to electronic signatures for commercial and other online activities. The Model Law on Electronic Signatures 2001 came as a sequel to the Model Law on Electronic Commerce (1996) keeping in view the increased acceptance of the Public Key Infrastructure (PKI) system in the area of electronic signatures. India, being a signatory to the UNCITRAL in 1996 came up with its first internet-specific legislation in 2000. Surprisingly enough, the Information Technology Act 2000(21 of 2000) did not mention the term "electronic signature" instead it used the term "digital signature." It is only in 2008 that the term "digital signature" wherever appearing in the Act was repealed and at the same places the term "electronic signature" was inserted. Thus, the amended IT Act gives the definition of electronic signature as "authentication of any electronic record by a subscriber by means of the electronic technique specified in the Second Schedule and includes digital signature [section 2(ta)]. The amended Act however retains the definition of 'digital signature' in section 2(p)." The main object of the Amendment Act 2008 is that in the unamended IT Act 2000 there was no mention of the word "electronic signature" which was a great lacuna. However, as the Model Law on Electronic Signatures 2001 urged its signatories to legislate on electronic signatures hence to meet this objective the IT Act was amended in 2008.

§2. Legal Effects of Electronic Signatures

125. In 2000, the digital signature through the IT Act 2000 got legal recognition and commercial activities started moving online. The Act had earlier recognized digital signatures based on asymmetric cryptosystems bringing them on par with manual signatures. However, the IT (Amendment) Act 2008 has now substituted the term "electronic signature" for the term "digital signatures."[128] With the popularity of electronic signatures globally there arose a need to provide electronic signatures with a legal framework so that they enjoy the same level of trust and confidence which has hitherto been the privilege of manuscript signature. In the history of electronic signatures the Utah Digital Signature Act 1995 was the first ever legislation

127. Isaac Bowman, *The History of Electric Signatures Laws,* ESign Laws.
128. Amendments to the IT Act 2000; s. 2. In the IT Act 2000 (21 of 2000)(hereinafter in this part referred to as the principal Act), for the words "digital signature" occurring in the chapter, section, sub-section and clause referred to in the Table below, the words "electronic signature" shall be substituted.

on the subject. There was growing legal skepticism about electronic signatures as it being a new technology and intangible too, raised a number of suspicions. A 2006 progress report on the European Union Electronic Signatures Directive shows that there was a slowing down of the spirit of users of electronic signatures. Factors, like security fears, cost, and complexity of the technology were some impediments to the acceptance of electronic signatures in the beginning. Countries such as Germany and Thailand have also reported low acceptance of electronic signatures.[129] Thus, it was felt that legislation would not hamper instead it will facilitate it; it is said that, "legislation can if properly written encourage rather than restrict, and promote rather than disable, the desirable policy goal of global e-commerce"[130] The formidable legal effect of electronic signatures globally can be categorized as follows:

- *The Evidentiary Issue*—It is a complex one. The mechanism to prove electronic signatures in the law court is not as easy. Most digital signature statutes even in India create a presumption that the person, who owns a particular key pair used to sign a document, in fact, did sign the document which is the ultimate purpose of PKI. But the difficulty arises from the fact that electronic signatures are impersonal by nature, and their originality becomes a challenge and always shrouded with doubt. Misuse of the private key cannot be ruled out. Even the original signor may often find it easier to escape from the legal noose and disown it easily.[131]
- *Absence of Originals*—It is difficult to ascertain the originality of the electronic signature because after all, it is a representation of some electromagnetic signals represented on the computer monitor.[132]
- *Absence of Physical Witnesses*—Electronic signatures cannot be proved with the help of natural witnesses, i.e., human beings. Hardly a person can testify that the particular electronic signature is the creation of a particular person with as much ease as he does in the context of manuscript signatures.
- *Absence of Handwriting Experts*, Thus, handwriting experts which were of great help to the courts are conspicuously absent in the context of electronic signatures.

Thus, evidentiary uncertainty is the strange effect of electronic signatures and their intangible nature; the requisition of a technician to prove it technically is also rare as techno-savvy is not easily available. Thus, in India too the IT Act 2000 made

---

129. *See*, eGovernmentNews, Take up of electronic signatures Remains Low in Germany EPRACTICE, EU (120302008), http://www.epractice.eu/document/1276; Pascal Prud'homme & Hassana Chiraphakul, *E-Commerce in Thailand: A Slow Awakening* February 2009 Thailand Law Forum, http:/ /thailawforum.com/articles/e-commerce.html.
130. Thomas J. Smedinghoff & Ruth Hil, Bro of Baker & McKenzie LLP, *Electronic Signature Legislation,* 14.
131. Chris Reed, *Authenticating Electronic Mail Messages-Some Evidential Problems,* Mod Law Review 52(5) (1989), 649, 650.
132. Lorna Brazell, *Electronic Signatures Law and Regulation* (2004) 1999, Stephen Mason, *Electronic Signatures in Law* (2007) 461.

relevant amendments in the century-old Indian Evidence Act 1872 to make it admissible in the court, regarding the presumption of electronic signatures, etc.[133]

§3. Use of Electronic Signatures by Public Administration

126. The IT Act envisages the use of electronic records and electronic signatures by public administration (section 6). It provides for the government and its agencies the use of electronic signatures. If any particular law requires (1) the filing of any application or any other documents with any governmental office, authority, body, or agency owned or controlled by the appropriate government or (2) the issue or grant of any license, permit, sanction, or approval or (3) the receipt or payment of money in a particular manner then the filing, issuance, grant, receipt or payment if effected by electronic means will be deemed to satisfy the requirements of law. The appropriate government is empowered to prescribe rules for the manner and format in which such electronic records shall be filed, created, or issued. It may also make rules for the manner or method of payment of any fee or charges for filing, creation, or issuance of any electronic record (section 6). The IT Act also permits the retention of documents, records, and information for any period of time in electronic form (section 7). The requirement of publication of a rule, regulation, etc., in the Official Gazette will be deemed fulfilled if it is published in the Electronic Gazette and the date of publication in the Electronic Gazette shall be taken as the date of its publication (section 8). However, no one can insist that any Ministry or Department of the Central Government or the State Government or any authority or body established under any law or funded by the Central or the State Government should be retained or preserved in electronic form or that any monetary transaction should be done in the electronic form (section 9).

133. Sections 65B, 67A, 73A, 85B of the Information Technology Act 2000.

Chapter 3. Trust Services (Certificates, Electronic Mail Services, Etc.)

§1. Importance of Trust Services

127. The entire world in this digital age is going manual free. Most of the human activities in the field of education, commerce, and medicine have taken to online. All the transactions are done electronically hence the traditional way of authenticating a document is becoming obsolete. Therefore, a need arises to make online transactions and documents reliable, authentic, and trustworthy. Thus trust services have been developed which include the methods for the creation, verification, and validation of electronic invoices, digital signatures, time stamps, certified electronic delivery, and website authentication certificates. This ensures not only the identity of the sender of the document but also verifies the originality of the matter and a promise that the document during its transaction has not been altered or tampered with. The most important beneficiaries of these trust services are the businesses and commercial transactions which help companies to digitize services hitherto done in the traditional way. The birth of electronic signatures though goes a long way in achieving this end, things are not fully trustworthy yet. Once an electronic signature is created and the data appending to it is thereby authenticated, the question remains regarding the tie of authenticity between the data and its signer, and regarding the reliability of the electronic signature. In public-key and private-key cryptography, the association of these pairs of numbers with a natural person or with the person who actually created it still remains a big question to be answered truly. Especially in the online surrounding where electrons and not men travel to finalize the deal, for the identity of the signer or the creator of the said electronic signature it was required that something more be done. There arose a need for the sake of national security, enforcement purposes, and also mutual trust of parties, to have an intermediary which could act as an agency between contracting parties, so that mistrust or doubt regarding the authenticity of electronic signatures could be done away with.

§2. The Trust Matrix in India

128. In 2000, digital signatures through the IT Act 2000 got legal recognition and commercial activities started moving online. The Act had earlier recognized digital signatures based on asymmetric cryptosystems bringing them at par with manual signatures. However, the IT (Amendment) Act, 2008 has now substituted the term "electronic signature" for the term "digital signature."[134] The Act provides

134. Amendments to the IT Act, 2000:

> *S. 2.* In the IT Act, 2000 (21 of 2000) (hereinafter in this part referred to as the "principal Act"), for the words "digital signature" occurring in the chapter, section, sub-s. and clause referred to in the Table below, the words "electronic signature" shall be substituted.

for the Controller of Certifying Authorities (CCA) who is entrusted with the responsibility of regulating the working of the certification authorities who are in turn given the responsibility to issue the Digital Signature Certificates (DSCs) for electronic authentication of users. The CCA certifies the public keys of Certifying Authorities using its own private key, which enables users in cyberspace to verify that a given certificate is issued by a licensed Certifying Authority. For this, it operates the Root Certifying Authority of India (RCAI). The CCA by virtue of section 20, IT Act 2000 maintained repositories that have now been deleted under the Amendment Act of 2008.[135]

By virtue of section 18(*b*) of the IT Act 2000, the CCA has established the Root Certifying Authority of India (RCAI) to digitally sign the public keys of Certifying Authorities. The requirements fulfilled by the RCAI include:

(1) The license issued to the Certifying Authority is digitally signed by the CCA.
(2) All public keys corresponding to the signing of private keys of a Certifying Authority are digitally signed by the CCA.
(3) That these keys are signed by the CCA and can be verified by a relying party through the CCA's website or Certifying Authority's own website.

The RCAI is operated using SmartTrust software. The Certification Practice Statement of RCAI guides the CCA personnel to perform Root Certifying Authority functions. The term "Root" signifies the entire Certifying Authority matrix including the software and its operations. The National Root Certifying Authority uses a 2048-bit RSA key pair and the Certifying Authority entity uses a 1024-bit RSA key pair.[136] Certifying Authorities (CA) have been granted a license to issue a digital signature certificate under section 24 of the Indian IT Act 2000. One can procure Class 2 or 3 certificates from any of the certifying authorities.

§3. Certification Agencies

129. Certification Agencies are appointed by the office of the Controller of Certification Agencies (CCA) under the provisions of the IT Act 2000. There are a total of twelve Certification Agencies authorized by the CCA to issue Digital Signature Certificates (DSCs). In India, as per the Ministry of Corporate Affairs following Certifying Authorities are licensed Certifying Authorities:

National Informatics Centre Certifying Authority (NICCA) is also one that is reliable and plays an important role in generating trust. It is an organization of the Government of India which issues certificates to government organizations for G2G transactions.

135. Formerly under the IT Act, the Controller had the job of maintaining a repository of all the Certifying Authorities in the country. The National Repository of Digital Certificates (NRDC) maintained it under S. 20.

136. Dr Sundeep Oberoi, "India PKI Forum," Presentation made at PKI Consortium Seminar, Nov. 8, 2007, 4.

Institute for Development and Research in Banking Technology (IDRBT) was setup by the RBI in 1996. It issues certificates for banks and financial institutions.

SafeScrypt—This Certifying Authority is the result of Sify Technology. It is the first Certifying Authority under the IT Act and a Versign Inc. affiliate for the Indian subcontinent offering Managed PKI Services to enterprises and digital certificates to end-users.

nCode Solutions—It is a Certifying Authority that delivers paperless and contactless DSC through the e-KYC method.

e-Mudhra Certification Authority—It is launched by InfoTech Consumer Services Ltd. It offers a variety of DSC solutions to individuals and organizations. The DSC is powered by the PKI technology, and *e-Mudhra* offers SSL certificates.

Centre for Development of Advanced Computing (CDAC)—It is a premier Research & Development Society of the Department of Electronics and Information Technology (DeitY).

130. National Securities Depository Limited (NSDL). NSDL e-Gov is now known as *protean.* It is the country's first depository services firm. It lays down the basic structure for e-governance in the country. It covers the fields of education and skill financing, old age security, cloud services, and identity authentication services.

Capricorn—It is a licensed Certifying Authority (CA) in India by the Controller of Certifying Authorities (CCA), i.e., Government of India under the Information Technology Act 2000. It provides digital signature certificates related to eSign, and PKI solutions. It gives safe and secure signing and encryption solutions and has a global span that aims at future cybersecurity frameworks. It supports the Digital India campaign of the Government of India.

Pantasign—It is a Certifying Authority incorporated in March 2019 under the Companies Act 2013. It promises to deliver DSC of the highest standard.

IDSign—It is a licensed Certifying Authority under the Government of India and provides DSC to consumers, corporates and government organizations, and individuals. IDSign CA provides a full range of PKI services that includes, certificate issuance, revocation list issuance, Online Certificate Status Protocol (OCSP), and Timestamping Authority (TSA).

Verasys—Verasys Technologies Private Limited provides legally valid electronic signatures as per the Second Schedule of the Information Technology Act and the guidelines of the CCA, Ministry of Information Technology, and Government of India. They provide *Aadhar*-based biometric Digital Signatures.

XtraTRust—Apart from certifying DSCs and managing PKIs it specializes in protecting smart connected systems by leveraging XtraTRust's comprehensive portfolio of IoT security technologies.

Moreover in India, the Premium SSL GenieGlobal Certification Authority is the first company to have global certification power in India. The Comodo SSL Premium is an Organization Validated (OV) Certificate that offers great value to company websites.[137]

137. It activates https and the padlock icon in the URL bar. It is protected by a $250,000 warranty. https://www.thesslstore.in/comodo/premiumssl.aspx.

Chapter 4. Online Financial Services

§1. Introduction and Importance

131. Economy forms the backbone of any country. It is the panoply of financial resources, revenue, export-import, the banking system, the industrial structure, and the commercial base of a country. It consists of a number of sectors like agriculture, financial services, and the like. Net proliferation has changed the face not only of banking but of the entire financial sector. It has revolutionized the entire financial services since it took to online.

§2. Internet Banking: The Formidable Online Financial Service

132. The dawn of the internet has marked the demise of traditional money. Banks have been the forerunners in harnessing the power of technology and are perhaps the biggest beneficiary of this great innovation. Ancient money apart from their notational value had its own market worth; for instance, gold coins or silver coins were valuable according to their weight as well. Today, technology has done away with even the paper's worth of money, and billions of transaction are being done notationally. The internet now forms the backbone of the entire banking system heralding the birth of transnational currency the world over. Wealth in digital form is the most striking feature of electronic banking. Electronic banking has silenced the great hassles of carrying money, transferring hard cash, and undergoing the prolonged and cumbersome process of money calculations. The payment system and money transfer is not even for a farthing, and above all the time taken is nanosecond. Internet banking, since its inception in the 1990s in the U.S. has swiftly moved on the path of progress globally as its main attraction for the consumer is increased convenience and the reduction of operational costs to the banks.[138] For all, internet banking is an altogether new experience. The major diversion from traditional banking to internet banking has been that the customer's signature being a promise of authenticity has been replaced by PIN, ID, and password which is hardly a biometric authentication. It is external to the customer and has easy transportability; the only thing is to have the knowledge of such external identification (ID and password, etc.). So long as this remains a secret, a problem does not arise but things change when there is a malicious transaction because of misappropriation of the means of identification.[139] In internet banking when a customer accesses his bank account with the help of user ID and password, then the customer's digital signature certificate is connected giving a signal to the bank that a valid entry by the customer has been made.

---

138. NP Singh, *Online Frauds in Banks with Phishing,* Journal of Internet Banking and Commerce 12(2) (August 2007), available at http://www.arraydev.com/commerce/jibc//.
139. AL Tyree, *Banking Law in Australia* (LexisNexis Butterworths, 2008) 351.

§3. Indian Scenario in Online Financial Services

133. India too though taking pride in the antiquity of the banking system has taken the glide path of digital banking. According to the Indian Central Banking Enquiry Committee (1931), money lending in India could be traced back to the *Vedic Period*, i.e., from 2000 to 1400 BC. Professional banking has its roots in 500 BC. *Kautilya's Arthshastra* dating back to 400 BC has references to creditors, lenders, and lending rates.[140] Ignoring the aspersions of internet banking like any other country, India has mirrored the technological temperament and has embarked upon the internet banking system in the country though a bit late. Computers replaced the bulky registers and even the Indian banks were purged of the piled-up ledgers. The Reserve Bank of India (RBI), the fountain of all banking activities and the supreme monetary authority in the country established in 1935, started issuing piecemeal regulations, circulars, and directives to catch up with the digitization of the banking system; the gradual transformation of Indian banks to internet banking was led by the RBI by setting up committees to define and coordinate banking technology. These are chronologically in the following order:

- In 1984, the Committee on Mechanization in the Banking Industry was formed.[141] Its main recommendation was the adoption of the MICR technology in all the banks in the metropolises in India.
- In 1988, the Committee on Computerization in Banks was set up. It focused, *inter alia*, on the computerization of the entire infrastructure and also suggested modalities for implementing online banking. As a result, computerization started in 1993 with the settlement between Indian Banks' Association and Bank Employees' Association.[142]
- In 1994, the Committee on Technology Issues Relating to Payments System, Cheque Clearing and Securities Settlement in the Banking Industry was set up. It emphasized electronic funds transfer (EFT) with the BANKET communication network as its carrier.
- In 1995, the Committee for Proposing Legislation on Electronic Funds Transfer and Other Electronic Payments was also formed.

All these initial activities undertaken by the RBI showed the upside movement of digitization of the banking system in the country. Resultantly, in 2007, the Payment and Settlement Systems Act 2007 (hereinafter called the Act of 2007) empowered the RBI to regulate various payments and settlement systems. It authorizes the RBI to permit both gross and net settlement procedures. As a sequel to the said Act, the RBI issued two important regulations, namely the Board for Regulation and Supervision of Payment and Settlement Systems Regulations, 2008 and the Payment and Settlement Systems Regulations, 2008. Dating back to the age of *Manu* down to the present scenario of chatbots, the Indian banking system has evolved as a strong

---

140. R Gandhi, *RBI Monthly Bulletin* (December 2014) 11.
141. Committee on Computerization-Annexure, RBI Publications, dated Dec. 12, 1998, available at https://www.rbi.org.in/scripts/PublicationsView.aspx?id=162.
142. *Indian Banking System* (IK International Publishing House Pvt. Ltd., 2006).

backbone of the country's economy and today it is a composition of various categories of banks catering to the needs of all classes of customers:

Banks	*Number of Banks*
Private Sector Banks	22
Public Sector Banks	18
Foreign Banks	46
Regional Rural Banks	53
Urban Cooperative Banks	1,542
Rural Cooperative Banks	94,384

Source: The Banking Network in India 2019.[143]

The Indian banking system is keeping pace with the fast-changing world of IT. The massive extent of the population has not been a drawback for the country and its impressive network of banks both scheduled and non-scheduled, public sector, and private sector have accepted the Electronic Payment System.

The Electronic Banking services in the country can be categorized as follows:

- *Internet Banking Services*—Balance enquiry and payment; transaction history; online transfer of funds; card to card transfer; Pre-paid mobile recharge; Buy and sell mutual funds; send money order anytime; open fixed deposit and recurring deposit; request of check book; stop payment request; request of debit cards; monthly bank account by e-mail; Reissue and debit of ATM Card; Link bank account to ATM Debit Card; renewal, premature closure of FD/RD; deactivate/ activate ATM Debit card; change password; Demat accounts; Loan details; interest rate updates; bills payment; online shopping; ticket booking; mobile top-up; share trading; online tax payments; convert to EMI; online loans; customer correspondence; demonstration of I-Banking; corporate internet banking.
- *Phone Banking Services*—Enquire about your balance account; request for funds transfer; stop check payment instructions; mobile banking registration; latest interest and exchange rates.
- *Mobile Banking Services*—Account balance; making payment; details of credit card balance; loan information; I-mobile; purchase and redemption of mutual fund units.
- Last three transactions.
- *ATM Services*—twenty-four-hour access to cash; transfer funds between accounts; view account balances and mini statements; pin change option.

143. Banking Sector in India—December 2019. Indian Brand Equity Foundation, https://www.ibef.org /industry/banking-india.aspx.

The Act of 2007 provides for the following special type of electronic services:

- Electronic Funds Transfer (EFT)—It is defined as the transfer of funds whereby a person instructs, authorizes, or orders the bank to debit or credit an account maintained with that bank through electronic means and includes point of sale transfers, automated teller machine transactions, direct deposits or withdrawal of funds, transfers initiated by telephone internet and card payment (section 2(1)(c); Act of 2007).
- National Electronic Funds Transfer (NEFT)—It is a nationwide funds transfer system to facilitate the transfer of funds from any bank branch to any other bank branch. The system has the concept of Centralized Accounting, and the bank's accounts that are sending or receiving the funds transfer instructions get operated only in Mumbai. The individual branches are spread all over the country.
- Real-Time Gross Settlement (RTGS)—It is a funds transfer mechanism where the transfer of money takes place from one bank to another on a "real-time" and on a "gross" basis. This is the fastest possible money transfer system through the banking channel. Settlement in "real-time" denotes that transaction is not subject to any waiting period. "Gross settlement" means the transaction is settled on a one-to-one basis without bunching with any other transaction.
- Payment systems—A Payment system is a mechanism that facilitates the transfer of value between a payer and a beneficiary by which the payer discharges the payment obligations to the beneficiary. It enables a two-way flow of payments in exchange for goods and services in the economy. Payment system includes systems enabling credit card operations, debit card operations, smart card operations, money transfer operations, or similar operations but does not apply to stock exchanges or clearing (section 34—Payment and Settlement Systems Act 2007).

§4. Payment Mechanism

134. A payment system is a mechanism that facilities the transfer of value between a payer and a beneficiary by which the payer discharges the payment obligations to the beneficiary. It enables a two-way flow of payments in exchange for goods and services in the economy. With the expansion of ICTs and economic liberalization, the traditional payment mechanism has undergone a revolutionary change and in a developing country like India also the wind of change is felt. The RBI indicated the mission to have a reliable, up-to-date, safe, efficient, and inclusive system of payment that is also compliant with international standards in this field. "The vision is to proactively encourage electronic payment system for ushering in a less cash society in India."[144] The formation of the National Payments Corporation of India (NPCI) in 2009 has set the stage for retail electronic payment systems in India which aims at a cashless society.[145] It is an umbrella organization

144. http://www.rbi.org.in.
145. Dhananjay Bapat & Suresh Chand Bihari, *The Electronic Banking Revolution in India:* Journal of Internet Banking and Commerce, 20(2), August 2015, 1–5.

for various retail payment systems in India.[146] Payment mechanisms include instruments through which payments can be made, rules, regulations, and procedures that guide these payments, the institutions which facilitate payment mechanisms, and legal systems that are established to facilitate the transfer of funds between different participants. The payment system includes systems enabling credit card operations, debit card operations, smart card operations, money transfer operations, or similar operations but does not apply to stock exchanges or clearing. (Section 34, Payment and Settlement Systems Act 2007).

The electronic banking services in the country are expanding constantly. It has taken myriad forms and techniques. More and more customers are joining the league of internet banking users. Notwithstanding the blues of Internet banking, the ultimate user as based on a study reveals the following: (1) consumers find internet banking friendlier than traditional banking; (2) public sector conventional banks lack speed; (3) ratings on various parameters are comparatively higher in case of frequent users and high-income groups.[147] There exists a difference in the usage pattern of consumers for the frequency of usage ($F = 7.503$) with high value for Indian private banks followed by multinational banks.[148] Banks too show an inclination toward resorting to offering internet banking services depending on the financial and technological standard of it. A bank that is a member of the bank holding company is more likely to take this path as the single website of the bank holding company can offer access to customers of many banks.[149] The RBI has recently issued a new set of rules regarding more safety and convenience in respect of debit cards and credit cards. These are issued under section 10(2) of the Payment and Settlement Systems Act 2007 w.e.f. March 16, 2020. In short, these are; the RBI has asked issuers of the card to give facility to the users to switch on and off their credit or debit cards at any point in time, cardholders should be given the choice to modify transaction limits as per their choice, and the users are also given the option to disable the card as per their choice.[150]

I. The Wallet Payment System

135. E-Wallets or Digital Wallets started in India in 2006 when the country was gradually catching up with the mobile spree. Wallet365.com was India's first wallet launched by the Times Group in association with YES Bank. Cashless is today's fashion. Traveling light is the mantra. E-wallets carry credentials and have successfully replaced the weighty wallets with multiple cards and coins. Consumer behavior in India is fast changing, it is *Fintech* or Financial Technology that is all set to

146. https://www.rbi.org.in/scripts/PaymentSystems_UM.aspx.
147. Sufyan Habib, *Internet Banking in India Consumer Concerns and Bank Marketing Strategies*, Research Journal of Management Sciences 1(3) (October 2012),20.
148. *Ibid.*
149. *Ibid.*, 22.
150. RBI/2019–20/142 DPSS.CO.PD No./0214.003/2019–2020. Jan. 15, 2020.www.rbi.org.in.

transform India into a digital and cashless economy.[151] Though still in the category of developing countries internet penetration in India has given leverage to mobile banking thereby technologies, like Digital Wallet, EMV,[152] Chip-based Cards,[153] and two-factor authentication via SMS-based One-time Password (OTP)[154] have taken center stage in the banking industry in India. These innovations have the goal of cyber security in the area of banking but fool proof security is yet a remote possibility. Smart phones have given a boom to the adoption of newer *Fintech* and both the customer and the banks are showing tremendous penchant and inclination to enter the world of Digital Wallet for various services, like mobile recharge, bill payments, money transfers, and online purchasing. Like any other payment mechanism, Digital Wallets are fraud-vulnerable and cybercrime susceptible. Digital Wallets, therefore, are more prone to the following inherent risks, like Phishing Fraud,[155] sniffing/intrusion/cyber attack[156] benefits through misconduct,[157] Fake KYC[158] and application manipulation by an authorized user.[159] Electronic Wallet is yet another name given to Digital Wallet which has dominated the payment mechanism the world over. "Electronic wallet refers to an electronic, internet-based payment system which stores financial as well as personal identity-related information."[160] Against the backdrop of the advent of ICT technologies and internet expansion, one big development has been in the marketplace, online or offline,

---

151. Today India is a digital economy with over a billion mobile phones 330 million internet users (c. 94% on wireless devices) and 240 smart phones. *Banking on the Future—Vision 2020*-CII-Deloitte. Confederation of Indian Industry. (CII). 18.
152. Euro Pay, MasterCard and Visa. It is the technical standard which ensures chip-based payment cards and terminals. These three companies originally developed the specifications in 1994.
153. On the directives issued by the Reserve Bank of India, Banks have issued EMV Chip Based Cards for secured transaction which is done by adopting following measures: the Card authentication verifies the Card credentials during transaction thereby guarding against counterfeit cards. Card holder Protection helps in identifying the right person i.e., the true card holder, Transaction authorization uses issuer-defined rules whereas the transaction is authorized either online or offline using issuer-defined risk parameters in the card. https://www.ijeas.org/download_data/IJEAS0201019.pdf.
154. One Time Password is a popular security mechanism which is a two-factor authentication (2FA). These OTPs are delivered by Banks through simple messaging service or SMS. However though the OTP mechanism is primarily meant for security and is used in beneficiary additions, money transactions purchase etc., yet it is not without risk. It is declared insecure by the National Institute of Standards and Technology (NIST). There is risk of interception of the OTP. There is a chance that pre-Registered Mobile Number (RMN) may not be attached with some mobile network and could be a VoIP service. Changing of pre RMN may not be possible without SMS-based OTP. Another risk is that the SMS may be delivered to an incorrect recipient in case the phone is lost or the number is changed by the user.
155. Fraudsters lure the customers with lucrative financial gains and induce them to share passwords, PINs and other sensitive information thereby phishing out wealth from the Digital wallet.
156. The criminals hack into the wallet, intercept traffic into the wallet between the digital wallet platform and the consumer thereby discover credentials and manipulate the wallet.
157. Regular customers detect application flaws which can be beneficial for them in specific scenarios and then they simulate same scenarios to exploit these limitations.
158. Customers can provide fake KYC information to gain access to some premium wallets which allow higher transaction value.
159. Employees having admin/super-user access can get into unauthorized transactions like pseudo virtual money generation on select wallets and other fraudulent tactics.
160. P Jinimol, *A Study on E-wallet*, International Journal of Trend in Scientific Research & Development 2(4) (May–June 2018), 1.

where payment mode has taken an innovative form. It is the virtual style which is an amalgamation of computer software and hardware system. Thus, "e-wallet is nothing but an online money account which does not require the use of a physical card for undertaking transaction remittance."[161] E-wallet carries valuable credentials like the personal and financial details of the user and the monetary value which empowers the user to purchase goods and services online.

II. Digital Wallet and Mobile Wallet

136. Quite recently the term Mobile Wallet (M-Wallet)has entered the retail market payment system which can be termed as a more innovative and improved form of Digital Wallet (D-Wallet). Both D-Wallet and M-Wallet store payment information and other credentials but they are implemented differently:

Digital Wallet or E-Wallet	*Mobile Wallet*
It contains payment information and is mostly used for online transactions. Users can complete transactions by using near—field communications (NFC)[162] technology.	When a Digital Wallet is used with a mobile it is called a Mobile Wallet. A Mobile Wallet is a type of Digital Wallet which is accessible via a mobile phone or a wearable device.[163] It uses NFC technology.
It allows users to store credit card and debit card numbers in the cloud, then they are accessed either from a laptop, tablet, or phone. The money stored in the wallet is used; it is like a place where users can store money online.	The use of smartphones, tablets, or smart watches has accelerated the use of Mobile Wallets. It is an app that stores credit cards, debit cards, and coupons. It contains payment information. Examples are Paytm, Apple Pay, Samsung Pay, and the like.
They are the main interface for using cryptocurrencies, like Bitcoin.[164]	
Does not require a physical bank account.	
These are global in nature and allow participation in the global financial system.	

161. *Ibid.*
162. The technology uses radio frequencies to communicate between devices. It uses the personal identification format which is created for the user to communicate the payment information to the POS (Point-of-service) terminal. Will Kenton: *Mobile Wallet,* May 9,2019, https://www.investopedia.com/terms/m/mobile-wallet.asp.
163. Susan Shain: *Mobile Wallets v. Digital Wallets: What Is the Difference?*, Nov. 29, 2019, https://www.creditcardinsider.com/blog/mobile-wallets-vs-digital-wallets-whats-the-difference/.
164. Julia Kagan, *Digital Wallet,* Feb. 13,20, https://www.investopedia.com/terms/d/digital-wallet.asp.

Digital Wallet or E-Wallet	*Mobile Wallet*
In a Digital Wallet money is already stored in the wallet for future use and there is no reference to the user's bank account.	Mobile Wallets use credit card or debit card directly for payment.
From the merchant's point of view in a Digital Wallet for online payment, some special code is required for the web store or app.	If a merchant is having an NFC terminal in a physical store then for receiving payment nothing extra is to be done and Mobile Wallets, like Paytm, Apple Pay, or Google Pay will facilitate payment easily.

Digital Wallet is a wider connotation that includes within it Mobile Wallet. Hence one can conclude that all Mobile Wallets are Digital Wallets but all Digital Wallets are not Mobile Wallets.

III. Unified Payments Interface (UPI)

137. UPI is an important step toward the achievement of a cashless economy. It is the easiest ever real-time payment system which is also claimed to be one of the safest ways to pay. Not only that, money is transferred instantly from one account to another but it is a single platform in which the various banking services are amalgamated under one umbrella. It is established by the NCPI and the RBI together with Indian Banks Association (IBA). The procedure of transferring money to another person now rests only on the registered mobile number (RMN) of the recipient and it does away with long and cumbersome details of the bank, like the IFSC code or account number of the recipient. The only condition being that the recipient's phone number must be linked to their bank account.[165]

§5. Changing Face of the Banking System in India

138. Despite the vulnerabilities and security glitches the banking network in India has reached its most advanced stage in the present decade. The changing face of the banking system in the country owes much to net proliferation and development of innovative technologies. Slowly, it is moving toward a digital future and is on the go. The Indian banking system consists of 12 public sector banks, 22 private sector banks, 44 foreign banks, 43 regional rural banks, 1,484 urban cooperative banks, and 96,000 rural cooperative banks, in addition to cooperative credit institutions. As on September 2021, the total number of ATMs in India increased to 213,145 out of which 47.5% are in rural and semi-rural areas. As of June 2022, the

165. Unified Payments Interface—Instant Mobile Payments—7.1.20, https://cleartax.in/s/upi-unified-payments-interface.

number of bank accounts opened under the government's flagship financial inclusion drive *"Pradhan Mantri Jan Dhan Yojana (PMJDY)"*reached 45.60 crore and deposits in the *Jan Dhan* bank accounts totaled INR 1.68 trillion (USD 21.56 billion). India is the largest market in the world for Android-based mobile lending apps, accounting for 82% of all online lenders worldwide. It currently has 887 active lending apps. The digital payment revolution has changed the financial behavior of customers whereas debit cards have widely replaced credit cards as the preferred payment mode in India. In May 2022, UPI recorded 5.95 billion transactions worth INR 10.41 trillion (USD 133.46 billion).[166]

166. Banking Industry Report, June 2022, https://www.ibef.org/industry/banking-presentation.

Chapter 5. Law of Evidence in the Digital Environment (Incl. Rules Regarding Electronic Archiving)

§1. GENERALLY

139. The main drawback of electronic evidence is LOVE or Lack of Visual evidence. Evidence in physical form remains a pet of the traditional law of evidence be it a document, an object, a photograph, a weapon, and the like. It was not only easy to preserve but easy to present in the law court and comparatively had a longer life. But with the digital revolution, all this changed and the production of electronic evidence in law courts became a challenge. The first computer evidence offered in the court was information generated by businesses. Long before computers became a household appliance, telephone companies and banks were using them to record, process, and report information that their businesses required.[167] But today, computers are no longer the exclusive appliance of commercial domains. They have reached the common man's table and thus they cover mines and mines of information stored in it giving birth to legal issues. Internet evidence is unique in the sense that it is so easy to create, alter, distort, modify, or even delete in nanoseconds. Collection of internet evidence and presenting it in court in its original form is yet another challenge faced by law enforcers. The Model Law on Electronic Commerce[168] apart from other subjects deals with the admissibility and evidentiary weight of data messages (Article 9(1)). The Article contains the rule that in legal proceedings, rules of evidence would not apply to exclude a data message either solely because it is a data message, electronic in format, or if it is the best evidence that the person adducing it could reasonably be expected to obtain on the grounds that it is not in its original form.

Indian Scenario—India being a signatory to the Model Law has imbibed most of the principles declared there in its legal provisions. Construction of new law provisions and amendments in existing laws continue. It not only attempts to define certain related terms but has given recognition to many of the electronic practices which lacked the same for quite some time. First, the traditional law defining the term "Evidence" has been amended to include electronic evidence as well by amending section 3 of the Indian Evidence Act 1872(1 of 1872). Section 3 thus say:

> 3 "Evidence" means and includes—
> (2) all documents including electronic records produced for the inspection of the court.

A separate section in the IT Act gives legal recognition to electronic records for the purposes of evidence. Legal Recognition of Electronic Records says that if the law requires any matter to be in writing or in typewritten form or printed form then even any information or matter which is contained in electronic form and is accessible shall be deemed to satisfy the requirement of the section (section 4). Thus, the

167. T Vikram, *Cybercrimes: A Study with a Case*, Indian Police Journal 80 (July–September 2002).
168. 51/162, Model Law on Electronic Commerce adopted by the UNCITRAL adopted on Dec. 16, 1996.

section is an attempt to supplement the traditional provisions requiring a document to be in "writing" by allowing the matter in the electronic form to be treated as "written" if the need arises. This is a commendable step as it will solve a good number of problems in the application of procedural laws as it is quite common that these traditional laws have known paper documents, and intangible or digital evidence are causing hardships in the path of investigation.

140. Apart from this, the IT Act 2000 has also added a new section 65-B to the Evidence Act regarding the admissibility of electronic records. The section says that any information in the electronic form whether printed on paper, stored, recorded, or copied in optical or magnetic media produced by a computer shall be considered as document and shall be admissible in evidence if it satisfies the conditions: First, the computer output containing the information was produced by the computer during the period over which the computer was used regularly to store or process information for the purposes of any activities regularly carried on over that period by the person having lawful control over it. Second, the information of the kind contained in the electronic record or of the kind from which the information so contained is derived, was during that period regularly fed into the computer in the ordinary course of the said activities. Third, throughout the material period if the computer was not functioning well or at all then such electronic record should have remained unaffected by such non-functioning, etc. Fourth, the information in the electronic record should have been fed into the computer as a regular activity (section 65-B). Thus, this amendment will help the prosecution and the defense where the evidence produced is electronic in nature. The applicable law for adducing Internet Evidence is section 65-B of the IT Act and the relevant amended provisions of the Indian Evidence Act 1872 (1 of 1872). The cumulative effect of both these provisions is that certain computer outputs of the original electronic record are now made admissible as evidence in law courts without proof or production of the original record. Thus, the matter on computer printouts, floppy disks, and CDs, whether original or downloaded from the internet is now admissible in law courts.

§2. Electronic Archiving

141. Everywhere, everything and everyone is changing to electronics. The digital revolution has digitized every facet of human life and all fields of knowledge, be it education, books, medicine, administration, businesses, sports, transportation, and all and sundry. But the mines of information contained in intangible form have a shorter life if not preserved in a proper way. The primary goal of digital archiving is the storage, retrieval, and access of rare documents with the aid of electronic technology for image capturing and reproducing. The main aim is to bring the entire treasure of knowledge as well the present bulk of information generated by the ICTs in such a compact digital form that it becomes easy, convenient, and time-saving to reach the particular piece of knowledge instantly and also to access it easily and quickly at the same time preserving it for future. Hence, electronic archiving can be termed as Repositories of digital information which would carry a nation's social, economic, cultural, and intellectual heritage forever.

I. Challenges of Electronic Information

142. Electronic information is volatile by nature. The mammoth amount of data in a system and the unfathomable information trove is of perishable nature. Other than normal information, the information in the form of evidence is all the more precious as its destruction will end in a gross miscarriage of justice. Its technicalities and presenting it in the form of evidence in law courts make the job of an investigator a complex one. Factors that are harmful to the originality of the data must be guarded against:[169] These are:

(1) as digital evidence is perishable: humidity, temperature, vibrations, physical mutilation, and magnetic fields created by a strong magnet over a disk or computer commands, such as "erase," or "format" can destroy the data;
(2) computer viruses or malicious programs can also destroy the data;
(3) improper handling during transportation may also cause loss or damage; and
(4) computer data can be destroyed by a strong magnetic field (low-density magnetic media is more susceptible to such interference than high-density media).

Thus, consequently, the question rises of maintaining its originality and preserving it for future use technically called "electronic archiving."

II. Electronic Archiving: Indian Way

143. In June 2011, the National Archives of India (NAI) signed an MOU with the "Centre for Development of Advanced Computing" (C-DAC)under the Ministry of Communication and Information Technology, New Delhi, for the digital preservation of electronic records. Under this Project, NAI developed its own digital preservation capabilities in fulfillment of the mandate of the Public Records Act of 1993 and took care of the electronic archives being generated in various Ministries / Departments of the Government of India electronically in a big way. Through this joint venture, NAI also designed a curriculum on digital preservation for training the archivists and record keepers who need to update their skills for managing electronic records. The Project continued up to 2017.

The Indian National Digital Preservation Programme, Department of Electronics and Information Technology (DeitY) approved the Center of Excellence for Digital Preservation project in 2011. It mainly aimed at:

(1) Conducting research and development in digital preservation to produce tools, technologies, solutions, and infrastructures to ensure that the digital information remains discoverable, accessible, readable, usable, reliable, authentic, and trustworthy on a long-term basis.
(2) Developing the digital preservation repositories.

---

169. SC Agarwal, *Cyber Crime: Prevention & Investigation*, Indian Police Journal 88(April–June 2002).

(3) Defining the digital preservation standards by taking the help of experts and disseminating the related information throughout India.
(4) Building the technical competencies required for the audit and certification of trustworthy digital repositories.

III. Digitalaya: The Archival System in India

144. The Human-Centered Design and Computing (HCDC) develops the e-Records Management and Archival System with the following objectives:

(a) E-records management.
(b) Long-term archival and preservation.
(c) Digital repository development.
(d) Controlled access to digital resources.

The HCDC Group developed the digital preservation "standard & guidelines" notified by the MeitY.[170] Apart from the above initiatives, a Conference was also held by the Center of Excellence for Digital Preservation in collaboration with European Alliance for Permanent Access (APA) in New Delhi in 2014. It highlighted national policy on digital preservation.

170. Notification No. 1(2)/2010-EG-II dated Dec. 13, 2013 applicable for all e-governance applications in India by the Ministry of Electronics and Information Technology, Government of India.

Chapter 6. Consumer Protection (Online Sales and Online Services)

§1. Introduction

145. E-Commerce has made possible, the impossible. Buying and selling from the comfort of home were unimaginable only a few decades ago. It was in the year 1994, August 11, when a man sold a CD by the band Sting to his friend through the website NetMarket, an American retail platform. He is recalled as the first buyer through the World Wide Web or e-commerce.[171] Since then the world transformed the physical markets into online sales and purchase platforms; the WTO defines it as, "ecommerce is the production, distribution, marketing, sales or delivery of goods and services by electronic means" E-Commerce comprises B2B, i.e., business-to-business transactions, B2C or Business to Consumer dealings (like Amazon, Flipkart, Jabong), C2C where consumers are in direct contact with each other, and C2B which is the reverse of B2C where a consumer can sell his products to a company or business organization. In India, the Information Technology Act 2000 governs the basic applicability of e-commerce. It is based on the UNCITRAL Model but is not a comprehensive legislation to deal with e-commerce-related activities in the country.

§2. The Consumer

146. The consumer is the pivot of the commercial world. The term consumer is not a new one though with technological advancement it has gained vital dimensions. In India, a number of laws have been protecting the consumer's interests, though in a sporadic manner, until 1986 when the law relating to retail commerce and consumer protection was consolidated into The Consumer Protection Act 1986. Before 1986, there were a number of Acts[172] that protected the consumer in a piecemeal manner and were quite specific in their application. Especially in the area of ICT, consumers availing services of not only a mobile telephone but of cable TV and other online services have reached millions. Thus, the TRAI has also come up with regulations and law to protect the interest of consumers in respect of communication services. Consumerism or the government's concern to protect consumer interest has also gained momentum. In the newly enacted Competition Act 2002 there has been a neo-wave concern for the consumer.

Consumer Protection Act 2019 was passed in July 2020, which aims at empowering consumers and protecting more and more of their rights. For this, the Act 2019 establishes a Central Consumer Protection Authority (CCPA) which is empowered to investigate the violations of the rights of consumers, order the recall of unsafe

171. Jyoti Langote, *E-commerce in India: An Analysis of Present Status, Challenges and Opportunities*, Journal of Emerging Technologies and Innovative Research 4(4) (April 2019).

172. The Code of Civil Procedure 1908, The Indian Contract Act 1872, The Sale of Goods Act 1930, The Indian Penal Code 1860, The Standards of Weights and Measures Act 1976, The Motor Vehicles Act 1988, The Monopoly and Restrictive Trade Practices Act 1969 (now repealed).

goods, and services, and order the discontinuance of unfair trade practices and misleading advertisements. There are provisions to impose penalties on manufacturers, endorsers, and publishers of misleading advertisements. There are rules under it to prevent unfair trade practices on e-commerce platforms. The Act 2019 is an all-embracing Act and it puts an obligation on e-commerce platforms to inform the consumers about return, refund, exchange, warranty, guarantee, delivery and shipment, mode of payment, grievance redressal mechanism, etc. In the earlier act of 1986, there was single point access to justice but this act gives the aggrieved consumer a cost-effective (no fee up to 5 million value matters), easier, and fast mode of resorting to justice and filing complaints electronically in the Consumer Disputes Resolution System. It empowers the District and State Commissions to review their own orders.

As a sequel to the Consumer Protection Act 2019 the Central Government notified the Consumer Protection (Jurisdiction of the District Commission, the State Commission, and the National Commission) Rules 2021. The Act of 2019 envisages a three-tier quasi-judicial mechanism at the District, State, and National levels for the redressal of consumer disputes. The product or services up to the value of 50 lakhs (5 million) rupees will be heard at the District level, products or services between 5 lakhs and 2 crore (20 million) will be heard at State level Commissions, and suits valuing above 2 crores will be heard at the National Commission. The Act of 2019 also allows filing suits electronically for which a portal named E-*Daakhil* has been set up. This will give the aggrieved consumer a hassle-free, inexpensive, and fast approach to justice. It includes an e-notice, document downloading facility, and video conferencing hearing link, etc. Normal disposal of cases is fixed at three months while those requiring laboratory testing, etc., will have to be disposed of within five months.[173]

§3. Consumer Protection

147. The protection of consumers online is being addressed by the legislations of the real world. The Indian Contract Act 1872 and the Consumer Protection Act 1986, and the Reserve Bank of India's continuous regulations and circulars also provide protection to the consumer. *Educating the user*: Making the users aware of the complicated technologies and at the same time keeping them updated on the changing technology in this field will help avoid the violations to some extent. The thrust area of user awareness is to make the user understand the importance of confidentiality and secrecy to be maintained by them in internet banking transactions. The responsibility mainly lies with the banks to start user awareness programs. The online users can be categorized as follows:

(1) Non-users who do not bank online.
(2) Users who bank online only to check accounts, etc., but do not transact.

173. Ministry of Consumer Affairs, Food & Public Distribution. Dated December 2021. Press Information Bureau. Delhi.

(3) Users who extensively use the online banking system and do online transactions.[174]

The non-users mainly have reservations about the security of their wealth and valuable information, lack of knowledge of computers that increase their dependency on others, and such lack of demo initiates them to avert internet banking. The second type or the non-transactors are apprehensive and find the entire online experience as a complex routine. They too felt the need to have more knowledge on operating their online accounts and on security issues. Lastly, the vigorous transactor looked for an error-free transaction, valued advanced options for time-saving, and expected more services from the bank.[175] Majorly, all three types of users give importance to three Ss: *simplicity, security, and service*. The online clientele commonly faces hardships with the new terminology used in internet banking: market gimmicks, payment through banking portals, the delicate nature of operations, like the click of a wrongly used button, etc.; actually need a full training course for the customers to transform the novice user to a satisfied and error-free one.

I. Rights of Consumer

148. Under the Consumer Protection Act 1986 the consumer has been accorded valuable rights among which is the right to be informed about the quality, quantity, potency, purity, standard, and price of goods to save the consumer from unfair trade practices (section 6(b)). Apart from this, the TRAI has specifically been formulating Regulations and issuing Directions[176] regarding providing prior information to the consumer as follows:

(1) All publications/advertisements of tariffs shall be in a specified format and shall provide certain essential information.
(2) The pulse rate/tariff for premium rate service shall be published in all communication/advertisements.
(3) The service providers shall inform customers in writing within a week of activation of service of the details of their tariff plans.
(4) The service providers shall provide in printed material, in English and Vernacular Languages to customers at the time of enrolment, the following:
   - Full and complete tariff information sheet.
   - The features of the service offered regarding rate and other value-added services.
   - The terms and conditions in simple wordings.
   - The rights of the consumers under TRAI.
   - The common charter of service agreed upon by the service providers.

174. Jhumkee Iyengar & Manisha Belvalkar, *Case Study of Online Banking in India: User Behaviour and Design Guidelines*.
175. *Ibid.*, 5.
176. Circular No. 301–9/2006-Eco. Dated May 23, 2006 issued by TRAI.

The Telecom Consumers Protection Regulations 2012 secures the rights of consumers and from 2012 to 2020 (11th Amendment) there has been a spate of amendments to it. The amendment of 2020 secures the consumers' rights to information regarding the activation of international mobile roaming service, its tariff, and other incidental matters regarding the use of mobile phones in foreign countries.[177]

§4. Online Sales

149. The Online Sale is an offshoot of e-commerce, it has revolutionized the marketplace when one opts for it, the marketplace is no longer a crowded place with weather battings, jostling, and elbowing. It is from the comfort of one's bedroom that marketing can be done using the internet and other electronic media to buy and sell products and provide services. With the use of a variety of websites, search engines, social media, and email one can do purchases to any financial limit. The sale comprises not only buying but also selling products. Amazon is a behemoth in the e-commerce space.

§5. Online Services

150. India though predominantly an agricultural country has moved fast on the internet highway and has left behind most of the developing countries of the world in the matter of utilizing the internet. Government policies including the one which allowed hundred percent foreign direct investments (FDI) and the Pandemic (COVID-19) served as a stimulus to expand the area of e-commerce in the country. This happens even though internet penetration is not very encouraging in rural area due to a lack of ICT infrastructure and computer literacy. The scene of e-commerce users in India is as follows:[178]

Active internet users (mostly mobile users)	February 2022	658 million
Active e-commerce penetration	76.7%	
Active social media users	February 2022	467 million
Online retail market size by 2022	73 bn USD	

E-Commerce Users in India

151. It is yet another big segment of e-commerce where the use of ICTs brings home a host of services both government and private. In reality, online government services are but another form of e-governance.

177. Telecom Regulatory Authority of India—Notification No. 301–20/2020-F&EA. New Delhi, Dated September 2020.
178. https://www.statista.com/topics/2454/e-commerce-in-india/ Dated Jul. 8, 2022.

MINISTRY OF FINANCE, e.g., Link *Aadhar* Card with Pan, Startup India Seed Fund Scheme, ePublishing, e-Auction India, G2C, etc.	**120 SERVICES**
MINISTRY OF PETROLEUM AND NATURAL GAS, e.g., Application for gas supply, booking of LTC Ticket, HP gas complaints, cylinder booking, etc.	**100 SERVICES**
MINISTRY OF HEALTH AND FAMILY WELFARE,- e.g., National Tele consultation service, Health ID, COVID-19 Sample Collection Management System, Guidelines for infection prevention, etc.	**71 SERVICES**
MINISTRY OF PERSONNEL, PUBLIC GRIEVANCES AND PENSIONS-Application for Family Pension, for Death Gratuity of Government Servant, Login on *Bhavaishya* Pension Sanction, etc.	**60 SERVICES**
TOTAL NUMBER OF SERVICES IN ALL THE STATES	**12317 SERVICES**

Instances of Government Online Services in India.[179]

The online services encompass G2B and G2C categories. The G2B services include: Broadcast *Seva* Portal, e-counselling, e-filling tax-return, information regarding goods and services tax, government e-market place, government portal for MSME registration, online application of ISBN for publications, and many more. The Government to Citizens Services include all information relating to: *Aadhar* or Unique Identification Numbers for individuals in India, Cybercrime Reporting Portal, Delhi Police Portal, e-India Information which provides political and geographical details of India, e-Visa which provides information about e-visa service of the Government of India, ICT innovations of the Election Commission of India, etc. There are also a number of citizen-centric Online Judicial Services in India which include :Indian courts and e-Governance initiatives, the Inter-operable Criminal Justice System, National Law Schools information, Pro Bono legal Services, etc.

179. National Government Services Portal, https://services.india.gov.in/service/ministry_services?ln=en&cmd_id=1859.

Chapter 7. Liability of Online Service Providers

§1. Liabilities Generally

152. "Every Internet transaction requires the participation of multiple intermediaries and may well involve more than two actors."[180] The internet seems to flow between the user and the host yet no transaction ends between the two parties exclusively. The postal carriers and telephone network are the predecessors of these online intermediaries though automated transmission marks the dividing line between the two. The internet is an amalgamation of human and non-human agencies that are equally important for its survival and when the question of liability regarding the dissemination of illegal content arises the human face of the internet is pinpointed for the arraignment. The virtual world of cyberspace abounded with all the echelons of human society, be it artists, statesmen, organizations, businesses, individuals, or so to say, criminals. Without the agency of the human hand, the virtual world will be reduced to non-existent. The ISPs are the first ones who come to a lawman's mind when the question of liability arises as they are "the 'glue' that binds the Internet together, via their supply of TCP/IP packet switching services, which allow third parties to communicate data packets across the 'network of networks'."[181] The liability of the ISPs is multifaceted and they are pinpointed not only for the content but are also held strictly liable for the harm caused to the victim apart from the civil and criminal liability they entail. With the changing of the technological scenario, it is being realized that the ISPs have taken multifold roles like that of access providers, network providers, and hosts and with it, the liability falls into different components depending on the particular role the ISP was involved in respect of the disputed act. Their liability basics are continuing to decline with the advent of automated technology; the greater the automation, the lesser the role of these intermediaries, and thus minimal is their liability area. The ISPs are the mediators, carriers of information, and online counterparts of telecommunications companies. Apart from serving individuals, ISPs also serve large companies providing a direct connection from the company's networks to the internet. ISPs themselves are connected to one another through Network Access Points (NAPs).[182]

I. Liability of ISPs in India

153. The liability of ISPs is determined by the IT Act 2000 and also by the guidelines issued on August 24, 2007,[183] further amended in 2010.[184] Thus, according to Clause 33, the guidelines are:

180. Chris Reed, Chapter 2: *From Each According to His Ability; Actors and Activities in the Internet World* in *Internet Law: Text and Materials* (Cambridge University Press, 2004) 24.
181. Chris Reed, *Computer Law* (Oxford University Press, 2003).
182. *See*, http//www.pcwebopedia.com;TERM/1/ISP.html.
183. Guidelines issued by DS Cell-DoT, Ministry of Communications and IT Government of India, New Delhi.
184. No. 820–1/2006/LR Vol. (II) Dated Jan. 25, 2010 *Ibid.*

(1) ISPs must prevent unlawful content and messages from being carried on the network. In case of a report of such obscene or objectionable content, the enforcement agencies shall prevent its carriage.
(2) ISPs must ensure that content carried by them must not infringe "international and domestic cyber laws."
(3) Use of an ISP network for anti-national activities would be construed as an offense under the Indian Penal code 1860.
(4) The ISPs are under obligation to follow the IT Act provisions failing which it will entail damages.
(5) ISPs must ensure and take care that their networks cannot be used to endanger or make vulnerable a networked infrastructure.
(6) ISPs must also ensure that their services are not used to break in or attempt to break into Indian networks.
(7) ISPs must provide without any delay all the tracing facilities to trace nuisance, obnoxious call messages, or communications transported through their network. Tracing facilities are to be provided to the Enforcement Department and to the Intelligence Department, etc.
(8) ISPs are also under the obligation to provide facilities to the government to counteract espionage, subversive acts, sabotage, or any other unlawful activity.
(9) The ISPs must also maintain communication of privacy over their network (Clause 34).

II. Liability of Electronic Communications Service Providers

154. The Telecom and Regulatory Authority of India is the main body that governs the liability of electronic communications providers. Telecommunication services under the TRAI Act 1997 have been defined as services of any description that includes electronic mail, voice mail, data services, audio text services, video text services, radio paging, and cellular mobile services and which are made available to the consumers by the transmission of signs, signals, wires, etc., or by other electromagnetic means but does not include broadcasting services (section 2(k)).

III. Liability of Information Society Service Providers

155. The IT Act 2000 is the sole law in India that explicitly mentions the law regarding the liability of ISPs. The law has undergone a massive change whereas the contours of the liability of the service providers have expanded; their obligations under the law are more defined and their exemptions circumscribed and conditional. The IT (Amendment) Act 2008 (10 of 2009), has inserted a catena of new sections connected with the liability of the intermediaries and their answerability before the law. Chapter XII comprising section 79 has been replaced and the term "intermediaries" is redefined. Apart from the IT Act 2000 rules made by the Central Government and the guidelines issued by the Telecom Department also circumscribe such liability within the legal framework when at the time of issuing the license to provide service, the ISPs are not only bound to follow the guidelines but they are also to abide by the security conditions of the licensor, i.e., the GoI. All these provisions define the limits of liability of the ISPs. An "intermediary" is defined under the Act as follows:

> "intermediary" regarding electronic records means any person who on behalf of another person receives, stores, or transmits that record or provides any service with respect to that record and includes telecom service providers, network service providers, internet service providers, web-hosting service providers, search engines, online payment sites, online auction sites, online—market places, and cyber cafes [section 2 (w)].

This definition of intermediary is an elaborate one and has explicitly mentioned even the different versions of service providers. It appears to be in consonance with the definition given by Graham J.H. Smith who for the first time identified the different roles the intermediaries play.[185] It is an improvement on the previous definition of the term given under the unamended IT Act in the sense that it has listed the names of various versions of the intermediaries and leaves no doubt regarding their existence. Moreover the term "cyber café" has also been separately defined in the Act to mean any facility from where access to the internet is offered by any person in the ordinary course of business to the members of the public (section 2 (na)). This definition makes it easier for law enforcers to fix the liability of an intermediary.

Exemption of Intermediaries, section 79 of the IT Act gives conditional immunity to the intermediaries. The intermediary shall not be liable for any third-party information (information dealt with by an intermediary in his capacity as an intermediary), data, or communication link available or hosted by him if the following conditions are satisfied:

(1) If the function of the intermediary is limited to providing access to a communication system over which information made available by third parties is transmitted or temporarily stored or hosted.
(2) The intermediary does not initiate the transmission.
(3) When he does not select the receiver of the transmission.
(4) The intermediary does not select or modify the information contained in the transmission.
(5) The intermediary observes due diligence and follows the guidelines issued by the Central Government or any of its agencies.

However, the intermediary will not get the benefit of exemption if:

(1) He has conspired, abetted, aided, or was induced whether by threats or promise or otherwise in the commission of the unlawful act.

185. Graham JH Smith & Bird & Bird, *Internet Law and Regulation* (4th ed. Sweet & Maxwell, 2007).

(2) Even after receiving information and actual knowledge about the unlawful act, the intermediary fails to expeditiously remove or disable access to the material and has also in doing so, not tampered with any object which could serve as evidence.

Thus, the exemption of the intermediary from being liable under the law rests on several conditions. It is obvious that if the intermediary is proven to be a partner in the posting of the incriminating material, his exemption is nullified. It is to be noted that to make the intermediary liable, it is not necessary to prove his *malafides* in cybersecurity matters and the intermediary cannot claim exemption on the ground that he was not aware of the malicious and incriminating material. In fact to get the exemption certain physical acts should be proved like he did not initiate the transmission, or did not select or modify the information.

New Legal Regime for the Intermediaries—The intention of the legislature behind the exemption of intermediaries is to encourage the free flow of information and that unnecessary restrain on them would hamper the growth of technological and communicational innovations. But the misuse of the internet and its criminalization has led to clothe this exemption with several safeguards. A perusal of the Amendment Act in the following sections shows that the scope of the exemption of the intermediaries has become limited and their freedom has to be enjoyed within defined legal limits:

- Section 6-A[186]—This section gives power to the Central Government or to the State Government to not only select the nature of service provided by the service provider but also to fix the service charges rates that are to be charged by such service providers. Thus, the service providers from the very beginning of their existence are not choosers and they have to abide by the orders of the government in this regard. The section on public interest also fixes the rates to be charged by them by law so that the innocent and the ignorant do not suffer at the hands of the service providers.
- Section 7-A—The section empowers the related authorities to inspect the related data and information which is in electronic form. Thus, by virtue of this section, whenever it is required by the Enforcement Department, the information stored or hosted by the intermediaries can also be the subject of audit and information.
- Section 43-A—A body corporate which possesses, deals with, or handles any personal data in a computer resource which it owns, controls, or operates is negligent in implementing security practices which results in wrongful loss or wrongful gain to any person then, such body corporate shall be liable to pay damages to the aggrieved.
- Section 67-A—The section puts an obligation on the intermediaries to take care of preserved data. For this, the Central Government is empowered to make rules in this regard. Any intermediary who violates such rules is held criminally liable; the penalty for which may extend to imprisonment up to three years and with a fine.

186. Inserted by virtue of s. 7 of the IT (Amendment) Act 2008 (10 of 2009).

- Section 69—The government has the power to order intercepting, monitoring, or decrypting any information on the ground of national security, public order, friendly relations with foreign States, etc., and all the intermediaries are under a duty to provide assistance and facilities to carry out the work of interception, monitoring, etc., failing which the intermediary may suffer imprisonment up to seven years and shall also be liable to pay fine.
- Section 69-A The government may order the blocking of information for public access on the ground of security of India, defense of India, friendly relations with foreign States, public order, or on the ground of prevention of any of these. For this, the government shall make rules and may order any intermediary or agency to block information failing which the intermediary may be punished with imprisonment of up to seven years and shall also be liable to a fine.
- Section 69-B—The government can order any intermediary or agency to monitor traffic data for the sake of cybersecurity for identification, analysis, prevention of intrusion, and spread of computer contaminant. The intermediary who does not obey or follow such orders may be punished with imprisonment of up to three years and may be liable to pay a fine.
- Section 70-B—The Indian Computer Emergency Team (ICERT) for the sake of cybersecurity can order any intermediary to take precautions to maintain cybersecurity in the country failing which the intermediary may be punished with imprisonment of up to one year or with a fine up to INR 1 lakh (0.1 million) or with both.
- Section 72-A—The dispelling of any information by the intermediary is rendered an offense. If any intermediary having entered into a contract with anyone to secure access to the personal information of such person discloses it to another person with the intention to cause wrongful loss or wrongful gain to someone then he will be punished with imprisonment of up to three years or with a fine which may extend up to INR 5 lakhs (0.5 million) or with both.

IV. Liability of Intermediary Service Providers

A. *Mere Conduits*

156. This categorized liability of mere conduits as initiated by the Electronic Commerce Directive[187] is not separately defined under the IT Act. However, this role of the intermediary is covered under the new definition of "intermediary" by the IT (Amendment) Act 2008—section 2(w) *supra.*

187. Liability of Intermediary Service Providers, European Union Directive (Feb. 8, 2000) also called E-Commerce Directive though not exhaustive on the point is yet a welcome step. It was to be implemented before Jan. 17, 2002. Ernst-Jan Louwers & Prpf. Corien E.J. Prins, *International Computer Law*, Vol. 2 (Lexis Nexis, 2004) 22–63.22.05[A].

B. Caching

157. This role of the intermediary also comes under the definition of "intermediary" in section 2(w) of the IT (Amendment) Act 2008.

C. Hosting, Hyperlinks, and Search Engines

158. Section 2(w) of the IT Act specifically covers the liability of "telecom service providers, network service providers, Internet service providers, web-hosting service providers, search engines, online payment sites, online auction-sites, online—market places, and cyber cafes."

V. Liability of Certification Service Providers

159. It is an era of electronic communication; the providers of certification services related to e-signatures are important in this regard. Electronic certificates are made trustworthy thereby. The EU directive 1999/93/EC introduces minimum liability regime to be adopted by various states.

VI. Liability of Domain Name Registrars

160. In India, no specific legislation is available for the liability of domain name registrars. However, cyber squatters are not uncommon in India and disputes do arise between the registrant and the domain name holder. The Information Technology Act 2000 and the IT (Amendment) Act 2008 also lack any specific provision on the subject. However, in India disputes regarding domain names have arisen which were mainly between the registrant and the domain name holder. For this, the courts in India have resorted to the ICANN Policy and have also applied the Common Law (Doctrine of Passing off, etc.). As domain names are treated in a similar way as trademarks, the law relating to trademarks is applied by the courts. A Registrar provides direct services to the Domain Name Registrants. The Registrar database contains customer information in addition to the DNS information contained in the Registry database. Registrars process name registrations for internet end users and send necessary DNS information to a Registry for entry into the Centralized Registry database and ultimate propagation over the internet, e.g., ERNET is the exclusive registrar for ac.in, edu.in, and res.in. .IN Registry is the official Registrar in India which facilitates the registration of domain names through its accredited registrars spread all over the world. The accredited Registrars in India fall under three categories: (1) IDN (Internationalized Domain Names) Accredited Registrars; (2) List of Registrars; (3) Government Registrars.

The ICANN has delegated IDN in seven Indian Languages to NIXI. These are (1) *Devnagiri; (2) Bengali; (3) Telegu; (4) Gujarati; (5) Urdu; (6) Tamil; (7) Gurumukhi (Punjabi*). The Registry has the authority to deny or suspend a registration if it conflicts with the sovereign national interest or public order. As no specific law is available hence if the registrar violates this direction then he will be held liable either under the law of tort or under the Indian Penal Code 1860 for offenses, like negligence, cheating, or mischief, as the case may be.

§2. The New Law Regarding Intermediaries

161. The Information Technology (Intermediary Guidelines and Digital Media Ethics Code) Rules, 2021[188] supersede the Information Technology (Intermediaries Guidelines) Rules, 2011. As online activity is expanding every day and the number and forms of intermediaries are changing every day hence the Government of India has come up with more Rules to regulate the activities of these intermediaries online. At the same time, it also categorizes the intermediaries as per their activity as below:

(1) Significant Social Media Intermediaries (SSMI) means a social media intermediary having such number of registered users (50 lakhs or more, equivalent to 5 million or more) in India above such threshold as notified by the Central Government. Section 2(1)(v).
(2) Social Media Intermediaries (SMI) means an intermediary which primarily enables online interaction between two or more users and allows creating uploading, sharing, disseminating, modifying, or accessing information using these services. Section 2(1)(w).

The Rules 2021 also lay down a Code of Ethics for the publishers of Digital Media content. The matter is discussed in detail under the heading Duties of Intermediaries *infra.*

188. The Gazette of India—Extraordinary—Part II—s. 3—Sub-s. (i)—No. 98 New Delhi, Thursday, Feb. 25, 2021/PHALGUNA 6, 1942.

Part IV. Intellectual Rights ("Digital Rights")

Chapter 1. Patent Law

§1. General Statement

162. Digital rights are the offspring of the digital world. They mainly imply the right to privacy and data protection. Information is the buzzword of today's world and many social and legal issues surround it. As per the Office of The High Commissioner of Human Rights 2021, there is a need to put a moratorium on the use of Artificial Intelligence (AI) which poses a threat to digital rights. These Digital rights are specifically recognized by various international organizations which can be enumerated below:

(1) The High Commissioner of Human Rights—It is the fountain of human rights for the entire mankind. The Office of the High Commissioner for Human Rights (OHCHR) advocated that human rights must be at the root of all the infrastructure for the use of technologies. Emphasis was laid on the inclusion of human rights when such technologies are used for surveillance and contact tracing in response to the COVID-19 pandemic.[189]

(2) European Union Commission Declaration on Digital Rights—The European Commission advocates for safe cyberspace and digital privacy for all the members of the European Union (EU).[190] It covers rights and principles for digital transformation and enjoyment of the digitization of the entire information technology while at the same time securing and enriching the rights of users and the masses. The principles aim at making every facet of human life, like their privacy, safe and affordable access and use of high-speed digital connectivity, access to comprehend information technology, and the like. The principles are deeply rooted in EU law. The Commission laid down its vision for Europe's digital transformation by 2030.

189. Annual Report of the United Nations High commissioner for Human Rights. 47th. Session. Jun. 21–Jul. 9, 2021. Agenda Item 2. A/HRC/47/54, para. 123, p. 15.

190. European Commission—Press release, Dated Jan. 26, 2022, https://ec.europa.eu/commission/presscorner/detail/en/IP_22_452.

§2. Digital Rights in India

163. Though India still lags behind in the digital literacy race yet there is a formidable chunk of the Indian population that uses digital technology. As such at this juncture, it becomes all the more necessary to save the digital rights of the masses who are still not aware of these valuable rights, namely the right to privacy, the right to data protection, etc. Part III of the Indian Constitution envisages a number of Fundamental Rights which throws a ring of protection around the citizen against the mighty state. Though there is always a whisper in the political corridors to secure the digital rights of the citizens yet it is felt and declared informally that digital rights are included in the Fundamental Rights. The law, namely the draft of the Data Protection Act 2019 which aims at securing the digital rights of the citizens, is still in the pipeline and the delay in its legislation is only delaying the legal protection of valuable rights.

§3. Patents

164. Patents play a constructive role in everyday life and they enrich life on earth; thus, "Patented inventions have pervaded every aspect of human life, from electric lighting (Edison and Swan) and sewing machines (patents held by Howe and Singer) to magnetic resonance imagining (MRI) (patents held by Damadian) and the iPhone (patents held by Apple)."[191] The person who invents or creates a thing of utility for the first time is given recognition by the state.

I. History

165. History of Patents in India—India too has sufficient legal provisions for the protection of patents. The granting of patents in India dates back to 1856 when George Alfred Penning, an engineer from Calcutta, was the first person to apply for a patent for "exclusive privilege" for his invention "an efficient *Punkah* Pulling Machine" and the then Government of India granted him the patent.[192] The 1856 Act was fashioned on the United Kingdom (U.K.) Act of 1852. The patent law in India passed through a long journey of reforms[193] until it reached its present state.

---

191. World Intellectual Property Organisation Report, p. 6. (WIPO) is an intellectual organisation established in 1970, the objective of which is to preserve and protect the rights of the owners of IP worldwide and the owners of such IP are given recognition and are also rewarded for their ingenuity.
192. Rajkumar S. Adukia, *Handbook of Intellectual Property Rights in India.*
193. In 1911, the Patents and Designs Act (Act II of 1911) was passed which later passed through several amendments in 1920, 1930 and in 1945. After Independence, the Government of India appointed a Committee under the chairmanship of Justice (Dr.) Bakshi Tek Chand in 1949 to review the patent law in the country. Thus, based on the recommendations of this Committee, the 1911 Act was amended mainly in relation to working of inventions and compulsory licence/revocation. Another amendment came in 1952 with the aim of providing compulsory licence for food, medicines, insecticide, germicide, fungicide, etc. Again in 1957, another Committee was formed under the chairmanship of Justice N. Rajagopala Ayyangar to have a relook at the patent law. However,

The Patents Act 1970 passed through piecemeal amendments made in 1994, 1999, and 2002 and lastly in 2005. These amendments attempt to make the law more exhaustive and encompassing.

§4. DEFINITION OF PATENTS

166. "Patents give temporary protection to technological inventions and design rights to the appearance of mass-produced goods."[194] "A Patent is defined as a group of exclusive rights that a national government can give to either an inventor or their assignee for a specific period of time, provided that he publically divulges the invention."[195] It provides an incentive to the creators of a novice; it gives them a reward for their contribution toward science or society. It denotes that creation by a person cannot be commercialized, used, distributed, or sold without the inventor's consent. Once the creator of a new thing gets a patent from the government it becomes his privilege to either sell it to others for gain or to allow its use. However, a patent is granted for a limited period depending on the particular law of a country, and the patent owner enjoys these rights only within such a period. Once the period expires, the creation enters the public domain and then the right of the patent owner comes to an end, also called "becoming off" patent. Patents protect technological innovation:

- once things such as machines and mouse traps and today things such as new molecules, plant varieties, and software. By describing his invention and showing that it is new, useful, and "nonobvious," an inventor can obtain a patent that gives him the right to prevent others from making, using, or selling the invention ... .[196]
- Patents are in fact a form of copyright and as often forwarded by some thinkers, they have a close affinity as "patents and copyrights approach, nearer than any other cases belonging to forensic discussion, to what may be called the metaphysics of law, where the distinctions are, or at least may be, very subtle and refined, and, sometimes, almost evanescent."[197]

---

the Bill based on the recommendations of this Committee lapsed in 1965. Later, on the recommendations of the Joint Parliamentary Committee an amended Bill was introduced in 1967 which was later passed in the form of Patents Act 1970 and which also declared the revocation of the 1911 Act for patents in India. The Patents Act 1911 continued for designs, Rajkumar S. Adukia, *Handbook of Intellectual Property Rights in India* 11–14.

194. WR Cornish, *Intellectual Property: Patents, Copyright, Trademarks and Allied Rights* (2nd ed., Sweet & Maxwell, Universal Law Publishing Co. Pvt. Ltd., 1997) 3.
195. Marcaria.com network, available at,http://www.marcaria.com/articles/trademark-and-other-intellectual-property-resource-guide.asp.
196. Amy Kapczynski, *Access to Knowledge: A Conceptual Genealogy* in Gaelle Krikorian & Amy Kapczynski (eds.), *Access to Knowledge in the Age of Intellectual Property* (Zone Books, New York, 2010) 23.
197. Arthur R Miller & Michael H Davis, *Intellectual Property: Patent, Trademarks and Copyright in a Nutshell* (3rd ed., West Group, 2000).

Chapter 2. Trademarks (Application in the Digital Context)

§1. General Statement

167. Trademarks in the commercial field give protection from imitation. The aim of trademark law is to protect words and symbols used in the commercial field by traders to identify their goods. This will give a distinct identity to the goods of the trader. "The symbol can be a word, phrase, design, image, sound, color, or even fragrance."[198] All these are regarded as the right of the particular trader. "To qualify as a mark, a symbol must 'identify and distinguish' the good or service."[199] The trademarks protect the use of a distinctive trade name in the commercial world where the holder of the mark (for e.g., Rolex) restricts its use most centrally to ensure that the consumers are not confused about the origin of a good.[200] Both the copyright and the trade mark belong to the same family and often overlap with each other. Both of these concepts are concerned with rights in intangible property but it is said that "a copyright is not a trademark and a trademark is not a copyright."[201] A copyright is a bundle of rights connected with the ideas of an author, artist, sculptor, and painter expressed in tangible form whilst a trademark affords its owner the right to use a specific mark to identify the source of the goods. Trade mark includes brand names, trade dress, service marks, certifications marks, and collective marks.[202] Thus, the key features of a trademark: the selected mark, symbol, or color, etc., should be capable of distinguishing such goods from similar goods of other manufacturers. It should be capable of being represented graphically (i.e., in paper form). It should be used or proposed to be used to mark in relation to goods for purposes of indication to express a relation between the good and the owner of it.[203] The trademark has many forms like service mark, collective mark, and certification mark. Trademark basically serves four functions:[204]

(1) It identifies the goods and services and their origin.
(2) It guarantees its unchanged quality.
(3) It advertises the goods and services.
(4) It creates an image for goods and services.

---

198. Stuart P Green, *Thirteen Ways to Steal a Bicycle: Theft Law in the Information Age* (Harvard University Press, 2012).
199. *Ibid.*
200. Amy Kapczynski, *Access to Knowledge: A Conceptual Genealogy* in Gaelle Krikorian & Amy Kapczynski (eds.), *Access to Knowledge in the Age of Intellectual Property* (Zone Books, 2010) 23.
201. Rashida YV MacMurray, *Trademarks or Copyrights: Which Intellectual Property Right Affords Its Owner the Greatest Protection of Architectural Ingenuity?* Northwestern Journal of Technology and Intellectual Property 3(2) (Spring, 2005), 112.
202. *Ibid.*, 121.
203. Rajkumar S Adukia, *Handbook of Intellectual Property Rights in India*, 66.
204. *Ibid.*, 67.

§2. Trademarks Law in India

168. The trademark law in India is more than a century old though the statutory law was made in 1860. The law was not exhaustive and before 1940 there was no trademark specific law in the country.[205] The questions of infringement and the law of *passing off* were solved by the application of section 54, Specific Relief Act 1877.[206] Later the trademark law in the country traveled through several changes.[207] The Indian Trade Marks Act 1999 is the present law which is in compliance with the TRIPS obligation and which gives better protection to the owner of trademarks, and which also lays down conditions for the acquisition of trademark and provides legal remedies in case of its violation. The Trade Mark Rules, 2002 are supplemental to the Act of 1999.

205. *Ibid.,* 14.
206. *Ibid.*
207. The declaration of ownership of the trademark was obtained under the Indian Registration Act, 1908. Later, Indian Trade Marks Act, 1940 was passed which was later replaced by the Trade and Merchandise Act, 1958.

Chapter 3. Design Protection (Application to Digital Products)

§1. THE INDIAN LAW ON SEMICONDUCTOR CHIPS

169. The Indian Law on Semiconductor Chips: Since the early 1970s, chip piracy became prevalent as its copying is easier and cheaper. A sui generis protection was thus badly required. Chip pirates without effort made considerable gains while the legitimate companies spending so much on research and development were not gaining accordingly. Thus, the Semiconductor Integrated Circuits Layout Design Act 2000 (SICLD) protects the layout design expressed in any manner which is original and which has also not been commercially exploited for two years from the date of application for registration and which is inherently distinctive and capable of being distinguishable from any other registered layout design which is protected (section 7). The Act defines the following:

- *"Semiconductor integrated circuit"* means a product having transistors or other circuitry elements, which are inseparably on a semiconductor material or an insulating material or inside the semiconductor material and designed to perform an electronic circuitry function (section 2(r)).
- *"Layout Design"* means a layout of transistors and other circuitry elements and includes lead wires connecting such elements expressed in any manner in a semiconductor integrated circuit (section 2(h)).
- *"Commercial exploitation*" in relation to SICLD means to sell, lease, offer or exhibit for sale or otherwise, or distribute semiconductor integrated circuit for any commercial purpose (section 2(e)).

Under the SICLD Act, protection is given to the layout design itself which will be different from protection in a chip product.[208] The Act in India however follows the IPIC Treaty's definition of "layout design"[209] as it requires strict adherence to the terms of the Treaty (Articles 2 through 7). Explanation to section 17 of the SICLD Act lays down that the right conferred by the registration of a layout design shall be available to the registered proprietor notwithstanding the fact that the layout design is incorporated in an article or not. Layout designs can be registered if they are (1) original; (2) inherently distinctive; (3) distinguishable from other registered layout designs; (4) not already commercially exploited for more than two years before the date of application for registration. Thus, not "novelty" but distinctiveness is the condition for registration under the Act. A layout design if it is the result of the creator's own intellectual efforts would be considered "original" for the

208. The US law follows a different pattern whereas a mask work is not eligible for protection unless it is fixed in a semiconductor chip product. Thus according to s. 901(a)(3) of the SCPA a mask work is "fixed" in a semiconductor chip product "when its embodiment in the product is sufficiently permanent or stable to permit the mask work to be perceived or reproduced from the product for a period more than transitory duration."

209. The IPIC Treaty defines it as "the three-dimensional disposition, however expressed, of the elements, at least one of which is an active element, and of some or all of the interconnections or an integrated circuit, or such a three—dimensional disposition prepared for an integrated circuit intended for manufacture." Article 2(ii).

purposes of registration. The Act recognizes that layout design will usually contain design elements already existing or protected in the semiconductor industry which is an important issue for semiconductor layout designs as they are in the vast majority of cases new compilations of well-known elements. Not only that "creator's own effort" is a condition but the Act also requires that such design should not be commonplace among the creators of layout designs and manufacturers. This can be evident by the original combination of elements of design that are not themselves original. Thus, a new topography can be the result of a combination of commonplace elements, which have not been combined in precisely the same way as before. There may also be a chance that any newly designed layout design will have at least some features or combination of features that are dissimilar to features that are already well-known in respect of semiconductor products. In a U.K. case[210] for the term "commonplace" Justice Laddie liked Counsel's submission that any design which is "trite, trivial, common-or-garden, hackneyed or of the type which would excite no particular attention in those in the relevant art is likely to be commonplace As for the second requirement under the Act, that it must be inherently distinctive or inherently capable of being distinguished from any other registered layout design although the terms that appear in the Trade Marks Act 1999 have different meanings. "Inherent distinctiveness" can be tested as follows:

- Even though well-known design elements may be there but in fact, the functions performed by it must be not only new but different from that performed by other layout designs.
- The elements and substances used in the manufacture of the layout—design should be novel in the industry.

This requirement of "distinctiveness" is peculiar to Indian law only.

The third requirement is with respect to commercial exploitation; thus any act of leasing, selling, offering, or exhibiting for sale in respect of a layout design is its commercial exploitation. The main test is to see if there is anything done for commercial purposes like distributing a layout design though not for money may also amount to commercial purposes.

In India like any other developed country law extends protection to the distinctive layout designs which are not previously commercially exploited and registration is the way to extend protection to it. There are elaborate provisions under the Semiconductor Integrated Circuits Layout Design Act 2000 (37 of 2000). The GoI is empowered under the Act to appoint a person as Registrar of Semiconductor Integrated Circuits Layout Design.[211] The GoI is also empowered to establish a Registry having a head office and several branches as the government fixes to carry out the functions under the Act. There shall for the purposes of registration be a register maintained by the Registry Office. Thus, the registration of a layout design will be done only if it fulfills the following conditions:

210. Ocular Sciences Ltd. Aspect Vision Care Limited [1997] RPC 289.

211. Section 3—*Chapter II Semiconductor Integrated Circuits Layout Design Act 2000* (37 of 2000).

- It is original.
- It is not commercially exploited anywhere in India or in a convention country. If a layout design has been commercially exploited for less than two years from the date of filing an application for registration in India or in any convention country then it will be regarded as not being commercially exploited for purposes of this Act (Proviso to section 7(1)).
- It is inherently distinctive.
- It is inherently capable of being distinguishable from any other registered layout design.

A layout design shall be considered to be original if it is the result of the creator's own intellectual efforts and is not commonly known to the creators of layout designs and manufacturers of semiconductor integrated circuits at the time of its creation. The Provision to section 7(2) says that a layout—design consisting of such combination of elements and interconnections that are commonly known among creators of designs and manufacturers of semiconductor integrated circuits shall be considered as "original" if such combination taken as a whole is the result of creator's own intellectual efforts.

The SICLID Act prohibits the registration of two or more persons who claim to be the creator of a layout design. This basic rule has an exception that when two or more persons claiming to be the creator of a layout design are so related to each other that:(a) both of them have put the combined intellectual effort in creating the design; or (b) both of them are connected in such a manner that their effort in creating the layout design becomes indistinguishable then both of them shall be registered as the joint—owner (joint proprietor) of the registered layout—design.[212] A registered proprietor in relation to a layout design is the person who is for the time being registered as the proprietor of the layout design (section 2(o)). A registered proprietor has the power to assign the layout design and to give effectual receipts for any consideration for such assignment (section 20).

I. Content of Exclusive Right

170. The registration of the layout design gives the registered proprietor of the layout design the exclusive right to the use of the layout and to obtain relief in respect of infringement. The right shall be available to the registered proprietor of that layout design irrespective of the fact as to whether the layout design is incorporated in an article or not.[213] The Act provides comprehensive protection to the layout designs of semiconductor integrated circuits as a recognized IP and also gives the proprietor a bundle of rights under it. There is one significant exception to this exclusive right; any person may reproduce the layout design "for the purposes of scientific evaluation, analysis research or teaching ..."[214] This is in consonance

212. Sections 14–17 *The Semiconductor Integrated Circuits Layout Design Act 2000*(37 of 2000).
213. Section 17 *The Semiconductor Integrated Circuits Layout Design Act 2000* (37 of 2000).
214. *Ibid.*, at s. 18.

with the fair dealing exception in copyright law. The Act also allows "reverse-engineer" layout designs for the purpose of analyzing the layout designs and incorporating the insights of their analysis into an original layout design of their own. Thus, for the sake of the development of creativity and also to follow the spirit of the IPIC (section 6(2)(b)) and the TRIPS Agreement this provision is made. This will also support the successful entry of the integrated circuit market segment with a new product that is compatible with established products. The registered proprietor also has the exclusive right to import, sell, or distribute for commercial purposes any semiconductor chip products in which the registered layout design is embodied.[215]

Enforcement of Exclusive Rights—The infringement of the layout design is regarded as an offense punishable with imprisonment up to three years or with a fine which should not be less than INR 50,000 and which may extend to INR 10 lakhs (1 million) or with both.[216] Although the Act does not provide for civil remedies but it also does not expressly rule out the application of civil remedies which means that resorting to remedies, like an injunction, accounts of profits, and damages to enforce rights regarding integrated circuit layout designs is possible. Section 16 explicitly says that "no person shall be entitled to institute any proceeding to prevent, or recover damages for the infringement of unregistered layout design" and it can be interpreted to mean that such remedies are available in respect of registered layout designs. The Act however exempts the innocent purchaser from infringing chip products who had no knowledge or any reasonable ground to know that such product is an incorporated or registered layout design. However, if after coming to know about it if the innocent purchaser continues with his acts in respect of such layout design then he will have to pay a royalty to the registered proprietor of the amount as settled between the two.[217]

II. Duration of the Protection

171. Protection under the Act extends for 10 years which is in conformity with Article 38(1) of the TRIPS Agreement. While the TRIPS Agreement and the IPIC Treaty are silent on the date of commencement of protection Indian law regards it as the date of first commercial exploitation anywhere in India or anywhere in the world whichever is earlier. Such protection shall extend up to a period of 10 years from the date of filing an application for registration or from the date of first commercial exploitation as given above (section 15).

215. *Ibid.*, at s. 18(1)(b) and Art. 6(1)(ii) of the IPIC Treaty and the TRIPS Agreement.

216. *Ibid.*, at s. 56. In respect of infringement of a layout design the registered proprietor can file a written complaint before the Magistrate Class I who is competent to take cognizance. The Court can order forfeiture of such goods and may also order its destruction in case of conviction.

217. *Ibid.*, s. 18(6).

Chapter 4. Copyright Protection in the Digital Context

§1. ORIGIN AND MEANING

172. The copyright protection in India dates back to 1847 when for the first time the 1847 Act secured this right to the author and for seven years thereafter.[218] In independent India, the present Copyright Act 1957 (14 of 1857) was passed and today the Copyright Act 1957[219] is the major law governing copyrights in the country. It is believed that "copyright is national in nature"[220] as the protection is limited to the boundaries of a country, but in the present scenarios of the Internet and Communication Technologies (ICTs) proliferation and a borderless world, protection seems to be transnational.

Meaning of copyright— Under the Copyright Act 1957[221] the term "copyright" encompasses the following acts:

(a) Regarding literary, dramatic, or musical work, not in the form of computer—
  - (i) to reproduce;
  - (ii) to issue copies;
  - (iii) to perform work in public or communicate to the public;
  - (iv) to make a film on it;
  - (v) to translate it;
  - (vi) to make an adaptation, etc.

(b) Regarding computer programs—
  - (i) to do any of the acts as specified in clause (*a*);
  - (ii) to sell or give on commercial rental or offer for sale or for commercial rental any computer program provided that such commercial rental does not apply in respect of computer programs where the program itself is not the essential object of the rental.

(c) Regarding artistic work—
  - (i) to reproduce the work in any material form including depiction in three dimensions of a two-dimensional work or vice versa;
  - (ii) to communicate the work to the public;
  - (iii) to include the work in any film;
  - (iv) to make any adaptation of the work, etc.

(d) Regarding cinematograph film—
  - (i) to make a copy of the film;
  - (ii) to sell or give on hire copy of the film;
  - (iii) to communicate the film to the public.

218. Rajkumar, *Handbook of Intellectual Property Rights in India*, 10.
219. Amended in 1999, the Copyright Rules, 1958 as amended in 1995 and the International Copyright Order, 1999 as amended in 2000. Last amended 2013.
220. Raman Mittal, *Copyright Law and the Internet* in SK Verma & Raman Mittal (eds.), *Legal Dimensions of Cyberspace* (Indian Law Institute, 2004) 115, Chapter 5.
221. Section 14, cls. (*a*)–(*e*).

(e) Regarding sound recording—
  (i) to make any other sound recording of it;
  (ii) to sell or give on hire such work.

§2. Copyright in Digital Context

173. Lawrence Lessig[222] refers to copyrighted work as "property" and says that it is a special type of property. Thus, though the form is intangible and cannot be perceived through our senses but like all the other rights the copyright also empowers the holder of it.[223] "Technology is an engine of change in the law of property."[224] It has opened new vistas for copyright owners, especially in the field of literature and scholarly writing. Technology has started redefining the contours of copyright, its content and effects. A new trend has emerged in this field as authors and writers no longer look up to publishers for the publication of their work. Authors and writers have started using the internet for the publication of their work and publishers offline fear a decline in their business. There is emerging a new concept of "open access." Traditionally speaking, "rights of exclusion are the core of copyright; copying, distributing or making some other privileged use of another's work is infringement absent author's permission."[225] This right of the author gets a blow with the Open Access Policy as the mandate in itself gives permission to publish the work without the author's permission.[226] The ICTs have mitigated the role of publishers, but at the same time, "copying" which is the hallmark of the computer has given birth to new copyright issues.

The Copyright Act 1957 gives "Copyright protection" to computer programs and databases as a "literary work." Sections 2 (ffb) and (ffc) define "computer" and also "computer program" respectively. However, the said Act has not been updated to meet the "myriad threats" posed by the digitization of the entire IPRs. The 1957 Act is still used to deal with modern changes which are not satisfactory. A refurbishing of the law is the need of the hour.

---

222. Lawrence Lessig, *Free Culture* (Free Culture Foundation, 2003–2013).
223. Paul Goldstein, *Copyright's Highway from Gutenberg to the Celestial Jukebox* (Revised ed., 2003).
224. Joshua AT Fairfield, *Virtual Property,* Boston Law Review 84 (2005), 1047, 1053, 1066.
225. *See*, 17 USC S. 106 (2011).
226. Harvard Faculty of Arts and Sciences, Open Access Policy, Harv U Libr. Off. for Scholarly Comm. (Feb. 12, 2008).

Chapter 5. Legal Protection of Software

§1. ORIGIN

174. Origin - The entire mechanism of a computer has two important facets: the discs or diskettes (part of the hardware) and the programs or instructions which are imbedded in it called the software. Usually, the programs are written in a language that is not intelligible for all and requires special expertise to comprehend it. Again the entire software is made up of the "source code"[227] and the "object code."[228] The source code and the object code are accompanied by certain manual and instructions by the producer for the better operation of the entire system and the source code, the object code, and the manual are collectively called the "computer program" or "software."[229] It is realized that the commercial value of an IP asset can be fully realized only through effective protection and monetization strategies. Apart from the commercial value of the software the literary or artistic work which it holds also has aesthetic and social value for the author.

The software industry in India and all over the world are soft targets of pirates. Because of their intangible nature, the software products are not only easy to copy and misuse but it is a tough job to contain the public tendency to piracy as well. Computer software is actually a set of mathematical representations, formulas, or algorithms or "a set of instructions expressed in words, codes, schemes or in any other form including a machine-readable medium capable of causing a computer to perform a particular task or to achieve a particular result[230] According to the World Intellectual Property Indicators Report 2013, the IP filing trends globally are at an all-time high.[231] As an indicator of the fact that the IT industry in India is gradually making a shift toward IP-driven products and services, the Annual Report of the Indian Patent office shows that there is five times increase in the number of Indian patent applications between the years 2009 and 2012. For the Indian IT-BPM firms, which are growing speedily by offering the value and proposition of cost savings and efficiencies in delivering business processes, the challenges are formidable and there is a need to move to an IP-led model. The IP in computer situation is tacit and peculiar by nature and legal protection is not enough but protective measures within the organization is a better option.

227. Program which appears on the screen or is taken out in the form of prints. *IP Handbook: Policy, Law and Use,* WIPO Publication No. 489(E) WIPO 2004 (2nd ed., 2008) 435.

228. This is yet another form of the program which is compiled into the digital values of "1" and "0." This is only machine readable expression. *Ibid.*

229. *WIPO IP Handbook: Policy, Law and Use,* WIPO Publication No. 489(E) WIPO 2004 (2nd ed., 2008).

230. Section 2(ffc) Copyright Act 1957. (India).

231. Pradeep Udhas (KPMG), Gary Matuszak, (KPMG) Chandrashekhar (NASSCOM); *Innovation Transforming the Growth Landscape*, 2.

§2. Computer Software

175. Computer Software under Indian Law: Although to date no specific law has been formulated in India for the protection of computer software, IP laws have been amended timely and suitably and software is protected under the copyright and patent laws and also through trade secrets. The legal provisions are as follows:

- *Software Protection under Copyright law:* section 2(o) of the Copyright Act 1957 says that "literary work" includes computer programs, tables, and compilations including computer literary databases. "Literary work" means an expression in print or writing and no importance is given to its merit. Thus, the expression can be not only in understandable words but it can also be in the form of symbols or notations, visible representations, etc. A computer program is defined under the Act as "a set of instructions expressed in words, codes, schemes or in any other form including a machine-readable medium, capable of causing a computer to perform a particular task or achieve a particular result." The Act however does not differentiate between the source code and the object code although they are covered under the Act as literal elements of a computer program. Computer software inclusive of program manuals, papers, printouts, punch cards containing information in a particular notation, magnetic tapes, discs required for operating computers, or any perforated media, and other data storage devices. Even magnetic discs, tapes and floppy discs which are recorded by means of electronic impulses are databases and are forms of literary work. However, the concept or idea of algorithms is not capable of copyright protection but programs that are operating computers are accepted to be within the ambit of artistic and literary work and thus protectable.[232]
- *Software Protection under Patent Law:* Patents can be used to protect the ideas in software to protect the functional aspects of the software and the law can be enforced against one who implements the patented feature by way of copying, reverse engineering, or by developing it independently. The TRIPS Agreement (Article 27.1) can be used for including computer programs but in the Agreement, there is no explicit direction to the Members regarding granting of patent protection to computer programs. The Patents Act 1970 did not expressly exclude the "computer programs" but under section 2(l)(j) a patentable invention was required to be non-living and tangible. Under this expression, the software in the form of a mathematical algorithm could not be patented as it was something not in tangible form. However, software combined with a machine or computer under its influence becomes a novel machine and thus could be regarded as "patentable." But again to fulfill the criteria of "patentability" it had to fulfill the condition of newness, inventive step, and capability to be an industrial application under section 2(l)(j) of the Patents Act 1970. However, under the pre-Revised Act, a software program on its own was not eligible for protection without hardware but the embedded system as a part of hardware was regarded as patentable. Thus, under the pre-Revised Act, IBM was granted two patents.[233] The Patents

232. SM Stewart, *International Copyright and Neighbouring Rights*, Vol. I (Butterworths, 1989), 57.
233. One granted in February 1996 (Patent No. 176178) and another in 2001.

(Amendment) Act 2002 excludes computer programs from patentability. Under section 2(k) "a mathematical or business method or a computer program per se or algorithms" are non-patentable. This section is in similarity to the European Patent Convention (EPC, section 52). However, although the EPO (1985), USPTO (1995), and JPO (1997) give guidelines there are no such guidelines by the Indian Patent Office. The question rests on the fact that what is the meaning and extent of the term "software program". Software patenting in India is thus hampered for the time being.

I. Subject Matter of Protection

176. Organizations in India have defined Intellectual Property on a wide spectrum of innovation ranging from reusable knowledge assets to high and software products. Based on the survey conducted by KPMG, there is felt a widely circulated idea that there should exist a clear ownership for the asset to be considered IP which could be achieved only through copyright and patent laws, and regulations. It is realized that the commercial value of an IP asset can be fully realized only through effective protection and monetization strategies. Apart from the commercial value of the software, the literary or artistic work which it holds also has aesthetic and social value for the author. In the beginning, software was sold as inseparable parts of the computer system but now software products have opened a new commercial counter where computer-readable forms, like diskettes, floppy disks, and CD-ROMs are separate from the computer hardware. The tangible forms of software, namely the disks and diskettes, etc., are different from the software embedded in them.[234] The queer nature of the software puts them in altogether a different category. It is not the tangible disk that is the subject matter of transfer /sale in such cases but actually, the owner passes certain rights in the use of the data therein. Computer software like biotechnology is subject to fierce competition[235] susceptible to easy mass copying with limited duration.

II. Conditions of Protection

177. The Indian Copyright law gives protection to all sorts of "literary work" including computer programs. To qualify for protection the "literary work" must be original. The term "originality" has been interpreted by the Indian courts in consonance with the interpretation of the British courts.[236] To be eligible for legal protection the expression of thought is given importance and not the originality of ideas; the expression of thought in print or in writing is given importance for purposes of legal protection. The degree of originality is not given as much importance as the labor, skill judgment, and finances which are spent on creation. To acquire a

234. R Matthan, *The Law Relating to Computers and the Internet* (Butterworths, 2000), 276.
235. SK Verma, *IP Protection of software and Software Contracts in India: A Legal Quagmire*, Journal of Intellectual Property Rights 17(July 2012), 284–295.
236. *RG Anand v. Deluxe Films*, AIR 1978 SC 1613.

copyright, it has to be registered with the Copyright Office by making an application in the prescribed form along with a prescribed fee to the Registrar of Copyrights. The registrar after holding inquiry may register the name of the author as owner of copyright in the Register of Copyrights.[237] In case of computer programs, the law does not require the mention of the source code and copyright software.

III. Ownership

178. According to section 17 of the Copyright Act 1957, the author of a work shall be the first owner of the copyright so possessed. This is true in respect of computer programs as well. The Act however differentiates between the "First Owners" in relation to a particular work or act done by the person concerned. Thus, section 17:

> *Ownership under Course of Employment:* Whereas the author does any literary, dramatic, or artistic work asked by the proprietor of a newspaper, magazine, etc., to be published in such newspaper/magazine under the contract or apprenticeship then in such a case the proprietor shall be the first owner if there is no contract which makes the author the owner and in case there is no such contract then the author shall be the first owner.
> *Creation for Consideration:* In such instances where a work such as a painting/ portrait drawn, a photo taken, or an engraving or film made is done at the request of a paying customer, then—in the absence of a specific contract bestowing ownership on the creator—the person on whose request the work is made shall be the first owner.
> *Course of Employment:* Where in cases the clauses A and B do not apply and there is a contract of employment between the employer and the author of some work then the employer will be the first owner.
> *Public Speech:* Where a person asks another to deliver a speech in public or to address the public then the person who asks such another shall be the first owner of such speech or address and the fact that the person who delivers such speech is employed by any other person will not affect the ownership of the person who asks to make such speech, etc.
> *Government Work:* Whereas the government has asked a person to do some work then if there is no contract to contradict it, the government shall be the first owner.
> *Public Undertaking Work:* Whereas any work is done on the direction of a public work undertaking then if there is no contract to the contrary then such public undertaking shall be the first owner.
> *Work of the International Organization:* Whereas any work of any international organization as per section 41 falls under any of these categories:
> – work is first done by or under the direction of it;
> – there is no copyright in that work in India at that time; or

237. Sections 44, 45—The Copyright Act 1957.

– if the work is published as a result of an agreement between the organization and where no right is reserved to the author.

In any of the above cases the international organization shall be the first owner. (Section 17(e)).

IV. Scope of Exclusive Rights

179. Under the Copyright Act 1957, copyright means the exclusive right to do or authorize the doing of any of the following acts in respect of a work or any substantial part thereof;[238] The Copyright Act 1957 also protects the author's economic rights in the copyrighted work (sections 14 and 57) which also includes the rights in computer programs. The owner of copyright thus has the following rights:

(1) All the copyrights: The Owner shall enjoy the following rights in respect of the computer programs to the exclusion of all others:
   - The right to reproduce the work and to publicize it, to make any film or sound recording of his work, to make translation or adaptation of the work, etc. (section 14).

(2) *Assignment of Copyright:* The owner of a copyright has the right to assign his copyright to another person in respect of some present work or some future work, partially or fully. The assignor of rights shall be the owner in respect of rights not assigned and the assignee shall be the owner in respect of rights so assigned. The representatives of the assignee shall be treated as assignees (section 18).

(3) Special Rights: Apart from the copyrights the author shall have the right to claim authorship of the work; to restrain or claim for damages in respect of any harm, distortion, mutilation, modification, etc., is done to his copyrighted work during the term of copyright and which at the same time harms his reputation. Such rights can also be exercised by the representatives of the author (section 57).

(4) *Rights of Owner in respect of infringed copies:* The owner of copyright shall have a right to retake or claim possession of the infringed copies from the person who makes such copies of the copyrighted work unauthorized. However, if the maker of such copies claims innocence regarding the author's rights and pleads "no knowledge" of the author's rights or denies any ground for having reason to believe that the copies are infringed ones then the owner cannot claim his rights (section 58).

Exclusion of owner's rights: In respect of computer programs certain acts have been excluded from the copyright area of the owner: the making of copies and adaptation of a computer program; to make backup copies of the work for security

238. Section 17—The Copyright Act 1957.

purposes; any act to obtain information necessary for the interoperability of any program if such information is not otherwise readily available; the observation, study or testing of any computer program to determine the ideas and principles which underline any elements of the program and where such acts are necessary for the functions for which the computer program was supplied; the making of copies from those copies which were made for non-commercial personal use (sections 52(aa)(ab), (ac), (ac)).

Limitations on the Scope of Protection

Although the Copyright Act 1957 has included computer programs within the term "literary work" for the purposes of according copyright protection to it, yet it has not simplified as to what in computer context is the literal part. The scope of infringement is connected with the act of infringement. The infringement of a non-literal part or the copying of computer design will constitute copyright infringement. The question in computer software cases has been with regard to the limits of substantial copying, and as to what portions come under copyright protection.[239] In India, the Copyright Act does not recognize the idea-expression dichotomy as expressed by TRIPS (Article 9(2)). In *RG Anand v. Deluxe Films*, the Supreme Court of India apart from the "look and feel" test also discussed the "abstraction test" as laid down by the U.S. Supreme Court.[240] The Court concluded that it was not proven that the similarities in the defendant's work were the result of copying but held that there was a common theme.[241] Thus, there is no precise test laid down by the Indian Courts to determine the area of infringement of copyright in computer programs. The "abstraction test" of "abstraction-filtration-comparison" (AFC) also has not been followed in India.[242] In computer programs the nature of the work is extremely technical hence an ordinary test is not suitable. Generally speaking, the copyright laws in software protect everything except when the expression is in an industry-standard or if the expression is functionally necessary to accomplish a functional task such as compatibility. Thus, icons by themselves are not protectable. Object code and source code are the literal portions of the program and are protected under the Copyright Act 1957.

V. Complementary Provisions

180. The Copyright Act 1957 is an elaborate law that circumscribes all the relevant matters connected with copyright in India. The entire Act by itself extends to even the software protection in the country. The holder of a copyright has inherent in it the right to allow any other person to make use of his work or creation. For

239. *Microsoft Corporation v. Vijay Kaushik and Another*, 2011 (48) PTC 127 (Del).
240. *Nichols v. Universal Pictures*, 45F.2d 119.
241. This was followed in *Barbara Taylor Bradford v. Sahara Media Limited* (2003) 47 SCL 445(Cal); *Raja Pocket Books v. Radha Pocket Books*, 1997(40) DRJ 791 (Delhi); *Zee Telefilms v. Sundial Communications*, 2003 (27) PTC 457 (Bom).
242. *Computer Associates v. Altai*, 982F.2d 693 (1992).

this, he is required to issue a license to such other person as per the provisions of the rules under Chapter IV of the Act read with Copyright Rules 2013.[243]

License by the Owner: The owner of a copyright, either by himself or by his agent can grant a right to another person in writing. This he can do for his existing or future work. The agreement must declare the duration, territorial extent, royalty, and other important matters relevant thereto (sections 19, 19-A). Where no duration is specified or where no territorial extent is specified then it shall deem to be five years from the date of assignment and India, respectively. The assignment usually provides for the possession of software for a specified period of time.[244] The assignor or the owner can retain his moral rights even after the assignment.[245] Section 57 of the Act also says that moral rights cannot be taken away by way of a license assignment. Section 52 however does not declare the assignment of "fair use" rights in the license agreement. The licensee cannot rent or lease the software for any direct or indirect profits as the right to rental, lease or lending, etc., is granted to the owner of the copyright in software (section 14(b)(ii)).

Compulsory License—Where there comes a question regarding the license for publication of work for the public good and an application is made to the Copyright Board[246] for grant of it then it must be accompanied with sufficient evidence to show that the owner has refused or allowed such republication and the reasons forwarded by it. The Board after hearing the applicant and the owner of the copyright shall if satisfied direct the Registrar of Copyright to issue the compulsory license to the applicant.[247]

Relinquishment of Copyright—The owner of a copyright of his own volition may give up or relinquish his right/rights in any copyrighted work (section 21). Such an act of the owner shall not affect the rights of other persons connected with it. The owner can relinquish his right in any one or more or all of his work which he will do by sending a notice to the Registrar of Copyrights. Such notice shall contain among other things the name, identity and nationality of the owner, the title of his work, its language, the rights he wishes to relinquish, the details of the publisher, the registration number, the date and time, etc. The Registrar of Copyright shall within fourteen days of publication of the notification in the official gazette post it on the Copyright website which will remain in the public domain for three years.[248] The rights of the owner shall cease to exist in the owner from the date of the notice (section 21(1)).

243. The Copyright Rules 2013, Notification. G.S.R. 172(E)-Gazette of India—Ministry of Human Resources, (Department of Higher Education), Government of India. New Delhi. Dated the Mar. 14, 2013.

244. SK Verma, *IP Protection of Software and Software Contracts in India: A Legal Quagmire,* Journal of Intellectual Property Rights 17 (July 2012), 288.

245. *Srimangal & Co. v. Books (India) Ltd.* AIR1973Mad.

246. Established under s. 11 of the Copyright Act 1957.

247. Rule 7(3), The Copyright Rules 2013, Notification. G.S.R. 172(E)-Gazette of India—Ministry of Human Resources, (Department of Higher Education), Government of India. New Delhi. Dated the Mar. 14, 2013.

248. Rule 4 & 5—The Copyright Rules 2013.

Chapter 6. Protection of Databases (Incl. "Data Ownership")

§1. INTRODUCTION

181. Databases are the offspring of technological advancements in machine-readable or other forms which by reason of the selection or other digitization of colossal data results into databases. Data that is already available is methodically collected in one place and is in an accessible condition. For purposes of copyright law, a database has been defined as a compilation of data arrangement of the contents that constitute intellectual creations.[249] Data can also be originally produced in digital forms which are readable as visuals, statements, texts, pictures, images, charts and tables, and spreadsheets and in the form of other visible representations. Digitization helps easy storage and easy accessibility of huge computer datasets. Databases such as a telephone directory are "compiled out of necessity." In the ordinary course of business the originators of many electronic databases take on the risks and tasks of gathering "raw data" and organizing it through an efficient search engine for easy access to data.[250] Databases may be "original" or "non-original." The copyright protection of compilations continues in the case of databases as well. One theory known as the "sweat of the brow" or "industrious collection" propounds that databases and compilations receive protection per se, i.e., without showing any authority or original authorship and that creativity is a concept that is alien to the requirements of "originality." If lots of money, labor, and time are invested into the creation of databases then such investment shall be sufficient to get copyright protection even if it lacks creativity. This theory advocates that it will give incentives to the compilers to develop new databases. The hard work which goes into compiling the huge yet structured datasets necessitates protection.[251] However, the advocates of the "modicum of creativity rule" interpret "original" as including a minimum level of creativity. The level of creativity, though minimal, requires that the work is original and not imitated and thus worthy of copyright protection. Note that an innovative character is not required.

Before 1996, the European Union countries had different levels of protection of databases and compilations while the U.K. recognized the "sweat of the brow" doctrine,[252] Germany required a higher level of creativity in order for works to qualify for copyright protection.[253] In 1996, the Directive unified the copyright criteria in the European Community and adopted the "modicum of creativity rule" in granting copyright protection.[254] With expanding ICTs India is becoming more capable in the database field which is opening commercialization possibilities for it.

249. Article 10.2, TRIPS; Art. 5 WCT.
250. JH Smith Graham, *Internet Law & Regulation* (3rd ed. Sweet & Maxwell, 2002), 246.
251. RG Nelson, *Seeking Refuge from a Technology Storm: The Current Status of Database Protection Legislation*, Journal of Intellectual Property Law 6 (1999), 453.
252. *BBC v. Wireless League Gazette Publishing Co.*,(1926) Ch. 433: *Independent Television Publications v. Time Out* (1984) FSR64; *Waterloo v. Reed* (1992), FSR 409: *Dun & Bradstreet Ltd. v. Typesetting Facilities Ltd.* (1992) FSR 320.
253. Fromm Nordemannet al., *Urheberrecht (Copyright Law)*, Commentary to ss. 2 and 4 of Copyright Act, 8th ed., 1994.
254. Article 3.1, Directive 96/9/EC of the European Parliament of databases.

§2. LEGAL PROTECTION OF ORIGINAL DATABASES

I. Subject Matter and Conditions of Protection

182. The Copyright law is subject to the requirements of "originality" and has protected collections of data as "literary works." In India, databases are protected under the generic category of compilations.[255] India being a member of the Berne Convention and TRIPS Agreement, the condition of "originality" is a special condition to accord copyright protection.[256] The Copyright Act 1957, does not define "originality" but to obtain copyright protection or the compilation it must have some sort of creativity in it; the Act insists on the original work of authors or creators. The Indian courts have also not been explicit on the concept of "originality" and each case is decided on the special "facts and circumstances" that it exhibits. Some of the verdicts have depicted the "sweat of the brow theory" and have rules that skill, labor, and judgment test are applied in copyright infringement of databases. In *McMillan v. Suresh Chander Deb,*[257] *Govindan v. Gopalkrishna,*[258] and in a number of other cases[259] the courts have held that a compilation developed through investment of time, money, labor, and expertise rises to the standard of literary work through it must have been retrieved from a common source. The underlying idea in all such decisions was that no one can make ill use of another's skill and labor and even a small amount of creativity attracts protection. A recent judgment in *Diljeet Titus, Advocate &Others v. Alfred A. Adebare & Ors.*,[260] the Delhi High Court has ruled that the copyright in a database prepared by an advocate in another employer's resources, expertise, and investment belongs to the employer-advocate. Referring to section 17(1)(c) of the Copyright Act 1957 the court held that work done during the course of employment or apprenticeship shall be the copyright of the employer, provided there is no contract to the contrary. Again in *Eastern Book Company v. Desai,*[261] the court held that in the case of compilations there can be a similar compilation prepared by another person but he cannot violate/infringe upon the "fruits" of the labor of the previous compiler. The court rejected the protection for "Head notes" prepared by the plaintiff holding that "protection of copyright must inhere in a creative, original selection of facts and not in the creative means used to discover the facts." Referring to the U.S. Court's decision in *Feist Publications, Inc.*

---

255. Section 2(1)(o) read with s. 13(1) Copyright Act 1957. The term "literary works" include compilations. India being a member of the Berne Convention and TRIPS Agreement, the condition of "originality" is a special condition to accord copyright protection.
256. Article 10(2), Agreement on Trade-Related Aspects of Intellectual Property Rights (Annex IC, Marrakesh Agreement Establishing the World Trade Organization) (Apr. 15, 1994), 33I.L.M. 81 (1994); Art. 2(5), Berne Convention for the Protection of Literary and Artistic Works (Jul. 24, 1971), (amend. Sep. 28, 1979).
257. I.L.R. 17 (Cal), 951, 961.
258. AIR 19565 Mad. 42.
259. *Shyamlal Paharia v. Gaya Prasad Gupta Rasal*, AIR 1971 All. 58; *Ganga Vishnu Shrikisondas v. Morishwar Bapuji Hegishte I.L.R. 13* (Bom), 358, 363 (1889); *Burlington Home Shopping Pvt. Ltd. v. Rajanish Chibber* (1995) 6 Entertainment Law Review 159 (Delhi).
260. 2006(32) PTC 609 (Del).
261. AIR 2001 Delhi 185.

v. Rural Telephone Service Co.,[262] the court said that there should be a modicum of creativity in the selection, arrangement, or coordination of the contents of a database to attract copyright protection.

II. Ownership

183. As an original database is given the same protection under the Copyright Act 1957 as a "literary work" in India, its rights of ownership are also on the same footing as the literary work.

III. Scope of Exclusive Rights

184. There is no specific law addressing databases in India. As databases and compilations come under the phrase "literary work," by analogy the exclusive rights of the owner in respect of original databases are the same as the one of the owners of a copyright of a "literary work." It thus falls under the category described under the Copyright law as follows:

- The owner has the exclusive right to: (i) reproduce the work or store it in electronic form; (ii) to issue copies of the work to the public; (iii) to use the work publicly; (iv) to make any cinematograph film, etc., with it; (v) to translate it; (vi) to make an adaptation of the work.
- To sell/give on rent such databases (section 14(b)(i)(ii) The Copyright Act 1957.).

However, the following acts shall not amount to copyright infringement in respect of databases (which are treated the same as computer programs):

(a) The making of copies or adaptation of the computer program for utilization of it for the purpose for which it was created.
(b) To make backup copies of it.
(c) The doing of an act necessary to obtain information essential for operating interoperability of an independently created computer program.
(d) The observation, study, or test of the computer program.
(e) The making of copy from a legally obtained copy for non-commercial personal use (sections 52(1)(11), (ab), (ac), (ad). The Copyright Act 1957).

IV. Duration of Protection

185. Duration of protection in the case of original databases; as the databases or compilations are included in the term "literary work" hence the protection given to

262. 499 U.S. 340 (1991).

such literary work logically applies to the original databases. Thus, if published during the lifetime of the author then the protection extends up to 60 years from his death, and if it is joint-authorship then for 60 years from the death of the last author (section 22, Copyright Act 1957).

§3. Legal Protection of Non-original Databases

I. Subject Matter and Conditions of Protection

186. The digital environment has called for a vast reform of the existing law regarding many subjects touching copyright. One of these is the need for a legal regime for non-original databases. Non-original databases involving substantial investment and effort denote databases that lack the prerequisite of originality or creativity to qualify for legal protection. It largely depends on the database industry in India to understand whether the developing countries including India need a sui generis protection of non-original databases. Eighty percent of the databases in India still emanate from the domain of the government out of which only 40% is available to the public. Only a small portion of the above data (about 40%) is available to the general public. The remaining 60% of data is either internal data that is department specific and therefore holds no relevance for the general public or "classified," as it includes sensitive information pertaining to atomic research, space research, defense research, etc. The types of database companies active in India are similar to those found in other parts of the world, e.g., databases containing legal information, medical and commercial information, traveling and tourist information, educational institutions information, and other compilations covering almost all the areas of public life. The potential for data creation in India and data wealth is mainly in the following areas:[263]

- *Traditional knowledge Data:* The government has established Traditional Knowledge Digital Library (TKDL). It contains all useful information connected with traditional medicinal (*Ayurvedic*) knowledge and cultural knowledge concerning folklore.
- *Genomic Data:*—The genomic industry in India is regarded as one of the "biodiversity" centers treasuring potential rich sources of animal /plant/microbial genomic data. It can fetch substantial revenue for the country.
- *Information Technology:* India has emerged as a strong IT superpower and consequently the IT industry and the ICT together give a big boost to the revenue collection of the country. Thus, the government has recognized this and has taken up "database creation" as one of its topmost priorities.

263. *Standing Committee on Copyright and Related Rights*-Seventh Session, Geneva-May 13–17 2002. WIPO-Study Prepared by Mr. Phiroz Vandrevala, Chairman-National Association of Software and Service Companies. (NASSCOM)—New Delhi—SCCR/7/5/.

To date, the country lacks a non-original (or even original) database-specific legislation. In the decision of the Delhi High Court in *Himalaya Drug Co. v. Sumit*[264] the court preferred to follow the First standard of "a modicum of creativity" and denied protection to copy-edited judgments. Thus, the said judgment indicates that the Indian copyright regime does not protect an "unoriginal" database and it is not even regarded as a separate tort under the unfair competition thus this common law right may not be available to protect the efforts of the Indian data base industry.

II. Ownership

187. There is no legislation on the subject in India.

III. Scope of Exclusive Rights

188. There is no legislation on the subject in India.

IV. Duration of Protection

189. There is no legislation on the subject in India.

264. Suit No. 1719 of 2000.

Chapter 7. Chips Protection

§1. General Statement

190. Chips, often referred to as "the crude oil of the information age,"[265] are the store house of massive information and data which can be easily and instantaneously transmitted the world over. As per an estimate by the Reserve Bank of India, the demand for electronic goods is expected to reach USD 400 billion by 2025.[266] The export of electronic items increased to USD 8,362.52 million during the period 2018–2019.[267] The Export-Import Bank of India (Exim Bank) in its recent study has estimated the size of the electronics industry in India to exceed USD 150 billion by 2015. Since 2005, the emergence of an IP regime in the country, India has come a long way in the field of establishing a viable patent system for its electronics industry. With the entry of international players, like *Flextronics, Elcoteq, Intel, Motorola, Texas Instruments, Nokia, and Samsung* the electronics industry has gained considerable importance. Innovations are continuing at an overwhelming pace and thus the GoI policy has been relaxed so that the electronics manufacturing industry covers the entire spectrum starting from components to subassemblies and—as the most important element—the integrated chips. Growth in all electronics goods received an impetus between 2013 and 2018 with mobile phones, industrial electronics, and consumer electronics partaking three-fourths part of this growth.[268] Electronic goods manufacturing forms an important part of the scheme of "Make in India" and "Digital India" which aims to achieve zero net imports by 2020.[269] Thus, electronic hardware production in the country is expected to rise from USD 20 billion in 2009 to USD 100 billion by 2014 and USD 400 billion by 2020 which includes exports of USD 4 billion in 2009 growing to USD 15 billion by 2014 and USD 80 billion by 2020. The semiconductor industry in India is also instrumental in these developments and is rightly called the "sunrise industry."

India has proven its expertise in chip design and where the activities used to center around mere testing and support, they then moved to product upgrading and have now matured into a full-fledged product development industry. This expansion into innovation-oriented industries highlights the crucial role Intellectual Property now has to play. Of the seven Intellectual Property Rights (IPRs): (1) copyright and related rights; (2) trademarks; (3) patents; (4) industrial designs; (5) layout designs of integrated circuits; (6) geographical indications; (7) Undisclosed Information apart from geographical indications and plant varieties, all others provide a fine interplay of protection in the electronics industry. IP can take many forms such as employment, contracts, nonconfidentiality agreements, firmware, software, IC

265. AJW Van de Gevel, *From Confrontation to Competition in the Globalized Semiconductor Industry*, May 29, 2000.
266. RBI Bulletin—Apr. 11, 2019. https://m.rbi.org.in/scripts/BS_ViewBulletin.aspx?Id=18172.
267. Annual Report 2018–2019. Department of Commerce. Ministry of Commerce-Government of India. 25.
268. Annual Report 2017–2018. Ministry of Electronics and Information Technology (MeitY)-Government of India.
269. *See,* https://digitalindia.gov.in/content/electronics-manufacturing.

designs, electronic ASIC, IC, MCM, board, systems designs and embedded components, core device components, company's brand, etc. A report from the Indian Trade and Patent Office indicated that out of every top ten foreign filers of patents nine are from the electronics industry. About 8,000 applications were filed from within the electronics industry alone, which shows about 35% increase in the last four years. Consequently, the protection of IPR in the field of Layout Design or semiconductor integrated circuits drew the attention of law makers. Thus, India being a signatory to the TRIPS Agreement and to the World Trade Organization (WTO) passed the Semiconductor Integrated Circuits Layout Design Act 2000 which fulfils the obligation of the TRIPS agreement (Articles 35–38) regarding the protection of semiconductor integrated circuits layout designs and also of the chips protection.

The subject of chip protection being covered by the SICLD Act 2000 has been discussed in Chapter 3 regarding Design Protection and it equally applies to chip protection hence its repetition is being avoided here.

Chapter 8. Protection of Internet Domain Names

§1. Introduction

191. To establish one's presence on the internet one has to have an address and a locating indicator. A domain name is the virtual equivalent of a postal address in the real world, i.e., a locator. Internet Protocols (IPs) are long numerical expressions to locate an organization or an individual on the internet which has its drawback in being legible only by the machine. To overcome this the linguistic version of the IP was established known as the "Domain Name System" (DNS).

192. The emergence of powerful search engines coupled with browsers that require only the identification of a part of a Uniform Resource Locator (URL) to locate the required site urged businesses to resort to domain names to reassert their presence on the internet. Consequently, the domain names became an exclusive identity of an organization ultimately becoming the online counterpart of classical trademarks. Today, domain names reflect the goodwill, reputation, and high recall value in respect of a business. As it gave an identity to the business houses and corporate giants, apprehensions regarding their piracy or misuse came up as the main issues. Legislators, therefore, started treating domain names at par with trademarks and legal protection to the same came as a necessity. This was done by the Internet Corporation for Assigned Names and Numbers. (ICANN).[270] The ICANN adopted the Uniform Domain Name Dispute resolution Policy (UDRP) on October 24, 1999. The policy offers an expedited administrative proceeding for trademark holders to contest "abusive registrations of domain names," and it gives to the registrar the power to cancel, transfer, or suspend a domain name in case of a dispute.

§2. The Indian Domain Name Policy

193. India has liberalized its domain name policy as in its previous policy only the commercial entity which was registered in India could apply for it. With the expansion of the commercial world there came repeated demands to allow foreign corporates to have a domain name in the country as it was not feasible for the foreign corporates to incorporate a local entity only for the purpose of holding a domain name registration in India. The highlights of the liberalized policy are as follows:

- New categories of the sub-domains, like gen.in., firm.in, and ind.in have been added.

270. It is a non-profit corporation that was established with the aim of allocating IP address for the assignment of protocol parameter and for root server system management functions. The registration process is done by the administrator of a Top-level Domain (TLD). The TLD gives unique number or address to the applicant so as to differentiate between various applicants and to maintain their identity.

- For a foreign entity to register a domain name in India the sub-domains would be co.in, gen.in, and firm.in.
- The co.in requirement to have a mandatory local presence in India has been done away with to some extent.
- The gen.in category has been added to facilitate foreign corporates who were unable to meet the local presence requirement.
- The previous condition that the name server should have a physical presence in India and that the domain name applicant should have permanent internet connectivity through an ISP has also been removed.

In India registration of.IN domain name has been allowed since 2005. Registration has been tremendously liberalized, has become cheaper, and is allowed to citizens and foreigners equally. This has paved the way for so-called cyber squatters. And thus there has been a steady rise in cybersquatting cases after the expiry of the sunrise period in January 2005. "IN" is India's top-level domain on the internet and-like.COM. IN can be used for email, websites, and other applications. Unlike other domains "IN" is the unique symbol of India in the world. IN Registry is the official.IN Registry appointed by the GoI to operate under the authority of the NIXI. The Department of Information Technology (DIT) in association with the Internet Service Providers Association of India (ISPAI) has promoted the NIXI as a not-for-profit company under section 25 of the Indian Companies Act 1956 with the aim of facilitating improved internet services in the country. NIXI aims at regulating internet traffic originating and having a destination within India and assuring its security. The Ministry of Communications and Information Technology through the Department of Information Technology has implemented the "New Policy for.in Internet Domain Name registration & National Internet Exchange" with effect from January 1, 2005. This policy basically governs the registration and administration of .in domain names in India. This policy is based on the internationally accepted UDRP as prescribed by ICANN and sets out the terms and conditions to resolve a dispute between the registrant and the complainant arising out of the registration and use of the .in Internet Domain Name.

Registrars—A Registrar provides direct services to Domain Name Registrants. The database of the Registry contains customer information and other valuable information regarding domain name registration. ERNET is India's exclusive Registrar for ac.in, edu.cin, and res.in. The Registrars first process the name registrations for internet end users and then send the necessary DNS information to a Registry for entry into the centralized Registry database and ultimate propagation over the internet.

Legal Status of Domain Names

With the proliferation of the internet, all the things associated with it increased; namely the domain name by itself became a soft target of cyber criminals. Ultimately, many legal issues raised their heads. In India, the sole cyber law under the title Information Technology Act 2000 (Amended 2008) does not address domain names. As domain names became identical with trademarks of the paper world in India the protection is accorded under the Trademarks Act 1999 though it has no extraterritorial jurisdiction. However, various judicial pronouncements in India regarding domain name issues and the legal protection accorded to it have become a good source of law on the subject. The time internet started getting a hold over the commercial and social world in India domain name disputes reached the doors of justice.

§3. Case Law

194. Case Law in India: In *Satyam Info way Ltd. v. Sifynet Solutions Pvt. Ltd.,*[271] the Supreme Court of India ruled that internet domain names are subject to the same legal norms as applicable to other IPs such as Trade Marks. The court held that "the use of the same or similar domain name may lead to a diversion of users which could result from such user mistakenly accessing one domain name instead of another. This may occur in e-commerce with its rapid progress and instant (and theoretical limitless) accessibility to users and potential customers and particularly so in areas of specific overlap." The court further said that ordinary consumers/ users seeking to locate the functions available in less than one domain name may get perplexed if they arrive at a different but similar-looking website that offers no such services. In such a situation the user could well conclude that the first domain name owner had misrepresented its goods and services through its promotional activities and the first domain owner would thereby lose their customer. In this case, the Supreme Court itself declared that there is no legislation in India that explicitly refers to dispute resolution in connection with domain names. The Trade Marks Act 1999 is not extraterritorial and is insufficient for the protection of domain names in the country.

In, *Yahoo! Inc. v. Akash Arora & Another,*[272] the Delhi High Court awarded relief to *Yahoo! Inc.'s* petition against the defendants who were attempting to use the domain name <yahooindia.com> for internet-related services. *Yahoo! Inc.,* who was the owner of the trademark *"Yahoo"* as well as the domain name <yahoo.com>, contended that by adopting the deceptively similar domain name <yahooindia-.com> the defendants had verbatim copied the format, contents, layout, color scheme, and source code of the plaintiff prior created regional section for India on the plaintiff's website. In this case, the court rejected the argument of the defendants that the provisions of the Indian Trade Mark Act 1999 would not apply to domain names on the internet. The court relied on the *Doctrine of Passing Off* and combined with an analysis of the working of the internet the court concluded that appropriation of the *"yahoo"* name by the defendants justified the action. The court held that though a general term yahoo has acquired identity with the business of the plaintiff company and has a strong association with the plaintiff's reputation and it thus needs maximum protection. The court thus granted an injunction restraining the defendants from using the word "yahoo" in its domain name.

Another landmark judgment *Rediff Communication Ltd. v. Cybertooth and Anr.*[273] deliberated upon the protection of domain names in India. The Single Bench

271. (2004 (28) PTC 566).
272. 1999 PTC (19) 210 (Delhi).
273. AIR Bom. 27.

judgment adds to the development of Indian Jurisprudence on domain names in India. The court ruled "a domain name is more that an Internet Address and is entitled to the equal protection as trade mark. With the advancement and progress in the technology, the services rendered in the Internet site have also come to be recognized and accepted and are being given protection so as to protect such service provider of service from passing off the services rendered by others as his services." Rejecting all the arguments, the court was convinced that there was clear "intention to deceive" on the part of the defendants as they deliberately used the term "<rediff>" to trade on the goodwill and reputation of the plaintiffs as their field of operation was also common and hence there were strong possibilities of confusion.

The Registration Procedure

195. The internet encompasses every facet of life on earth, be it communication, trade, education, agriculture, science, or technological development. It has reached the government departments as a symbol of good governance and has become an impressive medium in politics. India following closely and impressively the advanced nations of the world has embraced the new medium of the internet. Domain names come as a facilitating factor for the proliferation of the internet in any country. To make the proliferation of the internet easy and far-reaching, India adopted market-friendly liberal policies. Special consideration is to adopt the globally accepted policies and also procedure of registration so as to facilitate the addition of domain names.

196. In India, .in is the allocated country-code Top-level Domain (ccTLD). This helps not only the general masses but government entities, businesses, and organizations in establishing their Indian identity on the internet thereby using a short and unique Domain Name. The overcautious registration policy and absence of contemporary processes and infrastructure for registration have so far not favored the progress of the.in Domain. The government, therefore, took no time in revamping the.in Domain Name Registry in India to provide a greater thrust to its activities. Thus, the new policy has the following features:

- Unlimited generic.in registration will be offered at the second level of the domain name and also at the third level in the globally popular zones of the domain name, e.g., .co.in, .net.in, and .org.in.
- Registration shall be by Registrars who will be appointed by the.in Registry through an open process of selection which would be on the basis of transparent eligibility criteria.
- Registration shall be given by the Registrars following a competitive pricing policy and best market prices, and the charges shall be different but affordable for both the third and second levels.
- The.in Registry will adopt a uniform Dispute Resolution Policy (UDRP) and will be assisted by a Dispute Resolution Committee to resolve disputes involving the Registry. It will also appoint Arbitrators to address disputes between Registrars and registrants.

- The entire process of registration shall be online and should be completed in less than twenty-four hours of the receipt of the request from the registrant.
- The.in Registry will announce a "Sunrise Period" of ninety days to enable registered trademark owners, registered companies, and owners of intellectual property having a legitimate interest in protecting their brand to secure registration of their Domain Names after due verification.
- The zones for government, military, and educational institutions will be reserved for exclusive use by the respective organizations. Registrations for these departments will be offered by NIC, an organization nominated by the Ministry of Defense and ERNET.]
- The.in Registry will have the authority to deny or suspend any registration if it conflicts with the sovereign national interest or public order.
- The names of Constitutional Authorities, States/Union Territories, and specific names used by the.in Registry will constitute the reserved category of names inaccessible to the public.

The NIXI: The National Internet Exchange of India presents a unique domestic internet scenario in India with several large and small ISPs spread across a large geographical area. NIXI takes care of the concerns of large as well as the small ISPs at the same time keeping the larger national interest in mind by promoting domestic hosting of content as well as saving foreign exchange by keeping domestic traffic within India. The Traffic Routing and Tariff Policy are revised from time to time. NIXI is also given the responsibility of operating the .in Registry to implement the new policy framework for .in Domain Name by creating a .in Network Information Center (INNIC). The INNIC under NIXI operates as an autonomous body that implements various policies of the government; it maintains the .in Domain and ensures its operational stability, reliability, and security. The Registrars selected by the.in Registry are from among or utilize the services of the ISPs connected to NIXI nodes.

§4. Indian Domain Name Typology

197. In 2005, the policies were liberalized which allowed unlimited second-level registrations under.IN. The India Registry has formulated new policies for the registration and administration of.in domain names. The goal is to make.in domain names easier to use and a way of making the internet available to the common man. Following structure allows unlimited registration of domain names:

- in (available to anyone, used by companies, individuals, and organizations in India);
- co.in (originally for banks, registered companies, and trade marks);
- firm.in (originally for shops, partnerships liaison offices, and sole proprietorships);
- net.in (originally for Internet Service Providers);
- org.in (originally for non-profit organizations);
- gen.in (originally for general /miscellaneous use);

– ind.in (originally for individuals).

Six zones are fixed for use by prestigious institutions:

– ac.in (Academic institutions);
– edu.in (Educational institutions);
– ernet.in (Previously for educational and research institutions);
– gov.in (Indian government);
– mil.in (Indian military).

The domain nic.in is reserved for India's National Informatics Center (NIC) but other Indian agencies also use it.

I. Common Standards and Rules for the Registration of Second and Third-Level Domain Names

198. ERNET India is the Domain Registrars for all the educational and research institutes. It will register Domains at the second and third levels in the following zones:

– ac.in (Academic);
– edu.in (Academic);
– res.in (Indian Research Institute).

The Internet Domain Name Registry receives Domain Name Service (DNS) information from Domain Name Registrars, inserts that information into a centralized database, and then propagates that information in internet zone files on the internet so that domain names can be found by users around the world via applications such as the World Wide Web and email. .in Registry is the official .in Registry. It is appointed by the GoI and operates under NIXI.

II. Registration of Third-level Domain Names

199. Third-level domain names consist of three parts (like.in, .co, and .uk names). For instance in the third-level domain name—example.com.cn—CN will be the top-level part COM would be the second-level part and EXAMPLE would be the third-level part which is registered by the user/applicant. In India, there may be registration at the second level or at the third level beneath generic category second-level domains. There are no restrictions on who can register second-level domains or most third-level domains. Cancellation of Domain Name Registrations

Once the Registrant gets his domain name he becomes its rightful user. However, there may be disputes between the Registrar and the Registrant. In such a case the matter will be referred to the Arbitrator. The dispute shall be conducted by the Arbitrator in accordance with the Arbitration and Conciliation Act 1996 and in accordance with the .in Domain name Resolution Policy. The Cancellation of Domain name registration or its transfer shall take place in any of the following circumstances:

- First, at the end of the Arbitration proceedings the Arbitrator has the power to cancel the registration of the Registrant.
- Second, the Registrar has the right to cancel the transfer of domain name registration to another holder if the transfer is made in violation of paragraph 12 of the Policy.

§5. Out-of-Court Dispute Settlement

200. Domain names have rightful claimants. Disputes are bound to arise when there is a misuse of it by another or in other words cyber-squatting is committed. A person who considers that a registered domain name conflicts with his legitimate rights or interest may file a complaint to the .in registry on the following grounds:

- That registrant's domain name is either identically similar or confusingly similar to his trade mark or service mark over which the complainant has rights.
- That the registrant has no rights in respect of it.
- That there is bad faith on the part of the registrant to have the registration of such a domain name.

Thus, the registrant will have to submit to a mandatory arbitration proceeding in such a case and must follow the rules of the.in Registrar. The following remedies are available to the complainant:

(a) Cancellation of the domain name of the registrant.
(b) Transfer of the registrant's domain name registration to the complainant.

These remedies are however insufficient. The IT Act 2000 is also silent on the point. However, section 66D of the newly amended (2008) IT Act which makes cheating by personation or by any communicational device a punishable offense can be applied to cyber-squatting cases if the option of judicial courts is taken.

Part V. Cybersecurity Law

Chapter 1. Institutional Framework

> The five most efficient cyber defenders are: Anticipation, Education, Detection, Reaction and Resilience. Do remember: "Cybersecurity is much more than an IT topic."
>
> *Stephane Nappo*

§1. The Concept

201. The digital transformation also heralds an era where the digital population is growing exponentially with every passing day. There is about 7.77 billion population in the world and as of January 2020, there were about 4.5 billion internet users.[274] Surprisingly, the highest number of internet users is in Asia.[275] Though these figures would only show that human society is changing, and changing for the better and toward a more progressive life yet the more people are online the greater the danger of infractions and the higher the need for cyber security. According to the International Telecommunications Union (ITU) Connect 2030 there would be 70% internet connect by 2023 and 75% by 2025.[276] There is a shift toward the adoption of digital technologies which is prominent in developing countries such as India.[277] These adoptions are even faster in all nooks and corners of the country. The COVID-19 pandemic has further accelerated this adoption. This only opens the entire system to the risk of cyber attacks in the form of cyber crimes and cyber infractions. Such attacks affect the systems through viruses and hacking, and all systems are susceptible to such vulnerabilities irrespective of them being banks, industries, educational institutions, and commercial organizations. India became the

274. Worldwide digital population. Statista Published by J Clement, https://www.statista.com/statistics/617136/digital-population-worldwide/.
275. 50.3% are in Asia—15.9% are in Europe—11.5% are in Africa—10.1% are in Latin America and the Caribbean—7.6% are in North America—3.9% are in the Middle East—0.6% are in Oceania and Australia. Internet Stats & Facts (2020). https://hostingfacts.com/internet-facts-stats/.
276. Measuring the Information Society Report—Ch. 1—*The Current State of ICTs*—Key findings—Volume 1—2018. 2018 ITU—Geneva-Switzerland.
277. *Ibid.*

second most affected country due to cyber attacks from 2016 to 2018[278] so much so that it has urged industries and companies to opt for cyber insurance policies. India saw some 18 million cyber attacks and 200,000 threats in a day in the first quarter of 2022.[279] According to a United Nations Report, India has jumped 37 places to 10th position in the Global Cyber Security Index (GCI) 2020.

§2. THE CYBERSECURITY CHALLENGES IN INDIA

202. Being vulnerable to cyber attacks the country has seen some of the most harmful attacks, like the Union Bank of India Heist (2016) causing a loss of USD 171 billion; Wannacry Ransomware (May 2017), the global ransom ware attack affected thousands of computers in the country; data theft at Zomato (May 2017), data including names and passwords of 17 million users were hacked; and Petya Ransomware (June 2017), along with the world the container handling functions were affected, to name a few. Thus the challenges are numerous which are due to the following reasons:

- Diversity in devices—The devices used in the country make up of high-end mobile pieces and the most ordinary machines. The ordinary devices lack security mechanisms and throw a challenge to the law enforcers during an investigation.
- Lack of national level architecture—No such robust architecture exists in the country to check or prevent cyber attacks.
- Lack of separation—There is no boundary between various organizations, like banks, oil, and Natural Gas Commission (ONGC) thereby exposing these institutions to easy cyber attacks. To tackle this "technically equipped multi-agency organization" is required.[280]
- Lack of awareness—The population is less cyber literate and hence their understanding and precautions regarding cyber attacks are very low. A complete educative drive and guidance are required.

Cybersecurity is well received in the Information Technology Amendment Act 2008. There are a good number of provisions devoted to the cause of cybersecurity in the country. Realizing the ramifications of cyber incidents and the havoc they can cause to humans the government has formulated several precautionary measures in the IT Act.

---

278. https://inc42.com/buzz/cyber-attacks-india/.
279. Google's Royal Hansen—VP Engineering for Privacy, Safety and Security. August 2022. https://www.moneycontrol.com/news/business/india-saw-18-million-cyber-attacks-in-first-quarter-of-2022-google-executive-royal-hansen-9084911.html.
280. Milind Jain, *Cybersecuriy and Digitalization*. 2020. International Journal of Legal Science and Innovation 2(3), 132(ISSN 2581–9453). 139.

§3. Critical Information Infrastructure

203. Critical Information Infrastructure (CII) —The phrase "Critical Information Infrastructure" has been used in the Act to denote important military, intelligence, and medical and transport installations in India.

Section 70(1) explanation defines the term "Critical Information Infrastructure" in the following words:

- For the purposes of this section, "Critical Information Infrastructure" means the computer resource, the incapacitation or destruction of which, shall have a debilitating impact on national security, economy, public health, or safety.
- *Protected system* — The definition of the term "protected system" has been enlarged to bring within its ambit the CII as follows:

- Section 70(1)(Amended) — The appropriate government may, by notification in the Official Gazette, declare any computer resource which directly or indirectly affects the facility of Critical Information Infrastructure, to be a protected system.

Thus, the important and critical infrastructure in the country forming the backbone of the entire national life is a "protected system." Once an installation is declared as a protected system, the government takes extra precaution to safeguard it. The entry to such a protected system would be by the authority given by the government, and the government shall formulate separate rules and regulations to maintain the safety and security of such a protected system. Not only this but if anyone, without authority either enters such a protected system or attempts to enter they shall be punished with imprisonment which may extend up to ten years, and shall also be liable to a fine.

To address the threat the government issued Guidelines for the Protection of National Critical Information Infrastructure Protection Centre (NCIIPC) in 2015.[281] The guidelines recognize national security, economy, public health, and safety, as the key considerations in assessing whether the object of protection is critical. At present, the various sectors, like ICT and telecommunication, transportation, power, and energy; the Ministries of Home Affairs, External Affairs and Heavy Industries, and *Niti Ayog* (erstwhile Planning Commission) are regarded as CII. The Act also makes provision for any "appropriate government" to declare any computer system which directly or indirectly affects the facility of CII as a "protected system." Some of the "protected systems" are; TETRA Secured Communications Network, the UIDAI database, and the Long Range Identification and Tracking System. The guidelines define the functions of the NCIIPC as to "*take all necessary measures to facilitate protection of Critical Information Infrastructure, from unauthorized*

281. https://nciipc.gov.in/documents/NCIIPC_Guidelines_V2.pdf.

access, modification, use, disclosure, disruption, incapacitation or destruction, through coherent coordination, synergy and raising information security awareness among all stakeholders."[282]

National Nodal Agency (NNA) - To ensure cybersecurity in the country there is a provision for the establishment of a National Nodal Agency.

Section 70-A

(1) The Central Government may, by notification published in the Official Gazette, designate any organization of the government as the National Nodal Agency in respect of Critical Information Infrastructure Protection.
(2) The National Nodal Agency designated under sub-section (1) shall be responsible for all measures including research and development relating to the protection of Critical Information Infrastructure.
(3) The manner of performing functions and duties of the agency referred to in sub-section (1) shall be such as may be prescribed.

§4. Indian Computer Emergency Response Team

204. ICERT or CERT-In—According to section 2(*ua*), IT Act 2000 "Indian Computer Emergency Response Team" means an agency established under sub-section (1) of section 70-B.[283] The Central Government shall make arrangements for the establishment of a central entity to serve as ICERT. This will be a specialized body primarily to take care of the protected system in the country.

Composition

The Central Government shall appoint an agency of the government to be called the ICERT. There shall be appointed a Director General of the agency and such other officers and employees as the government may prescribe. The salaries, allowances, and terms and conditions of the office bearers and staff of the agency shall be prescribed by the government. The appointment of such agency shall be notified by the government in the Official Gazette.

Functions

The ICERT shall be the national agency for cybersecurity and shall be responsible for all measures including research and development relating to CII. It will perform the following functions:

(a) collection, analysis, and dissemination of information on cyber incidents;
(b) forecast and alerts of cyber security incidents;
(c) emergency measures for handling cyber security incidents;

---

282. Guidelines for the Protection of Critical Information Infrastructure—Version. 2.0—2015—Executive Summary—para. 2. p. 1.
283. Inserted by s. 36 of the IT (Amendment) Act, 2008 (10 of 2009).

(d) coordination of cyber incidents response activities;
(e) issue guidelines, advisories, vulnerability notes, and whitepapers relating to information security practices, procedures, prevention, response, and reporting of cyber incidents; and
(f) such other functions relating to cybersecurity as may be prescribed.

The government shall lay down the manner of performing such functions and the related duties of the agency. The agency is empowered to issue directions to or ask for information from any of the service providers, intermediaries, data centers, body corporate, and any other person. If any such person or entity fails to follow the directions so issued, it shall be held guilty under the section and be punished with imprisonment which may extend to one year or with a fine up to INR 1 lakh or with both. The court shall take cognizance of an offense under this section only after the complaint is filed by an officer of the agency (sections 70-B(1)–(8)).

205. Monitoring, interception, and decryption of data — Elaborate provisions are made under the Amendment Act to intercept incriminating data, or to screen it off from public view not only on the grounds of cybersecurity but also for the sake of decency, morality, and life values. Sections 69 (Directions for interception or monitoring or decryption), 69-A (Blocking for public access), and 69-B (Monitoring and Collecting traffic data) empower the government to authorize any agency to take these steps as per the rules prescribed by the government. As a result, the government has formulated the Information Technology (Procedure and Safeguards for Monitoring and Collecting Traffic Data or Information) Rules, 2009.[284] There are also certain state and sectoral CERTs which include FinCERT for banking and RailCERT for railways.

§5. Government Initiatives: The Latest

206. The Global Cybersecurity Index 2018 discussed *supra* has listed India among the countries that have shown high commitment toward the five pillars of cybersecurity. The initiative has been since the proliferation of the internet in the country at the turn of the millennium. The IT Act 2000 is a stepping stone in this direction. Thereafter, a number of initiatives were taken from time to time which are as follows:[285]

284. *Vide* G.S.R. 782 (E), Oct. 27, 2009.
285. Indian Prime Minister in his speech at the Asia Society, New York on Sep. 22, 2003 on the Indo-US relations in the emerging global environment expressed common concern of India and the US on terrorism, transnational crime and cyber crime and proposed to establish ties in this area. Again, during the Summit of Bay of Bengal Initiative for Multi-Sectoral Technical and Economic Cooperation (BIMSTEC) held at Bangkok on Jul. 31, 2004, the Prime Minister deliberated on mutual cooperation in the field of combating the menace of international terrorism and transnational crimes.
In August 2005, in the ASEAN Regional Forum, India reiterated its standpoint on cooperation against international terrorism and it also endorsed the establishment of an ARF Inter-Sessional Meeting on Counter-terrorism and Transnational Crime which is active on the job.

(1) Indian Cyber Crime Coordination Centre (I4C) is established to contain other cyber crimes. Measures are also taken to prevent cybersecurity attacks. These are as follows:
   - To protect against cyber attacks on the critical infrastructure in the country the government established National Critical Information Infrastructure Protection Centre (NCIIPC).
   - It is made mandatory for all institutions and organizations who provide digital services to report any cyber attack to the Computer Emergency Response Team (CERT) promptly.
   - Cyber *Swachhta Kendra* (Botnet Cleaning and Malware Analysis Center) is established to help in the detection of malware attacks and to provide tools for their removal.
   - The CERT regularly issues advisories to remain alert and also issues measures to tackle them.
   - Chief Information Security Officers (CISOs) are given guidelines regarding their responsibilities and compliance with orders.
   - There is also a provision for the auditing of websites and their regular checking.
   - Organizations are established for Information Security Best Practices and for security auditing.
   - There is a provision for Crisis Management Plan to counter cyber attacks and cyber terrorism.
   - Cybersecurity mock drills are also done to safeguard important government structures and to enable preparedness for any cyber onslaught.
   - Training programs for Chief Information Security Officers (CISOs) are also held to train them in securing important IT structures of the country.

India thus shows immense interest and urge to become relevant and impressive in the area of IT.

The India—US Joint Statement delivered in New Delhi on Mar. 2, 2006 while vying for global safety and security laid stress on counter-terrorism cooperation between the two nations. They reaffirmed their commitment to a Maritime Cooperation Framework to prevent piracy and transnational crime at sea. It also laid emphasis on the growing electronic interdependencies to protect critical infrastructure from cyber crime, terrorism and other malicious threats.

Chapter 2. Sector-Specific Obligations (E.g., Financial Sector, Health Sector, Etc.)

§1. GENERALLY

207. India is moving neck and neck with other developed countries of the world to harness the benefits of the ICTs and at the same time to build up a Digital India with safe harbors for netizens. As per McKinsey's Report 2019 approximately 1.2 billion users are registered on India's digital ID program, "*Aadhaar.*" Thus the more the number of internet users the greater the threat of cybersecurity. Since digitization, India has faced "over 6.07 lakh cyber security incidents" just in the first half of 2021.[286] Thus more the dependence on digitization the greater the vulnerability. Not only is privacy of individuals affected but the economy of the country is also adversely affected. According to a 2021 IBM Report, the global average data breach cost in 2021 was USD 4.24 million. In FY 2022–2023, the government allocated INR 515 crores (5,150 millions) for cybersecurity which is the amount to be used by the Computer Emergency Response Team to monitor cybersecurity incidents in the country for issuing advisories on cyber threats and also for measures to counter it. Both the public and private sectors have launched their own programs to contain the menace of cyber attacks.

I. Private Companies

208. About 80% companies have decided to upgrade their cybersecurity budget. They also opt for insurance coverage against cyber attacks. The solutions include the full range of potential vulnerabilities, including web and mobile applications, cloud infrastructure security, and IoT security so that they are not required to pay the endless price of unpreparedness.

II. Financial Sector

209. Banks, in any country, have been the forerunner in harnessing the fruits of ICTs and digitization. So also in India, the entire banking system has been overhauled or digitized which exposed them to greater computer glitches and cyber attacks. But the cyber infractions in banks are about 50 years old and the banks have been fighting the borderless battle since.[287] "Digitisation will likely be the key for banks to run operations efficiently, improve productivity, remain competitive, and

286. As per the written reply of the Minister of State for Electronics and information technology submitted in the Lower house of the Parliament.
287. Cyber security in Indian banking Industry: Part I. Deloitte—November 2020. p. 05. https://www2.deloitte.com/in/en/pages/financial-services/articles/in-fs-cybersecurity-in-the-indian-banking-industry.html.

thrive."[288] The ease with which banks are operating in the digital environment is not without challenges and grim risks. The deadly COVID-19 Pandemic caused havoc not only in the lives of human beings around the world but as per VMware Carbon Report, "cyber attacks against banks and financial institutions globally increased 238% amidst the COVID-19 crisis between February 2020 and April 2020." India was not an exception; the Reserve Bank of India (RBI) sounded a red alert in July 2020 regarding cybersecurity issues. The financial stability report[289] underlined the challenges arising due to increased cyber attacks. The national lockdowns necessitated people to transact more through internet banking thereby making the system more vulnerable. Hackers caused 40,000 cyber attacks in India within five days in the last week of June.[290]

A. *Major Cyber Attacks in Indian Financial Sector*

210. More sophisticated cyber attacks in the banking industry in India are making headway since 2016. These are shown below:[291]

Year	*Nature of Attacks*
2016	Government-owned Indian bank's server was compromised
2017	World's biggest "ransomware" attack, Wannacry and "Notpetya" where USD 10 billion were lost.
2018	Pune-based leading cooperative bank suffered a loss of USD 13.8 million in cyber attacks
2019	The server of Indian cooperative banks was attacked and USD 0.1 million stolen. Another Mumbai-based bank suffered a loss of USD 4.1 million from a cooperative bank

288. Cyber security in Indian banking Industry: Part I. Deloitte—November 2020. https://www2.deloitte.com/in/en/pages/financial-services/articles/in-fs-cybersecurity-in-the-indian-banking-industry.html.
289. Reserve Bank of India, RBI releases the financial stability report, July 2020, Jul. 24, 2020, https://www.rbi.org.in/Scripts/BS_PressReleaseDisplay. aspx?prid=50122.
290. Press Trust of India, *Rise in cyber attacks from China, Over 40,000 Cases In 5 Days: Official* NDTV, Jun. 23, 2020, https://www.ndtv.com/indianews/rise-in-cyber-attacks-from-china-over-40–000-cases-in-5-days-official-2251111.
291. *Supra* Note 291, p. 06.

Year	*Nature of Attacks*
2020	During the COVID-19 outbreak, Banks and Financial Services Industry (FSI) cyber attacks increased 238% between February and April 2020. Global hackers caused some 40,000 cyber attacks on the IT and Indian banking industry in the last week of June 2020

A Glance: Cyber attacks in the Indian Banking Sector.

B. Digitization of Indian Banks

211. The Indian banks embrace more complex technologies, like mobile and internet banking, and improved employee intranet, and adopt hybrid cloud technology thereby giving way to steady cyber attacks. Most of the banks before COVID-19 preferred to go for strategic digitization of their customer services and experiences. Four pillars of the banks in India are; *customers, vendors, business partners, and employees*. Changes in the behavior of urban customers, millennials, and the middle-income population who desired faster solutions and improved customized services necessitated the entry of digitization in banking systems. Among the other three pillars, namely the vendors, business partners, and employees, digitization was slow and steady. However, in the post-pandemic period the digitization process was due to the following reasons:

– The banking sector is employee-intensive, and the lockdowns, work-from-home trend, and various other restrictions during the pandemic affected business operations and resource availability. As a result, banks have become prone to disruptions and distractions. A resilient information technology architecture and adoption of digitization become a compelled option.
– Customer outreach is to be achieved as the banks in India are dealing with a variety of customers, rural, urban, technology savvy, and customers with personal preferences. There is increased demand for contactless transactions and virtual services. Digitization becomes inevitable.
– Banks like any other business prefer cost-effective services. As per the RBI's latest financial stability report, macro stress tests for credit risk indicate that the gross Non-Performing Assets (NPA) ratio of Scheduled Commercial Banks (SCBs) may increase from 8.5% in March 2020 to 12.5% by March 2021.[292] Thus rising NPAs will increase financial stress and credit costs. Digitization will help the banks to run their operations effectively.

292. Reserve Bank of India, RBI releases the financial stability report, July 2020, Jul. 24, 2020, https://www.rbi.org.in/Scripts/BS_PressReleaseDisplay. aspx?prid=50122.

Technological Solutions and government Initiative
Banks have a storehouse of Personally Identifiable Information (PII) and hence are the first target of cyber criminals and hackers. More and more banks are resorting to Cloud and Internet of Things (IoT) technologies. Managing data privacy becomes their foremost job for which they adopt data sharing mechanisms, data lifecycle management, and data ownership. The RBI envisages an account aggregator's platform (AA ecosystem) because aggregators are responsible for transferring data without storing customer credentials. Data life-cycle management entails using data as per need and using technological means against its misuse. Data ownership requires rules to retain and dispose customer information. Increasing use of multiple devices by customers to access bank services exposes them to a grimmer risk of cyber attacks and cyber crimes. Like any other part of the world India faces a shortage of cybersecurity professionals The Data Security Council of India (DSCI) predicted in 2015 that India will need 1 million cybersecurity professionals by 2020.[293]

212. The Government of India under the aegis of the National Security Council Secretariat initiated formulating the National Cyber Security Strategy 2020 (NCSS 2020) for the next five years (2020–2025) to ensure a "safe, secure, trusted, resilient, and vibrant cyberspace." Supervision by the fountain authority, namely the RBI makes the path of the banks more difficult in achieving cybersecurity. Since March 2020, the RBI has issued more than 10 advisories/alerts on various cyber threats and best practices to supervised entities while some of them have been issued in coordination with the ICERT.

III. Health Sector

213. The Indian health industry is fast resorting to technological advancements, like remote health monitoring, electronic health records, and the IoT thereby making it more prone to cyber attacks. The data collected by CloudSEK shows that there have been 1.87 lakhs (18.7 million) attacks in the first four months of 2022. The CloudSEK Report says "India recorded the second highest number of attacks with a total of 7.7% of the total attacks on the health care industry in 2021."[294] The country since the COVID-19 Pandemic has seen a boom in virtual healthcare, tele consultations, telemedicine, wearable technology, and email prescriptions thereby opening the industry to newer vulnerabilities. #BeCyberSmart slogan gives an awakening call to the healthcare industry as the loss of data will cost not only the life of patients but also their trust. The volume of critical data being transferred and stored every day calls for an integrated, unified, end-to-end security portfolio to help address privacy requirements, improve threat detection, and reduce management

293. Data Security Center of India, "Cyber security: 1 million cyber security professionals needed by 2020," Press Release, DSCI News Center, August 2015.
294. Cyber attacks on Indian healthcare Industry second highest in the World: CloudSEK.PTI. Sep. 20, 2022, https://www.thehindu.com/sci-tech/technology/cyber-attacks-on-indian-healthcare-industry-second-highest-in-the-world-cloudsek/article65914129.ece.

complexity.[295] Sophos's The State of Ransom ware in Healthcare 2021 Report indicates 34% of healthcare organizations were hit by ransom ware last year. The widespread flaws offer a greater opportunity to ransom ware cyber criminals.

214. In the healthcare sector, apart from fortification of data safety cybersecurity entails privacy, integrity, and well-being of the patients. Digitization and emerging technologies require updating the entire healthcare infrastructure by adopting and incorporating blockchain, IoTs, etc., to reduce the chance of infringements, give better healthcare to patients, reduce casualties, and upgrade the level of healthcare in the country. The Data Security Council of India (DSCI) is a premier data security body in the country which is committed to making cyberspace, safe, secure, and trusted by establishing best practices, standards, and initiatives in cybersecurity and privacy.[296] As there is an increased focus on digital transformation the pharma companies in India are giving more attention to cybersecurity in the field of healthcare and pharmacy; as ransomware attacks and IP and data theft are becoming the top cybersecurity concerns in the country. India is marching toward becoming a "World Pharmacy" and is bent upon leveraging the power of technology and digital transformation. It is recognizing cybersecurity as the key lever while enhancing security around data, and operational technologies (OT) and across the supply chain.[297]

Role of the government
The healthcare level in the country is not satisfactory in view of the present-time needs of patients. Expenditure of the government as per various reports is estimated to be 1.5% of the total GDP which is low as far as the population of the nation is considered. The initiatives taken by the government in the field of maternal health come under the National Health Policy 2017 apart from providing good healthcare services in other medical areas.

IV. Transport Sector

215. Transportation in the country is a mosaic of railways, roads, sea, and airlines. By this time all these facets are fully IT-enabled and digitized. Different ministries tackle their respective departments, and apart from the IT Act provisions of cybersecurity, frequent advisories and notifications are issued to tackle the onslaught of cyber attacks. Innovative technologies, like IoT and artificial intelligence (AI), though are the drivers of digital transformation in the transport and logistics industry but at the same time, they make the systems more prone to cyber attacks. The CERT-In is the main organization that takes care of cyber attacks in various sectors. Cyber attacks are a reality now and call for not only legal or ministerial measures but in the latest context, technological measures have also become mandatory. In 2021, many of the government systems were compromised, while by

295. Nandita Vijay—Indian healthcare to prioritize cyber security and place robust data privacy framework. November 2021, http://www.pharmabiz.com/NewsDetails.aspx?aid=143687&sid=1.
296. Deloitte, News Release. Data Security Council of India Report 2022, https://www.dsci.in/sites/default/files/Press%20Release%20-%20DSCI%20Pharma%20Report.pdf.
297. G Shukla, *Partner and Leader, Deloitte India. Ibid.*

way of preparedness the Ministry of Road Transport and Highways received an alert from the Indian Computer Emergency Response Team regarding "targeted intrusion activities" directed toward Indian transport with possible malicious intentions. The Ministry, therefore, asked the sector to strengthen the cybersecurity posture of their infrastructure. Thus various agencies, like the National Informatics Center (NIC), National Highways Authority of India (NHAI), National Highways Infrastructure Development Corporation (NHIDCL), Indian Roads Congress (IRC), Indian Academy of Highway Engineers (IAHE), and Public Works Departments (PWDs) of states are advised to have IT audit by CERT-In certified agencies.

Railways—The digitalization of railways services in India began with ticketing, freight operations, train operations, and asset management, which are now heavily reliant on IT systems. *Rail Cloud* and *Rail Saathi* (Train Companion) are some of the measures used by the Railways to enhance passenger safety and experience which aims as an integrated platform to facilitate ticket booking, inquiry, onboard cleaning, ordering meals, etc. Recently, the Government of India sanctioned a 5-year plan to implement 4G technology for modernizing communication networks and to improve safety in the trains. Rapid digitization enhances infrastructure, systems, services, rolling stock, and signaling along with improving operational efficiency. Technological capabilities invite cyber threat challenges; it calls for a new cybersecurity framework.

V. Cyber Security in Armed Forces

216. "When we talk of Digital India we also talk of Digital Armed Forces."[298] So to say, technology is the new normal. The Armed Forces see cyberspace from the perspective of Command, Control, Computers, Communications and Intelligence (C4ISR).[299] From the age of industrial warfare, the world is drifting toward information warfare. Cyber warfare if resorted to will be within the four contours of the Constitution of India, international laws, and treaties to which India is a signatory.[300] Cyber weapons such as Stuxnet, DuQu, Flame, WannaCry, Petya, Non-Petya, and a long list of Advanced Persistent Threats (ATPs) are early signs of large-scale cyber war. Like any other aspect of the Armed Forces cybersecurity takes a grimmer form and a breach of cybersecurity in the domain of Armed Forces would not sit to count the loss but it will engage in war to thwart the attempts made by the enemy country. Though the Defense Department is still not equipped to launch a cyberwar yet there is full preparedness to prevent it. "From cyber-crimes to cyber espionage to cyber terrorism to social engineering to cyber war and now cognitive dimension … "[301] today the ICT smears the entire battlefield from land and sea to air and outer space everywhere there is the digital environment which has changed the basics of these sectors. Thus in "this shadowy battlefield, victories are fought

298. Prime Minister of India—March 2019.
299. VIF, 94.
300. Credible Cyber Deterrence in Armed Forces of India—Vivekanand International Foundation Task Force Report. March 2019.
301. *Ibid.*, at 45.

for with bits instead of bullets, malware instead of militias and botnets instead of bombs."[302] However, even the Armed Forces opine that cybersecurity is a continuous process to deal with and only one sector alone cannot combat the menace. It is the interaction and cooperation among, the government, all stakeholders, industry, and academia. Public-Private Partnerships and government-funded research will yield promising results in the Armed Forces sector.

§2. International Framework

217. Cybersecurity is contingent on international cooperation in which India must participate. In 2015, a group of 25 international experts commissioned by the UN General Assembly (UNGA) urged that "International engagement is an important aspect of India's cyber policy."[303] India has cyber engagements with over 15 countries, including the U.S.A., U.K., Russia, Japan, Germany, France, and member nations of ASEAN. Recently, India signed cyber agreements with the U.S.A., Israel, and Russia. The Indian Computer Emergency Response Team has also entered into some ten Memorandums of Understanding (MoU) with its overseas counterparts. UN Secretary-General Antonio Guterres has said, "Episodes of cyber warfare between states already exist. What is worse is that there is no regulatory scheme for that type of warfare, it is not clear how the Geneva Convention or international humanitarian law applies to it." To ensure capacity building and for cybersecurity, it is suggested that India must have at the earliest an "Integrated National Cyber Doctrine," developed jointly by the civil authority and the Armed Forces with "Cyber Security" dealt by the civil authorities and "Cyber Power" by the Armed Forces.

§3. Indian Scenario: Combined Effort

218. Institutional support to achieve assured cybersecurity is paramount. The borderless nature of cyberspace calls for national movement and participation from all stakeholders. Though India responded promptly to the call of the UNCITRAL document of Model Law and passed the IT Act 2000(Amended 2008) yet the law is mainly civil in nature and regulates e-commerce. Then there was National Policy on Electronics 2012 and National Cyber Security Policy 2013. These very comprehensive documents deal with almost all facets of cybersecurity but do not talk about the creation and application of cyber power, and the role, organization, equipping, and training of the Indian Armed Forces. The government though expressed the desire to digitize the Armed Forces yet there has not been a serious effort in this direction. Toward capacity building, the Government of India established the Defence Cyber Agency (DCyA) in November 2019, which works under the Ministry of Defence and is a joint effort of the tri-services (Army, Air Force, and Navy) and would aim to achieve the "national objectives" regarding cyber space. This is

302. *Ibid.*, at 46.
303. *Ibid.*, at 102.

to strengthen cybersecurity in the country and to upgrade its position from 21st among 30 countries that desired to become a cyber power as per the report of the "National Cyber Power Index" released in September 2020.[304] However, the IT Act 2000 establishes Indian Computer Emergency Response Team (CERT-In) with similar organs at state and in the defense sector. There has been a constant effort by the government to ensure cybersecurity in the critical information infrastructure with the cooperation of public-private partnerships and the use of ICT technologies. The entire cybersecurity structure in this regard can be explained below:

- Operation-Operationalization of a National Critical Information Infrastructure Projection Centre (NCIIPC).
- The Ministry of Electronics and Information Technology (MeitY) established National Cyber Coordination Centre (NCCC) for cyber threat management and information sharing.
- For testing, evaluation, and cyber audit there is a Cyber Security Assurance and Certification Body.
- A Research & Development Fund is also formed to enhance research in the field.
- There is a public-private partnership on cybersecurity measures.
- Capacity building and creation of 500,000 cyber professionals.
- The National Security Council Secretariat (NSCS) coordinates cybersecurity issues. There is a Cyber Security Coordinator at NSCS who is given the task of coordinating and encouraging cybersecurity efforts.

Armed Forces Initiative

219. The Defense Forces aim at focussing on two aspects: first, to concentrate on capacity building of the Armed Forces; and second, integration with the national cybersecurity architecture at a macro level.[305] The task force, therefore, suggests that cyber power of the Armed Forces be based on the following seven pillars:

(1) Policy and strategy for development and employment of cyber power.
(2) Adoption of the Indian Armed Forces Doctrine for use of cyber power.
(3) Organization of cyber deterrence, synergy, and staffing and adaptation of cyber force.
(4) Human resource training and certification.
(5) Technology, R&D standards, and integrity of data.
(6) Development of concepts for effective cyber deterrence.
(7) International engagement and legal framework.

However, there exists a gap when it comes to managing cyber power in the Armed Forces. The Armed Forces Computer Emergency Response Team works in collaboration with the CERT-In. There must also be real-time communications between CERTs of the Armed Force and CERT-In.

---

304. Abhinandan Mishra; *India's cyber offensive capabilities still not top-notch*—August 2022. https://www.sundayguardianlive.com/news/indias-cyber-offensive-capabilities-still-not-top-notch.
305. *Supra* Note 304 at 50.

Chapter 3. Liability and Remedies

§1. General Statement

220. The CERT-In Rules, however, disown any responsibility (thus accountability) for the CERT-In to maintain cybersecurity or adequately respond to the same. The Government of India launched[306] cyber crime portal (www.cybercrime.gov.in) so that the victims find an easier way to file complaints in which especially women and children are the main targets. Thus reporting procedures regarding degrading crimes like Child Pornography/Child Sexual Abuse Material, rape/gang rape imageries, or sexually explicit content have been made easier and within reach of these victims.

306. Steps Taken to Deal with Cyber Crime and Cyber Security—Press Information Bureau, Government of India Ministry of Home Affairs—Jul. 17, 2019. Press Information Bureau. Delhi.

Part VI. Cybercrime

Chapter 1. Application of International and Regional Agreements (E.g., Status of the Council of Europe Cybercrime Convention, Law Enforcement Cooperation Agreements, Etc.)

§1. Generally

221. Law experts all over the world though categorize cyber crimes under different headings and the number of categories may not be the same, but one common thread binds them all as almost all of them recognize that old crimes are being transformed by the use of the internet and new crimes are being created in the digital environment. To accord uniformity to laws governing cyber crimes, various attempts are made by international institutions and forums, such as the G8 Member States, to achieve a concerted effort to legislate against cyber crimes. These can be enumerated in the following section. The first major attempt was under the auspices of the Organisation for Economic Co-operation and Development (OECD). It published a report in 1986, which listed five categories of offenses that it believed should constitute a common approach to computer crime.[307] Yet another significant institution, the Council of Europe has also embarked on categorizing and listing various computer-related offenses in order to achieve harmony among the signatory States in the field of cyber-criminal law.[308]

---

307. Ferrera, Lichtenstein, Reder, August & Schiano, *Cyber Law: Text and Cases* (West Thomson Learning, 2001) 297 ("Computer-Related Criminality: Analysis of Legal Policy in the OECD Area" (Report DSTI-ICCP 84.22 of Apr. 18, 1986)); Ian Walden, Chapter 9: *Computer Crime* in Chris Reed (ed.), *Computer Law* (3rd ed., Oxford University Press, 2003) 314.

308. In 1985, a Select Committee of Experts, the European Committee on Crime Problems was established under the auspices of the Council of Europe to consider the legal issues raised by computer crime. The final report was published in September 1989. As part of the Committee's work, it produced guidelines for national legislatures on a "Minimum List of Offences Necessary for a Uniform Criminal Policy." The offences were: computer fraud; computer forgery; damage to computer data or computer programs; computer sabotage; unauthorized access; unauthorized interception; unauthorized reproduction of a computer program; and unauthorized reproduction of topography. These eight offences were seen by all Member States to be critical areas of computer misuse that required provisions in criminal law. In addition, the report put forward an "optional list" of four offences that failed to achieve consensus among Members, but was thought to be worthy of consideration. The Report was published with a Council of Ministers' recommendation urging governments to take account of the Report when reviewing and initiating legislation in this field. Recommendation No. R (89) 9, Sep. 13, 1999. *Ibid.*

§2. Council of Europe Cyber Crime Convention 2001

222. In November 2001, the Council of Ministers adopted the Cyber Crime Convention, which addresses the issues of substantive and procedural criminal law, on which Member States are obliged to take measures to implement it in their national laws as well as in addressing the issues of international cooperation.[309] Section 1 of the Convention distinguishes three categories of offenses:

(a) "Offenses against the confidentiality, integrity and availability of computer data and systems": Illegal access, illegal interception, data interference, systems interference, and misuse of devices. (Articles 2–6).
(b) "Computer-related offenses": forgery and fraud. (Articles 7–8).
(c) "Content-related offenses": child pornography and infringement of copyrights and related rights. (Articles 9–10).

The Cyber Crime Convention 2001, also known as Budapest Convention, to date remains the most significant document in the internet era regarding the crime committed in the new ambiance. It has been the first guidance in the matter of prosecution of such crimes now known as cyber crimes. Not only to European countries it has shown the way to the entire world how to deal with the new born crimes which are a clear deviation from traditional crimes. It has achieved uniformity in criminalizing online behavior and has been a great contributor in giving shape to the innovative criminal acts committed through a computer.

Present Status of the Convention

223. The Convention was negotiated by members of the Council of Europe as well as Canada, Japan, South Africa, and the U.S.A. It is open for accession by any State, and an increasing number of countries of Africa, the Americas, and the Asia/Pacific region are making use of this opportunity in the interest of effective criminal justice action on cybercrime.[310] The Convention comprises not only Parties who are signatories but also those who are invited to accede. By May 2020, there were 76 states including the Parties and invitees. The Convention is open to the world and helps the states in structuring their domestic laws along the roadmap shown by it and it also encourages international cooperation in this field. Thus, the impact of the Convention has yielded the following results in the last two decades:

- About 177 states from all over the world adopted it in their domestic legislation.
- 153 Members of the United Nations adopted it for reforms in their national legislations.
- 106 states adopted specific domestic provisions corresponding broadly to the substantive criminal law articles of the Convention. Mainly the African countries came out as the main beneficiaries of the substantive criminal law provisions.

309. *Ibid.*, 315.
310. The Budapest Convention on Cybercrime: Benefits and Impact in Practice, Strasbourg, Jul. 13, 2020, https://rm.coe.int/t-cy-2020-16-bc-benefits-rep-provisional/16809ef6ac.

- As for the procedural laws, some 82 states applied the general procedural laws to investigate cybercrimes as reformation in this field and making specific procedural laws as per the guidance given in Articles 16–21; and adopting the safeguard given in Article 15 of the Convention appeared to be a difficult task.

"Second Additional Protocol to the Convention on Cybercrime on enhanced co-operation and disclosure of electronic evidence" was approved by the Committee of Ministers on November 17, 2021. It realizes that the availability of electronic evidence becomes difficult in the present scenario as the evidence is often found in different and unknown jurisdictions hence the prosecution escapes justice. The Protocol thus provides a legal basis for disclosure of domain name information, direct cooperation with service providers, cooperation in emergencies, etc., to accelerate and make enforcement procedures effective.[311]

311. Details of Treaty No. 224. Full list (coe.int).

Chapter 2. Specific Computer Crimes (Unlawful Access, Identity Theft, Online Fraud, Online Sabotage, Forgery)

§1. General Statement

224. The Rise of Computer-Related crime—The internet has a global face. Computers hand-in-hand with the internet swept the globe in less than two and a half decades. It invaded every nook and corner of life on earth and today life is unimaginable without computers and the internet. Technological innovations had already started perforating the legal fabric by the middle of the twentieth century. The evolution of computers had taken the path of sophistication and technical excellence. The first-ever Electronic Numerical Integrator and Computer (ENIAC) was switched on in February 1946. The invention of computers is a boon yet the "cases of computer abuse began to be documented from the outset."[312] By the late 1970s, "crime by computer" was a serious enough problem to merit new criminal statutes[313] but the internet proliferation and unstoppable growth of technology did not have such an impact as it is having today. Slowly and gradually, computers were emerging as indispensable household gadgets but at the same time, they also became a new weapon in the hand of criminals. The year 1960, can be called the genesis of the field of computer law; it was the time when large mainframe computers were dominated by IBM and other seven companies[314] which together were termed by Douglas W. Jones as *Snow White and the Seven Dwarfs.* Also, this was the year when the first legal article on computer law by Roy N. Freed was published.[315] The article depicts the awakening of the legal mind to the importance and relevance of computers in the legal world. Following are the different forms of computer crimes:

I. Unlawful Access

225. Information and data stored in the computer are the subject matter of crimes that are computer-related. It is a new-age crime and can be committed in two ways: by internal means and by external means. Hacking is the most common and oldest way to make illegal access to the data stored in the system. The Indian law though does not define the term "hacking" yet the various actions comprising it have been made punishable. Section 43 of the IT Act 2000 says that if an act (i) destroys, deletes, or alters any information residing in a computer resource or diminishes its value or utility or affects it injuriously by any means or (ii) steals, conceals,

312. Donn B Parker, *Crime by Computer* (Charles Scribner's sons, New York 1976); Martin Wasik, *Crime and the Computer* (Oxford University Press, 1991).

313. Richard C Hollinger, *Computer Crime* in Clifton D. Bryant (ed.), *Encyclopedia of Criminology and Deviant Behaviour* (Vol. II, Brunner-Routledge, Taylor & Francis Group, 2000), 76–81.

314. Often referred to as BUNCH; Burroughs, Univac, NCR, Control Data, Honeywell, plus GE and Xerox make it seven.

315. Roy N Freed, *A Lawyer's Guide Through the Computer Maze* (The Practical Lawyer, November 1960).

destroys, or alters or causes any person to steal, conceal, destroy or alter any computer source code used for a computer resource shall be liable to pay damages by way of compensation not exceeding INR 1 crore (10 million). This section is to be read with section 66 of the IT Amendment Act 2008 which says that if a person does any act as defined under section 43 *dishonestly*[316] *and fraudulently*[317] then he shall be punished with imprisonment of up to three years or with a fine which may extend to INR 5 lakhs (0.5 million) or with both. Previously under the IT Act 2000, the illegal access entailed only civil action by way of damages but in the amended Act 2008 if the access has been done dishonestly and fraudulently then it is declared as a punishable criminal offense.

II. Identity Theft

226. Computer-related crimes are committed mainly by causing injury or harm to the data stored in the computer. However, the IT (Amendment) Act 2008 introduces a number of other related crimes which are often committed along with or as a result of computer data interference. These are:

- Identity theft—Anyone who fraudulently or dishonestly uses any electronic signature, password, or unique identification figure of another is said to commit the offense of identity theft. The offense is punished with imprisonment of up to three years or with a fine of up to INR 1 lakh (0.1 million) (section 66-C).
- Cheating by personation—It is a traditional offense as defined under the India Penal Code 1860 when a person disguises himself as another and by doing so causes wrongful loss to another. The offense when committed by using computer resources or communication devices then the offense is punishable under the IT Act with imprisonment of up to three years and with a fine of up to INR 1 lakh (0.1 million) (section 66-D).

III. Online Fraud

227. Jack Blum says, "International fraud, commercial fraud, money laundering and tax evasion will be the most important enterprise crimes of the future."[318] Unlike the U.S. and the U.K. where fraud or "wire fraud" has been separately defined and dealt with,[319] there is no separate provision for "wire fraud" in the IT Act 2000. This can be analogized with the fact that under the Indian Penal Code

316. "Dishonestly" means—Whoever does anything with the intention of causing wrongful gain to one person or wrongful loss to another person is said to do that thing "dishonestly" s. 24 the Indian Penal Code 1860.
317. "Fraudulently"—A person is said to do a thing fraudulently if he does that thing with intend to defraud but not otherwise s. 25 The Indian Penal Code 1860.
318. Sherry I Louise, *Crimes and Corruption in the Digital Age,* Journal of International Affairs (March 1998).
319. Recommendations of the U.K. Audit Commission and the Computer Fraud and Abuse Act (US 1986).

1860 which is the major substantive penal in India, "fraud" is neither defined nor is it considered a separate offense under the Code. Under Indian penal provisions, fraud is not an offense but it is taken as a mental condition that is present in many other crimes. Under IPC a person is said to do a thing fraudulently if he does that thing with intent to defraud but not otherwise (section 25, The Indian Penal Code 1860). In the words of Sir James Stephen, fraudster's own "advantage" is the principal object whether or not the victim has suffered some loss or injury. The IT Act 2000 has no mention of the word "fraud" or "fraudulently" but in The IT (Amendment) Act 2008 section 66 read with section 43(i) reveals that to commit an offense under it, one has to prove that the act of intrusion into any computer data was done dishonestly and fraudulently. Section 415[320] of IPC defines cheating and can be compared with the U.S. law regarding wire fraud in the Computer Fraud and Abuse Act 1986 which enumerates "false pretenses" and "intent to defraud" as ingredients of the offense of fraud with the use of interstate wire communications as yet one more ingredient. As IPC is a traditional law, only an amendment in section 415 can bring it along the lines of the U.S. law where "the use of interstate wire communications" is included as one of the ingredients of fraud committed via the internet. After the amendment, section 415 should read as this; "Whoever, by deceiving any person, fraudulently or dishonestly, by electronic communication or otherwise, induces … " section 415 can then be independently applied to Internet Fraud where there has been no concomitant computer intrusion. However, in cases[321] where fraud is committed by vandalizing the communication system and by infusing malicious programs and codes, section 415 read with sections 43, 65, or 66 whatever the case may be can be applied.

IV. Online Sabotage

228. A company's success depends on its good will and reputation. But nevertheless, competition exists in the market and there is a run to overshadow others. Online sabotage has become a way of sabotaging or harming the reputation of businesses. It consists of discrediting products and services with negative comments and evaluations. No definite mention of this term is found in the IT Act 2000.

V. Forgery

229. Online forgery is an offense that needs little effort as compared to offline forgery. It is usually not resorted for money but it is also employed for "glory or a

320. Section 415—Whoever by deceiving any person, fraudulently or dishonestly, induces the person so deceived to deliver any property to any person, or to consent that any person shall retain any property, or intentionally induces the person so deceived to do or omit to do anything which he would not do or omit if he were not so deceived, and which act or omission causes or is likely to cause damage or harm to that person in body, mind, reputation, or property, is said to cheat.

321. The most popular of such cases is credit card fraud. Then there are bogus online investment schemes and market manipulation schemes where fraud is committed by hacking into the computer system of other users.

spirit of devilment, cocking a snook at experts and purchasers."[322] Like other countries, in India too forgery has been an offense under substantive criminal law. It is defined under section 463 of the Indian Penal Code 1860 as making a false document with any one or more of the intents mentioned in the said section. The traditional offense has a reference to "document" or "part of a document" in the said section. The technological boom and the instances of forgery through computers rendered the said section inadequate for the purposes of digital forgery as the term "document" could be applied to computer data and information stored therein which was transient in nature. Thus, to make the said section workable in the online situation as well, amendments were made in the said section by the IT Act 2000. These amendments made electronic records as also an instrument of the offense of forgery. The relevant section 470 says Forged[323](document or electronic record).—A false (document or electronic record) made wholly or in part by forgery is designated "as forged document or electronic record." Thus, not only paper documents but an electronic record which is intangible in nature can be the object of forgery.

Section 463, Forgery—[324] Whoever makes any false document or false electronic record or part of a document or electronic record, with intent to cause damage or injury, to the public or to any person, or to support any claim or title or to cause any person to part with property, or to enter into any express or implied contract, or with intent to commit fraud or that fraud may be committed, commits forgery.

This definition after the amendment includes "the making of any false electronic record or part thereof with intent to cause damage or injury to the public or to any person." Traditionally speaking, the offense of forgery is said to be committed when the maker of it knows that the document is not genuine but represents it as genuine with the object of defrauding someone. When such false making is done using digital means such as "desktop publishing systems, colour laser and inkjet printers, colour copiers and image scanners" which "enable crooks to make fake, with relative ease checks, currencies, passports, visas, birth certificates, ID Cards, etc."[325]

Section 464 of the Indian Penal Code 1860 is also amended by the IT Act 2000 and also by the IT (Amendment) Act 2008. The amended section describing the "making of false document" says that a person is said to make a false document or false electronic record when the person dishonestly and fraudulently makes, signs, or seals a document or its part, or makes or transmits any electronic record or affixes any electronic signature on any electronic record, or who makes any mark to give authenticity to any document or electronic record. The section also regards the cancellation, alteration of any document or electronic record, or affixing of an electronic signature on it to be taken as made by any person living or dead as making of a false document or electronic record. In the third place, the section also regards the making of a document when anyone causes a person of unsound mind, or a person under intoxication, or a person under deception to put his signature or electronic signature on any document. Thus, the section comprehensively covers the case of digital forgery where it also clarifies in Explanation 3 that the expression

322. "Caslon Analytics Profile Forgery, Fraud and Forensics," http://www.caslon.comau/siteuse.htm.
323. Substituted by the IT Act, s. 91 & Schedule I for document.
324. *Ibid.*
325. Steven Furnell, *Cybercrime: Vandalizing the Information Society* (Addison-Wesley, 2002) 235.

"affixing electronic signature" shall have the same meaning as it appears in section 2(I)(d) of the IT Act 2000. The effect of technology on the offense of forgery has been tremendous as computer technology by its very nature reduces the burden of handwritten documents and simplifies the job of the writer. Mass copying which hardly can be termed as copy requires nanoseconds and the identical replica of the original makes the job of a law enforcer a challenging one.

Chapter 3. Traditional Crimes in a Digital Context

§1. General Statement

230. The internet proliferation has given birth to a new generation of crimes now commonly known as "cyber crimes." Simultaneously the internet has become an easy tool for committing those crimes which existed since the inception of this world. That said, the traditional crimes, almost all of them have been not only speeded up by the net proliferation but even their face, content, and result has undergone a magical transformation. Writers, like Ian Walden, DS Wall, and others opine that the internet has given wings to traditional crimes making them more complex to investigate as they are now committed in an intangible environment with the help of computers and the internet. Some of these crimes are examined below.

I. Online Obscenity

231. Pornographic content on the internet calls for a separate category of content-related crimes.[326] Aberrant activities online have provided an easy opportunity for criminals to make money with total disregard for the cultural and moral ethos of human society. Obscenity comes up as the most popular crime committed online and which has given a bad name to the blissful internet. Obscenity is not a new offense and traditionally speaking no civilized society regards indecent expressions, visuals, representations, or acts as acceptable. This is because such obscene acts drive one to commit similar crimes. Cockburn CJ in R. Hicklin in 1868, said the test of obscenity is "whether the tendency of the matter charged as obscene is to deprave and corrupt those whose minds are open to such immoral influences, and into whose hands a publication of this sort may fall."[327] The Supreme Court of India in *Ranjit D. Udeshi v. State of Maharashtra*[328] has observed that the test of obscenity laid down by Cockburn CJ should not be discarded and held that obscenity in India is treating sex in a manner appealing to the carnal side of human nature or having that tendency. Under the traditional Indian Penal Code 1860, sale of obscene material is regarded as an offense (section 292).

232. Online Obscenity—The IT Act 2000 was deficient in addressing obscenity which is committed online but the IT (Amendment) Act 2008 has done away with this lacuna and obscenity and other sex-related offenses have been added as new sections to address these crimes. The earlier section 67[329] was the only section that

---

326. Cybercrime Convention 2001.
327. (1868) LR 3 QB 360,371.
328. AIR 1965 SC 881: (1965) 2 Cri LJ 8.
329. Section 67—(IT Act 2000)—"*Publishing of information which is obscene in electronic form.*—Whoever publishes or transmits or causes to be published in the electronic form, any material which is lascivious or appeals to the prurient interest or if its effect is such as t tend to deprave and corrupt persons who are likely, having regard to all relevant circumstances, to read, see or hear the matter contained or embodied in it, shall be punished on **first** conviction with imprisonment of either description for a term which may extend to five years and with fine which may extend to

dealt with obscenity in a limited manner and it also did not distinguish between child pornography and mainstream pornography. The section was deficient in many ways; it said nothing about the knowledge of the offender, i.e., it says nothing about whether in cases where such an offending material is hidden in the cache memory of a system of which the offender is unaware, what will be his liability in such case. Secondly, the section uses the word "persons" and omits to mention the age of such a person. It only means that A who is a matured person of age 50, if the material published depraves, and corrupts his mind, hearing, or reading such an offending material, the offense is not committed. Does the section aim at a particular application? Here the prosecution may take the help of section 293 of the Indian Penal Code 1860. Thirdly, the section also omits to clarify as to what is "obscenity."

The IT (Amendment) Act 2008 (10 of 2009) has reformed the law of online obscenity in India to a greater extent. The combined effect of sections 66-E, 67, 67-A, and 67-B is that online obscenity has been brought within the legal regime and it also differentiates between "child pornography" and "mainstream pornography." Section 67 provides punishment for publishing obscene material in electronic form. The new section 67 in a descriptive manner is the same as the old section but it differs from it in two ways: First, in the marginal heading the word "transmitting" is inserted.; Second, the quantum of punishment has been changed as the term of imprisonment has been decreased while the amount of fine has been increased in both the first and second convictions. The section is deficient in the fact that like the traditional section 292 of the Indian Penal Code 1860 the present section 67 too does not define the content of the term "obscenity." As regards the punishment, it is not only two-fold but also stringent, i.e., for the first time of commission of the offense the punishment includes both a fine and imprisonment, and for a subsequent commission the quantum of this punishment is doubled which is more severe as compared to the Indian standards. Like fraud and other crimes, in the matter of internet obscenity too, the provisions of traditional obscenity laws as contained in section 293 of the Indian Penal Code 1860 will be helpful when it comes to prosecuting persons dealing in cyber pornography that is applicable to persons under the age of 20 years. Other Acts like the Indecent Representation of Women (Prohibition) Act 1986 and Young Persons (Harmful Publications) Act 1956 can also be invoked in the matter of internet obscenity.

Section 67-A—The section inserted by the IT (Amendment) Act 2008 comes out with the explanation that an act that depicts sex-appealing activities in electronic form is also punishable. The new section thus enlarges the area of obscenity and includes within it, the depiction of sex activities. It is for the first time that any Indian law defines such type of offense thereby indicating indirectly that depiction of a sex-related act in public is intolerable, prepares the weak-minded to commit an offense, and is morally degrading and hence an offense. The punishment given here is two-tier which only shows that the fear of graver punishment may deter the criminal to commit the offense for the second time.

INR 1 lakh and in the event of a **second** or subsequent conviction with imprisonment of either description for a term which may extend to ten years and also with fine which may extend to INR 2 lakh."

Section 67-B—The section inserted by the IT (Amendment) Act 2008 differentiates between "child pornography" and "mainstream pornography." The section is an exhaustive one and dwells well on the subject of child pornography. It elaborately describes what constitutes child pornography and is a pioneer law provision in the country in the sense that the time-tested IPC the term "child pornography" does not occur. The reason is well understood in the context of India as India is a religiously dominated society where morality and spirituality are deep-rooted. Going to the extent of indulging in physical exploitation with the underage is though not ruled out but publicizing the same and making it a profession was hitherto unknown to it. While those underage are physically and economically exploited such acts before the public eye and their depiction for the public show have been scant in India. A law on such a subject was not so eagerly required until the internet made it not only common among the masses but the foreign websites aided in its popularization. Section 67-B makes an offense not only the publication or transmission of it but also the creation of, and the browsing and downloading of these objectionable materials though posted by others as an offense. The section provides grave corporal punishment (five years imprisonment on the first conviction and seven years imprisonment in the case of the second conviction). The pecuniary punishment is also heavy, with a maximum of INR 10 lakhs (1 million) in both types of convictions. As under section 292 of the Indian Penal Code 1860 section 67 of the IT Act and also under provision to section 67-B the exceptions are the same which say that the provisions of sections 67 and 67-A shall not extend to any book, pamphlet, paper, writing, drawing, painting, and representation of the figure in electronic form if the publication is justified for the public good or is in the interest of science, literature, art, or learning, or other objects of general concern, or which is preserved for bonafide heritage or religious purpose. These exceptions are inserted in view of the rich cultural heritage of India which is the spirit of India and in this respect, no distinction is made between obscenities in the virtual and the real world.

II. Hate Speech

233. Free speech is the quintessence of democracy and hence it is guaranteed under the Constitution of India. It is an expression that is likely to cause distress or offend others. The oral words which express hatred toward others not only hurts sentiments but often becomes a law and order issue. The term however is not defined in any of the laws in India but there are a good number of laws that criminalize the hateful words so much so that in 2014 the Supreme Court of India urged the Law Commission of India in the case *Pravasi Bhalai Sanghthan v. Union of India and others*[330] stating, "we request the Law Commission to also examine the issues raised herein thoroughly and also to consider, if it deems proper, defining the expression 'hate speech' and make recommendations to the Parliament to strengthen the Election Commission to curb the menace of 'hate speeches', irrespective of

330. AIR 2014 SC 159.

whenever made." The Commission's Report No. 267 titled "Hate speech" came up with a number of suggestions for amendments and additions in the various criminal provisions to curb the menace.

Hate Speech in the internet Era

234. All this continued for some time in the physical world but then the arrival of the internet gave unbounded freedom to the netizens who knew no limit. In the first case of *Delfi v. Estonia,*[331] the applicants approached the court against the order of the Estonian Court, wherein the applicants (owners of the internet news portal) had been made liable for user-generated comments posted on their website. The court insisted on the need to "harmonise these two conflicting realities" emphasizing that freedom of speech cannot be enjoyed at the cost of the rights of others as enunciated in the Convention.[332] However, in the latest case of *Shreya Singhal v. Union of India,*[333] the court adjudicated upon section 66A of the Information Technology Act 2000 and declared it invalid ruling that the section "did not establish any proximate relationship between the restriction and the act." The court differentiated between discussion and advocacy which are the essence of Article 19(1)(a) and said that both of these will call for restriction only if they amount to incitement. Quite recently hate speech online has let loose a spate of violence against immigrants, and racial and lingual minorities.

Legal Regime to Combat Hate Speech in India

235. In India, free speech is a constitutional right but it is laced with certain restrictions, and the concomitant penalties are provided under various laws of the country. The term "hate speech" though remains undefined in the legislation but its effect which goes against societal interest and against individual rights is met with criminal consequences. This has happened since the very start of the legal provisions though there are no specific provisions to deal with online hate speech. The provisions are piecemeal as given below:

- The Indian Penal Code 1860.

  It has the following sections which penalize the harmful effect of hate speech:

  (1) Section 124A penalizes sedition or expression of hatred toward the Government of India or the country.
  (2) Section 153A penalizes hateful speech which promotes enmity among racial, lingual, religious, and regional groups of citizens (five years of sentence and fine).
  (3) Section 153B—Imputation, insult to members of a certain religious, racial, regional, or lingual group in a place of worship (five years of sentence and fine).

331. *Delfi AS v. Estonia*, Application no. 64569/09 (2015).
332. *Ibid.*, at para. 110.
333. AIR 2015 Sc 1523.

(4) Section 298—Uttering of words deliberately to outrage the religious feelings of any group of citizens (one year or fine or both).
(5) Section 505(1) & (2)—Circulating any statement or, rumor causing public mischief, enmity, or hatred (five years and fine).

The Representation of Peoples Act 1951

(1) Section 8—Illegitimate use of freedom of speech (Disqualifying from contesting elections).
(2) Section 123(3A) and section 125—Promotion of enmity among religious, lingual, racial, or regional groups is regarded as a corrupt practice.

The Protection of Civil Rights Act 1955
Section 7, Fostering social disabilities through word of mouth and speech encouraging one to practice "untouchability" (One to six months sentence and fine of INR 100–INR 500).

The Cable Television Network Regulation Act 1995
Section 19—The authorities can prohibit the transmission of any program or channel if it is destined to promote enmity among religious, regional, and lingual groups or if it is against the public interest.

The Cinematograph Act 1952

236. Sections 4, 5B, and 7 empower the Board of Film Certification to restrict or stop exhibiting of any film if through its characters and their dialogues and speech the film promotes enmity against the country and the sovereignty of the State and its integrity or if it inculcates enmity among people and is harmful to public interest.

The Code of Criminal Procedure 1973

(1) Section 95—It empowers the State to forfeit any material, book, or magazine which violates sections 124A, 153A, 153B, 292, 293, 295A, etc., of the Indian Penal Code 1860.
(2) Section 107—Empowers the Executive Magistrate to prevent a person from making such statements which may be a violation of public order and tranquility. The Magistrate can ask him to produce a bond of good behavior.
(3) Section 144—The Magistrate can pass any prohibitory order to stop anyone from making any hateful speech to incite and offense or to disturb the peace.

The Information Technology Act 2000(Amended 2008)
Section 69 (A)—Empowers the Government of India to restrict and block the social media intermediaries if the content they post/host is against the sovereignty and integrity of India, or against the defense and security of the State, harms

friendly relations with foreign states, violates public order, etc. The action presupposes a procedure under which a Committee first glances at the anomalies which then finalizes the directions.

The Twitter Case

237. On July 7, 2022, the Government of India through its Ministry of Electronic and Information Technology blocked the Twitter account. Consequently, Twitter moved the Karnataka High Court against the multiple blocking orders and sought relief. The grounds taken were: that the government has not given any specific reason for blocking and how it harms the public interest; no notice was given for it and there was no compliance with the Rules to block the accounts; and that some of the accounts blocked were of certain political parties as a result of which the freedom of speech suffers. Twitter pleads for setting aside the order. The High Court has issued notice to the Government of India.

III. Defamation Generally

238. "One who steals my purse steals trash, but he that filches from me my good name robs me of that which not enriches him and makes me poor indeed."[334] It is one of the cardinal rights of human beings and its strangeness lies in the fact that it is a crime that can be committed even against the dead. The crime presupposes a man with a reputation, a good name, and a halo of prestige around him. So to say, it exists since mankind and it is one of the oldest crimes in the law books. Anyone who tries to tarnish the name of a person be it by words of mouth or by words written by pen becomes guilty under the law. This crime is as old as the mountains and hence all the traditional laws of the world define it as a punishable offense.

Indian law for the traditional crime of Defamation

239. In India, defamation is regarded both as a crime and as a tort. As a tort, it is still uncodified. The main crux of the crime of defamation is its tendency to cause pain to the victim who is the object of unfavorable sentiments of his fellow-creatures and those inconveniences to which such victim is exposed.[335] The classical definition is a "false statement about a man to his discredit."[336] The Delhi High Court in *Imtiaz Ahmed v. Durdana Zamir* held as follows:[337]

> the test of defamatory nature of a statement is its tendency to incite an adverse opinion or feeling of other persons toward the plaintiff. A statement is to be judged by the standard of the ordinary, right thinking members of the society at the relevant time. The words must have resulted in the plaintiff to be shunned

334. William Shakespeare (1564–1616) through *Iago* in *Othello*. Act 3, Scene 3, 155–61.
335. Note R, of Lord Macaulay Report, p. 175.
336. *Scott v. Sampson*, (1882) LR 8 QBD 491.
337. 2009 SCC OnLine Del 477: (2009) 109 DRJ 357: 2009 INDLAW Del 119.

or evaded or regarded with the feeling of hatred, contempt, ridicule, fear, dislike or disrespect or to convey an imputation to him or disparaging him or his office, profession, calling, trade or business.

In India, under civil law when defamation is taken as a tort it has the following elements:

(1) The statement must be defamatory.
(2) It must refer to the plaintiff.
(3) Must be published or made known to the person other than the one defamed.
(4) It must be false and frivolous.

The aggrieved is compensated in monetary terms. The criminal liability is met with a sentence and fine. The wrong of defamation is of two kinds: first, it can be in the form of libel which is the permanent form like in writing, printing, pictures, or effigies. The other is slander which is in the form of spoken words, or in some transitory form, whether visible or audible such as gestures or inarticulate but significant sounds.[338] The Indian Penal Code 1860 does not recognize any distinction between libel and slander.[339] The offense of defamation is defined under section 499 of the Code and has the following ingredients as also approved by the Calcutta High Court:[340]

- Imputation by words written or spoken, through signs or through visible representation.
- Making or publishing such a statement.
- Making or publishing with the intention or knowledge of harming the reputation of a person.

The Explanations appending to the section further extend the nature of such a statement. It will amount to defamation if:

> *Explanation I*—Even if it amounts to maligning the reputation of a dead person.
> *Explanation II*—Imputation can be of a company or legal person.
> *Explanation III*—An ironical statement that imputes will amount to defamation.
> *Explanation IV*—Nothing is defamatory unless it lowers the victim in the eye of others, or lowers him in his caste or, calling; or renders him in a loathsome state. The Indian Penal Code 1860 has a number of grounds from Exception 1–10 appending to section 499 which can serve as a defense for the accused.

338. Salmond, *Law of Torts* (16th ed.) 140–41.
339. Ratanlal Ranchhoddas & Dhirajlal Keshavlal Thakore, *The Indian Penal Code* (31st ed., Reprint 2007) 2255.
340. *Sunilakhya Chowdhury v. H.M. Jadwet*, 1967 SCCOnLine Cal 83: AIR 1968 Cal 266: 1968 Cri LJ 736.

Defamation in Digital Context

240. Like a good number of other traditional crimes defamation also got a limitless arena to flourish since it is a crime that is committed with the help of words and not with the aid of a sword. Internet, emerging as the strongest medium of communication, gives a ripe field for the offense of defamation to flourish as publication, which is the main ingredient of defamation, and communication which is the heartbeat of the internet, complement each other to pave the way for the commission of this offense online:

> the Internet affords the man on the street with a unique opportunity to have his thoughts often off the cuff, published instantaneously throughout the world. The main legal issue in this section does not, however, concern the primary defamer; nothing is special about the law as it relates to a person defaming over the Internet. What is legally special is that to "publish" on the Internet, one generally must submit the material in an electronic form to a third party; it is thus third party that in effect publishes the material.[341]

The ever-enlarging social media, Facebook, Meta, Twitter, WhatsApp, Instagram, emails, intranets, and mailing lists, have all become game changers in this field where digital defamation can be committed not with the stroke of a pen but merely by pressing a key on the keyboard with a feather touch, so easy and so quick, defamation was never so weird and fast. However the term "defamation" gets new overtones in the form of digital defamation and is given the name "cyberbullying." It is the negative use of technology and contains the following important features:

(1) Men are present in using technology to malign or harm the reputation of others.
(2) *Anonymity*—Like any other online activity the perpetrator who is guilty of cyberbullying cannot be traced easily.
(3) *Unrestricted use*—In the digital environs the sender and the receiver of various text messages and chats are the only actors involved and generally speaking there is no in-between monitoring.
(4) *Isolation*—Cell phone takes the form of a highly personal device; the victim is usually the only person who handles it and when he falls victim to cyberbullying, he suffers and broods alone. Thus, it can "create simultaneous sensations of exposure (the whole world is watching) and alienation (no one understands)."[342]
(5) *Global face*—Cyberbullying once taken place online and once the defamatory material is posted online it becomes known to the entire world; it is "published" and any user can either preserve it or publish it

341. Clive Gringras, *The Laws of the Internet* (Butterworths, 1997) Ch. 3, "Tort" 91.
342. Puar Jasbir, *Ecologies of Sex, Sensation and Slow Death* (Peniscope, Social Text, retrieved Dec. 15, 2011).

(6) *Counter attacks*—Anonymity is the biggest advantage online. This often helps the victim too to retaliate and place a counterattack. Thus, "unfortunately students who retaliate against bullies online can be mistakenly perceived as the source of the problem. This can be especially true under circumstances where the original victimization left no tangible evidence, but the cyber bullying did."[343]

Indian Response

241. The main criminal law of the country, the Penal Code 1860 is often supplemented with the provisions of the Information Technology Act and often direct amendments are made to meet the exigencies of cyber crimes committed by the use of the internet. The addition of section 66-A by the Information Technology (Amendment) Act 2008 met the offense of cyberbullying to some extent but it is now declared unconstitutional by the Supreme Court. The Supreme Court in *Shreya Singhal v. Union of India,*[344] took a sagacious view of section 66-A, Information Technology Act 2000 (amended 2008). The response has been stern and curt and it is regarded as an "open-ended and constitutionally vague" provision. It was a controversial law, a grey area curtailing the freedom of speech and expression online, and is struck down as being violative of Article 19(1)(a) guaranteeing free speech to its citizens. With the quashing down of section 66A of the IT Act, a vacuum is created regarding the prosecution of digital defamation. Earlier it was clubbing of section 501 of the Indian Penal Code 1860 and section 66A of the IT Act to deal with offensive and defamatory material sent via the internet. A need arises therefore to replace the repealed provision with a more specific one that has the wording of section 501 of the IPC but at the same time addresses defamation committed through electronic means.

343. Nancy E Willard *Cyberbullying and Cyberthreats* (2nd ed., Research Press, Jan. 18, 2007).

344. (2015) 5 SCC 1. The judgment came in the wake of a PIL filed by a law student Shreya Singhal after two girls from Palghar were arrested in 2012 for posting a comment on the *Bandh* called in the aftermath of the demise of Shiv Sena leader Bal Thackeray. Seven other petitions including those *by People's Union for Civil Liberties, Mouthshout.com* and the *Internet and Mobile Association of India* were clubbed together and heard by the Supreme Court. The observations came on Mar. 24, 2015.

Chapter 4. Criminal Procedural Aspects (Incl. Data Retention, Interception of Electronic Communications, Network Search, Seizure of Data, Duties of Intermediaries)

§1. General Statement

242. The IT Act has subsumed the substantive law regarding computer crimes and has also at the same time declared that wherever the said Act is deficient in any procedure, the Code of Criminal Procedure 1973 and the Evidence Act 1872 (amended 2000) will be followed.

§2. Data Retention

243. In the digitized world mammoth amount of information can be easily preserved. The question arises then as to of what use will be such preserved information. Basically, for law enforcement agencies the world over, data retention is a favored practice. As it helps in the investigation and collection of evidence. This being a serious objective, data retention is favored but an established standard is required for it. In 2006, the European Union passed the Data Retention Directive which requires European ISP to retain telecom and internet traffic data from customers' communications for at least six months and up to two years. The GoI has established a data retention regime[345] in which retention requirements for service providers are found in the ISP and UASL licenses which are grounded in the Indian Telegraph Act 1885.

ISP License, According to the ISP license[346] eight categories of records are required to be retained for security purposes in which the duration of retention is also often indicated. Thus, according to the ISP License, each ISP must maintain the following:

- Users and services—A log of all users and their services will be made available to the Telecom Authority in real-time (section 34.12).
- Outward Login and Telnet—A log of every outward login or telnet through an ISP's computer shall be made available in real-time to the Telecom Authority (section 34.12).
- Packets—Copies of all packets originating from the Customer Premises Equipment of the ISP must be available in real-time to the Telecom Authority (section 34.12).
- Subscribers—A complete list of subscribers must be made available on the ISP website with password-controlled access available to the authorized Intelligence Agencies at any time (section 34.12).

345. Elonnai Hickock, *Data Retention in India*, Posted Jan. 30, 2013.

346. Government of India—Ministry of Communications and IT; Department of Telecommunication. License Agreement for Provision of Internet Services.

- Internet Leased Line Customers—A complete list of Internet leased line customers and their sub-customers consisting of the name of the customer, IP address allotted, the bandwidth provided, address of installation, date of installing/commissioning, and name of a contact person with his email, etc., must be given. This should be available on a password-protected website (section 34.14). The password and login must be furnished to the various authorities in the Department of Telecommunication (DoT). The information must be accessible to authorized government agencies (section 34.14).
- Diagram records and reasons—A record of the complete network of set up at each of the internet leased line customer premises along with details of connectivity must be posted on the website of the service provider. Details of other communication links, like the PSTN, NLD, ILD, WLL, GSM, and reasons for taking the links by the customer must be recorded by the service provider before activation of the link. These records are also subject to inspection (section 34.18).
- Commercial Records—All such commercial records must be maintained for a year (section 34.23).
- Location—The service provider should be able to provide the geographical location of any subscriber whenever asked for (section 34.28(x)).
- Remote Activities—A complete audit record of the remote access activities must be retained for a period of six months and must be furnished to the Licensor when asked for (section 34.28 (xv).)

244. **UASL License—**[347] For security purposes, customer transactions are required to be preserved and there are about twelve categories of such information. In some cases, the duration of retention has been indicated while in others merely the presentation of records on the orders of the authorities has been directed. Thus, the ISPs are directed to retain the following information:

- Numbers—Calling /Called Party mobile /PSTN numbers are to be furnished when required (section 41.10).
- Interception Records—Time, date, and duration of interception is to be provided (section 41.10).
- Location—Location of target subscribers, Cell ID should be provided for the location of the target subscriber when required (section 41.10).
- All Call records—It includes: (1) Failed call records;(2) Roaming subscriber records (section 41.10).
- Commercial Records—All commercial records regarding communications exchanged on the network must be retained for one year (section 41.17).
- Outgoing Call records—A record of checks made on outgoing calls made by the customer who is making large outgoing calls day and night to various customers must be maintained (section 41.19(ii)).
- Calling Line Identification—A list of subscribers including address details using calling line identification should be preserved in a password-protected website accessible only to government agencies (section 41.19(iv)).

---

347. Government of India—Ministry of Communication & IT—DoT—License Agreement for Unified Access Service after Migration from CMTS, Amended Dec. 3, 2009.

- Location—the Service Providers must also provide the geographical location of the subscriber when asked for (section 41.20 (x)).
- Remote access activities—Full audit trail for six months of the remote access activities pertaining to the network in India must also be retained (section 41.20(xv)).

Data Retention Practice in India

245. On September 10, 2012, the Center for Internet and Society sent an RTI to MTNL and BSNL regarding certain queries. In response to this BSNL replied that it stores at least three types of information including: IP session information—connection start/end time, bytes in and out (three years offline), and Bill copies for post-paid and recharge/top-up billing details for pre-paid for six months. MTNL responded that it retains five types of information including :text message details for one year, Call detail records for one year, Bill copies for post-paid for one year, recharge details for pre-paid for three months, and the location of the mobile number if it has used the MTNL/GSM/3GCDMA network for one year.

Interception of Electronic communications

246. The IT (Amendment) Act 2008 empowers the Central or State governments to authorize its officers to order interception or monitoring of any information generated, transmitted, received, or stored in any computer resource. The grounds of interception are (1) in the interest of sovereignty; (2) integrity of India; (3) defense of India; (4) security of the State; (5) friendly relations with foreign States; (6) public order; (7) prevention of incitement to the commission of any offense; (8) for investigation of any offense. The procedure of interception shall be prescribed by the government. The subscriber or intermediary or any other person is under an obligation not only to facilitate access to the computer resource but also to intercept or monitor or decrypt the intended information. The intermediary who fails in it shall be punished with imprisonment of up to seven years and shall also be liable to a fine (section 69). The government can on the above grounds order the blocking of public access to any information which is being transmitted. The intermediary who fails in it shall be punished with imprisonment of up to seven years and shall also be liable to a fine (section 69A).

Both the Indian Telegraph Act 1885 (ITA) and the Telegraph Act (TA) also provide for interception. The TA creates two levels of circumstances that must be met before the interception of communications can take place. It is mainly for the sake of public emergency, or safety, or for the sovereignty or integrity of India for preventing incitement of an offense. The ITA allows interception for the investigation of an offense also. The ITA allows for the interception, monitoring, and decryption of information while TA allows only for the interception of communications. The ITA makes it obligatory for the intermediaries for disclosing decryption keys if so asked by the nodal officer. The intermediary must also destroy records pertaining to the interception within two months of discontinuance unless it is required further for some investigation, criminal complaint, or legal proceedings. If an interception is required beyond the jurisdiction of a State Government then the secretary in charge of the Home Department will request permission from the secretary of the Ministry of Home Affairs.

§3. NETWORK SEARCH AND SEIZURE OF DATA

247. The IT Act 2000 envisages special procedures for the investigation of computer-related crimes. It empowers the officer of the rank of Inspector to handle the investigation in the amended section 78 which states:

> Section 78—Power to investigate offenses (amended 2008)—Notwithstanding anything contained in the Criminal Procedure Code 1973 (2 of 1974), a police officer not below the rank of Inspector shall investigate any offense under this Act.

The words "Deputy Superintendent of Police" has been replaced by the term "Inspector" which shows that the investigation of computer-related crimes will be as easy and expedited as any other ordinary crime so that the lack of willpower to prosecute, commonly found in the people, is reduced to some extent. The section is merely a declaratory one that reposes senior officials from the responsibility of investigating such computer-related crimes. There is a felt need to have a technology expert and a computer-savvy person to handle the job of investigation and an otherwise competent officer but with amateur skills in the field of computer technology could inadvertently but irretrievably damage the data.[348] Search and seizure, being an inseparable part of the investigation are treated separately in the IT Act 2000. In traditional crimes too when the suspects do not easily cooperate in the investigation then coercive methods are adopted. The Code of Criminal Procedure 1973 initially sends summon to the person concerned to produce the required evidence. If the summons does not work then the court can issue orders to the police for the search and seizure of documents and things.[349] Computer-related crimes though committed in the intangible world, have some physical appliances, like hard disks, CPU, monitor, magnetic tapes, and software which could be quite valuable in reaching an investigative conclusion. Thus the IT Act 2000 in Chapter XIII, section 80 envisages certain rules regarding the search and seizure of such incriminating objects in which the power of Police officers and other officers to enter, search, etc., (amended)[350] are given. The section authorizes a police officer, not below the rank of an Inspector whether authorized by the Government of India or by any of the State Government to enter, search, and arrest any person without a warrant who is reasonably suspected of having committed an offense under the Act. The term "public place" includes any public conveyance, hotel, shop, or any other place where the

348. SC Agarwal, *Cybercrime: Prevention & Investigation*, Indian Police Journal 85 (April–June 2002).
349. Prof. KN Chandrasekhran Pillai & RV Kelkar, RV Kelkar's *Criminal Procedure* (3rd ed. Eastern Book Co. 1993), 140.
350. The words "Deputy Superintendent of Police" are replaced by the word "Inspector" by the IT (Amended) Act 2008.

general public has free access. The person so arrested shall then be presented before a Magistrate having jurisdiction or before the Officer-in-Charge of a police station. The section also allows the application of the relevant provisions of the Code of Criminal Procedure 1973 to entry, search, or arrest made under this section (section 80 IT Amended Act 2008). The mention of the word "public place" in the section presumably excludes a private home from it. The section is conspicuously silent on the point of domestic homes understandably for the reason that in the year 2000 computer systems were not so easily used or available in the homely surroundings. India is on the path of information superpower and today even a humble domesticity can boast of having a computer set in the house. In such cases, the search and seizure operation may suffer a setback if one goes by the true wording of the section. In such situations, the traditional provisions contained in section 47 and section 100 of the Criminal Procedure Code 1973 will need to be applied. The said section 100 has three important aspects: first, it makes it obligatory for the occupant of a closed place to afford facilities to the investigative authorities; second, the authorities should be armed with proper authority to conduct the search; and third, procedures have been designated "to obtain as reliable evidence as possible of the search and to exclude the possibility of any concoction, or malpractice of any kind."[351] Thus the traditional law too insists upon the originality of the material collected.

The most crucial question in computer-related crime investigations is the reliability of digital evidence. This is the work less of a law expert and more of a technology expert. The 2008 Amendments in the IT Act have given due importance to this fact and thus section 45-A has been inserted in the Indian Evidence Act 1872 (1 of 1872) whereby the opinion of the Electronic Evidence Expert (EEE) has been made admissible by the court. Handling information and data and keeping it in its original form until it reaches the court needs extra care and precautions. There is the danger of the evidence being manipulated at the hands of a dishonest but technologically expert person. The trustworthiness of the evidence depends much on the way it is collected. For this, computer forensics is being recognized as a new branch of forensic science and which "is the scientific collection, examination, analysis and presentation of information held on or retrieved from storage media in such a way that it can be used as potential legal evidence."[352]

Duties of Intermediaries

248. The internet is a chain of players human and non-human. "Every Internet transaction requires the participation of multiple intermediaries, and may well involve more than two actors."[353] They are not only indispensable for the working of the net but they are also often the contributors not only in the good of the internet but in "principal actors"[354] who have something to contribute toward the commission of a crime. The postal carriers and telephone network are the predecessors

351. *Emperor v. Balai Ghosh*, AIR 1930 Cal 141.
352. *Morgans v. Director of Public Prosecutions* (2001) 1 AC315.
353. Chris Reed, Chapter 2: *From Each According to His Ability: Actors and Activities in the Internet World* in *Internet Law: Text and Materials* (Cambridge University Press, 2004) 24.
354. *Ibid.*, 24.

of these online intermediaries though automated transmission marks the dividing line between the two. Online intermediaries are unconscious actors in internet transaction and they have no pre-existing legal relationship with other actors.[355] With the proliferation of technological innovations, like AI, Big Data, IoT and, the like there is a greater and more quality use of the internet in recent times. This has given the ISPs even greater opportunity to come in contact with the personal data of users. Earlier at the onset of the internet the job of the ISPs was of limited nature, e.g., to merely transfer data over the entire spectrum of the net like through emails, websites, etc., but then the world has seen a boom of social networking platforms. These are the endless number of platforms and social networking sites, like Facebook, WhatsApp, YouTube, emails, Amazon, eBay, and many others. This growing importance of the intermediaries calls for their grimmer responsibility and thus the legal activities are on to pinpoint their accountability and to make them more responsible.

Intermediaries under the Information Technology Act 2000(amended 2008)

249. The IT Act 2000 is the sole law in India that explicitly mentions the law regarding the liability of the ISPs. The law has undergone a massive change whereas the contours of the liability of the service providers have expanded; their obligations under the law are more defined and their exemptions circumscribed and conditional. The IT (Amendment) Act 2008 (10 of 2009), also known as the Amendment Act has inserted a catena of new sections connected with the liability of the intermediaries and their answerability before the law. Chapter XII comprising section 79 has been replaced and the term "intermediaries" is redefined. Apart from the IT Act 2000, rules made by the Central Government and the guidelines issued by the Telecom Department also circumscribe such liability within the legal framework when at the time of issuing the license to provide service, the ISPs are not only bound to follow the guidelines but they are also to abide by the security conditions of the licensor, i.e., the Government of India. All these provisions define the limits of liability of the ISPs. An intermediary is defined under the Amendment Act under section 2(*w*) as follows:

> (*w*) "intermediary," with respect to any particular electronic records, means any person who on behalf of another person receives, stores or transmits that record or provides any service with respect to that record and includes telecom service providers, network service providers, Internet service providers, web-hosting service providers, search engines, online payment sites, online-auction sites, online-market places, and cyber cafes.

355. Chris Reed, Chapter 2: *From Each According to His Ability: Actors and Activities in the Internet World* in *Internet Law: Text and Materials* (Cambridge University Press, 2004; Universal Law Publishing, First Indian Reprint, 2005) 89.

Duties of Intermediaries: New Law

250. As the internet has entered every nook and corner of human life and as the role of intermediaries in the internet arena grows day by day, thus with this proliferation more and more grievances are expected hence the Government of India recently came up with a number of rules to circumscribe the duties of the intermediaries. The Information Technology (Intermediary Guidelines and Digital Media Ethics Code) Rules, 2021[356] supersede the Information Technology (Intermediaries Guidelines) Rules, 2011. With the involvement of social media networks and their growing popularity, the Rules proceed to define digital intermediaries in the following manner:

- Significant Social Media Intermediaries (SSMI)—means a social media intermediary having such a number of registered users (50 lakhs or more equivalent to 5 million or more) in India above such threshold as notified by the central government section 2(1)(v).
- Social Media Intermediaries (SMI) means an intermediary which primarily enables online interaction between two or more users and allows creating, uploading, sharing, dissemination, modification, or access to information using these services section 2(1)(w).

251. Thus the Rules 2021 provide for a good number of obligations and certain code of ethics and makes it incumbent upon the SSMI and SMI to follow them with due diligence (Part II of the Rules). A failure to observe these duties would entail liability under the relevant provisions of the Indian Penal Code 1860 (Rule 7).

Duties of the Intermediaries under the Rules:

252. The Rules 2021 require both the significant social media intermediaries and the social media intermediaries to observe the following duties with due diligence:

- Publication of details of the code of conduct for the users on its website. This includes the publication of rules and regulations for posting, user agreement, and privacy policy (Rule 3 (a) & (b)).
- The user should be informed about the code of conduct once a year with the declaration that the intermediary reserves the right to terminate the user's access or for removing any objectionable material from the platform (Rule 3 (c)).
- Intermediaries must not accommodate any unlawful material on their platform and if ordered by the government must remove such material as mentioned in Rule 3(i)-(x).
- When notified by the court or by the government under section (3)(b) of section 79 of the IT Act 2000 the intermediary must diligently and promptly remove the objectionable material and disable defaulting user's access to the platform.

---

356. The Gazette of India—Extraordinary—Part II—s. 3—Sub-s. (i)—No. 98 New Delhi, Thursday, Feb. 25, 2021/PHALGUNA 6, 1942.

- Preserving information: It is the duty of every intermediary to preserve the information which has been removed and also the registration of such a defaulting user for about 180 days. (Rule 3(g) & (h)).
- The intermediary must secure its computer resource following the reasonable security practices as provided in Information Technology (Reasonable Security Practices and Procedures and Sensitive Personal Information) Rules, 2011.
- Duty to provide information—The intermediary shall provide to the government such information as ordered by the government, within seventy-two hours of receipt of such order either from the government or from any authorized agency, the order being in written form (Rule 3, (j)).
- The intermediary shall not deploy, alter, or modify the technical configuration of the computer resource within its control (Rule 3, (k)).
- The intermediary has the duty to report cybersecurity incidents and share related information with the Indian Computer Emergency Response Team in accordance with the policies and procedures as mentioned in the Information Technology (The Indian Computer Emergency Response Team and Manner of Performing Functions and Duties) Rules, 2013 (Rule 3, (l)).
- The intermediary has the duty to publicize the mechanism regarding registering grievances and also the name of the Grievance Officer. The Grievance Officer is to acknowledge any complaint received by him and dispose it of within fifteen days (Rule 3, (2)).
- The intermediary within twenty-four hours of receipt of the complaint must remove or disable access to content that depicts the private area of an individual, shows him in nudity or involved in any sexual conduct, or contains morphed images.(Rule 3, (2)(b)).

Additional Duties of Significant Social Media Intermediary

253. Rule 4 provides for "Additional due diligence to be observed by significant social media intermediaries." Ministry concerned can extend the additional due diligence to intermediaries who do not fall under the category of significant social media intermediaries (Rule 6). They have the duty to appoint the following officers:

- Chief Compliance Officer: Chief Compliance Officer means key managerial personnel or another senior employee of SSMI who is residing in India. His duty will be to check compliance with such Rules and the IT Act.
- Nodal Contact Person: Nodal Contact Person will be an employee of an SSMI who resides in India. He should cooperate with enforcement agencies 24x7.
- Resident Grievance Officer: He is an employee of the SSMI who is resident in India. He is made responsible for performing functions relating to sub-rule (2) of Rule 3, i.e., with regard to the grievance redressal mechanism (Rule 4 (a)-(d)).
- The intermediary providing messaging services must disclose and provide the identity of the originator of the message when required to do so by the order of a court or by the order of a Competent Authority under section 69 as per the Information Technology (Procedure and Safeguards for interception, monitoring, and decryption of information) Rules, 2009. When providing such identification the

said intermediary must not disclose the contents of an electronic message or any other information related to him. In case the first originator is in foreign land then the person who first discloses the information must be regarded as the first originator (Rule 4(2)).

- An intermediary under Rule 4 is under obligation to deploy such tools or other mechanisms to proactively identify information regarding, rape, child sexual abuse, or any other content which has been previously removed by it and must notify any user about it who is attempting to access such content (Rule 4(4)). In this regard, care is to be taken by such intermediaries regarding the rights of free speech and privacy of users.
- Such an intermediary must have and display the physical address of a contact in India (Rule 4 (5)).
- It must deploy a proper mechanism to register a complaint and also provide a tracking facility to the complainant (Rule 4 (6)).
- The significant social media intermediary shall enable users who register for their services from India, or use their services in India, to voluntarily verify their accounts by using any appropriate mechanism (Rule 4(7)).
- When an intermediary on its own accord moves or disables access to a particular content then it must notify the user who has uploaded, created, and disseminated such information. Also, the Resident Grievance Officer must provide such a user with an appropriate platform to entertain any dispute arising out of it. Government can call for any additional information when it deems it proper (Rule 4 (8)).

Duty regarding Additional Due Diligence

254. As regards the publishers of news and current affairs content the intermediary must inform them that in addition to the usual terms of agreement with the users, the publishers shall furnish details of their accounts with the intermediary before the government as required under Rule 18. The intermediary shall then provide such a publisher with a demonstrable and visible mark of verification as being publishers. (Rule 5).

Code of Ethics for Digital Media (Rules 2021)

255. The Digital Media in the country like any other part of the world has been expanded and there is a trove of news and current affairs and online curated content. The Rules 2021 also envisage certain Code of Ethics for such publishers. It will apply to the following categories of persons or entities:

(1) Publishers of news and current affairs content.
(2) Publishers of online curated content (Rule 8).
(3) Such rules will apply to the publishers who operate in India or conduct the systematic business activity of making their content available in India. The Code of Ethics falls under the following categories:

> Level I—Self-regulation by the publishers; This entails a grievance redressal mechanism and a Grievance Officer to be appointed by the publisher in India to address any grievance received with respect to its content.
> Level II—Self-regulation by the self-regulating bodies of the publishers; this includes a self-regulating independent body of publishers the head of which will be the retired Judge of the Supreme Court or High court and six more members comprising eminent persons from the field of child rights, broadcasting, entertainment, media, etc. Such a body will note adherence by the publishers of the Code of Ethics, etc.
> Level III—This entails an Oversight Mechanism by the Central Government. The Ministry shall coordinate and facilitate the adherence to the Code of Ethics by publishers and self-regulating bodies and develop an Oversight Mechanism. It will establish a Departmental Committee for addressing grievances.

Thus the government is getting more sensitive and strict day by day to control the growing power of electronic media and a spate of notifications and advisories have become a routine.

Selected Bibliography

Government Publications

The Gazette of India. Extraordinary. Part II—section 1. No. 56 NEW DELHI, FRIDAY, AUGUST 9, 2019/SHRAVANA 18, 1941 (SAKA).

NeSDA 21 Report-Ministry of Personnel, Public Grievances and Pensions, Press Information Bureau-Delhi, June 2022.

Lok Sabha, BULLETIN Part II-(General Information Relating to Parliamentary and other matters). Nos. 3293–3304. Tuesday November 2021.

Ministry of Consumer Affairs, Food & Public Distribution. Dated December 2021. Press Information Bureau. Delhi.

Telecom Regulatory Authority of India—Notification No. 301-20/2020-F&EA. New Delhi, Dated September 2020.

National Government Services Portalhttps://services.india.gov.in/service/ministry_services?ln=en&cmd_id=1859.

The Gazette of India—Extraordinary, PART II—section 3—Sub-section (i), No. 98] New Delhi, Thursday, February 25, 2021/Phalguna 6, 1942.

RBI Bulletin—April 11, 2019. https://m.rbi.org.in/scripts/BS_ViewBulletin.aspx?Id=18172Annual Report 2018–2019. Department of Commerce. Ministry of Commerce-Government of India.

Annual Report 2017–2018. Ministry of Electronics and Information Technology (MeitY)—Government of India.

Reserve Bank of India, RBI releases the financial stability report, July 2020, July 24, 2020.

Steps Taken to Deal with Cyber Crime and Cyber Security, Press Information Bureau-Government of India Ministry of Home Affairs, July 17, 2019. Press Information Bureau. Delhi.

India 2014-Publications Division, Ministry of Information and Broadcasting, Government of India. New Delhi.

National Telecom Policy 2012-Ministry of Telecommunications, Government of India.

The information Technology (Electronic Service Delivery) Rules 2011-Notification GSR-316 (E)-(Part II section 3(i)) The Gazette of India Extraordinary-Dated April 11, 2011.

The Information Technology (Amendment) Act 2008-(Part II section I). The Gazette of India Extraordinary-Dated February 5, 2009.

Selected Bibliography

The Information Technology (Procedures and Safeguards for Interception, Monitoring and Decryption of Information Rules 2009. Notification G.S.R. 780-(E)-Dated October 27, 2009. Clarification on the Information Technology (Intermediary guidelines) Rules 2011. Department of Electronics and Information Technology—Ministry of Communications and Information Technology, Dated March 18, 2013.

Clarification on IT (reasonable Security Practices and Procedures and Sensitive Personal data or information) Rules 2011. Press Information Bureau—Government of India-Ministry of Communications and IT—New Delhi dated August 24, 2011.

Books, Journals and Papers

Chaudhary RN & Singh SP, *Law Relating to Telecommunications and Broadcasting*, 4th ed. Reprint 2013-Orient Publishing Company, New Delhi-Allahabad.

Chris R, *Computer Law* (Cambridge University Press, 2003).

Fatima T, *Cybercrimes*, 3rd ed. (Eastern Book Company-Lucknow, 202).

Kamath N, *Law Relating to Computers Internet & E-Commerce*, 2nd ed. (Universal Law Publishing Company Pvt. Ltd, Delhi, 2005).

Rachhoya RN, *International Technology Law& Cybercrime* (Kirti Publications, Jaipur, 2003).

Raghavan V, *Communications Law in India*, 1st ed. (Lexis Nexis Butterworths, 2007).

Rashid MA, *Law Relating to Electronic Transfer of Money.* 1st ed. (Lexis Nexis. Butterworths Wadhwa Nagpur, 2010).

Singh A, *Company Law* (Eastern Book Company 2019).

Singh A, *Competition Law*, 1st ed. (Eastern Book Company 2012).

Singh A, *Law of Contract* (Eastern Book Company 2021).

Verma & Mittal eds., *Legal Dimensions of Cyberspace* (Indian Law Institute-New Delhi, 2004).

Papers

Annual Report of the United Nations High Commissioner for Human Rights. 47th. Session. June 21–July 9, 2021. Agenda Item 2. A/HRC/47/54.

European Commission, Press release, Dated January 26, 2022.

Press Release, European Commission https://ec.europa.eu/commission/presscorner/detail/en/IP_22_5374 Dated September 15, 2022. Document 52017DC0476-EUR, Access to European Union Law.

India Brand Equity Foundation IBEF—November 2021.

Indian Brand Equity Foundation—March 2022.

Banking Sector in India—December 2019. Indian Brand Equity Foundation.

TRAI Report of July 19, 2022.

Rahul Bajaj, Towards a Framework for Scrutinizing Combinations in the Digital Market: A Roadmap for Reform. VIDHI—Centre for Legal Policy. January 2022.

Anand Kumar Bajaj, MD, CEO. Nachiket Kelkar: Digital India Has Nudged Indians into Adopting New Technology, August 21, 2022.

E-Health Laws and Regulations—Samisti Legal, *Advocates & Legal Advisers*, April 11, 2020.

Manisha Wadhwa, *Electronic Health Records in India: ITC India Working Paper* March 25, 2020.

Mustafa Rajkotwala, *E-voting to Become Reality Soon? Here's What Election Commission Should Do Before Going for Blockchain Polls*, October 9, 2021.

Ramya G, Kumarean Perumal: Online Voting system Using Cloud—International Conference on Emerging Trends in Information Technology and Engineering. Conference Paper, February 2020.

Banking Industry Report—June 2022.

Internet Stats & Facts (2020). https://hostingfacts.com/internet-facts-stats.

Google's Royal Hansen—VP Engineering for Privacy, Safety and Security. August 2022.

https://eurlex.europa.eu/legalcontent/EN/TXT/?qid=1505297631636&uri=COM:2017:476:FIN.

Cyber security in Indian banking Industry: Part I. Deloitte—November 2020.

Press Trust of India,—Rise in cyber attacks from China, Over 40,000 Cases in 5 Days: Official—NDTV, June 23, 2020.

Cyber attacks on Indian healthcare Industry second highest in the World: CloudSEK.PTI. September 20, 2022.

Deloitte, News Release. Data Security Council of India Report 2022.

Abhinandan Mishra; India's cyber offensive capabilities still not top-notch—August 2022. https://www.sundayguardianlive.com/news/indias-cyber-offensive-capabilities-still-not-top-notch.

The Budapest Convention on Cybercrime: Benefits and Impact in Practice—Strasbourg, July 13, 2020. https://rm.coe.int/t-cy-2020-16-bc-benefits-rep-provisional/16809ef6ac.

Bhattacharyya Manas, *Telecom Sector in India: Vision 2020,* Background Paper submitted to the Committee on India: Vision 2020.

First Analysis of the Personal Data Protection Law in India—Final Report—Prepared by CRID-University of Namur, Report delivered in the framework of contract JLS/C4/2005/15 between CRID and the Director General Justice, Freedom and Security.

Gopalakrishnan Veena, *Government Contracts*—Legal Service India.com.

Gupta Apar, Protection of Databases in India: Copyright Termination sui Generis Conception, Journal of Intellectual Property Rights—Vol. 12, July 2007, pp. 422–427.

Gupta Atul, Integrated Circuits and Intellectual Property Rights in India, Journal of intellectual Property Rights—Vol. 10, November 2005, pp. 474–479.

Maggon Harsh, *Legal Protection of Databases: An India Perspective*—Journal of Intellectual Property Rights—Vol. II, March 2006 pp. 140–144.

Nollen Stanley, *Intellectual Property in the Indian software Industry: Past Role and Future* (June 2004) International Intellectual Property Institute-George Washington University, McDonough School of Business, Washington DC. U.S.A.

Rai Gulshan, *Our IT Rules are not Draconian*-Business Standard, July 27, 2014.

Securus-Strategic Trade Solutions, Copyright Securus Strategic Trade Solutions, LLC.

Selected Bibliography

Swarup Mridushi, *Protection of Databases-An Analysis of the International Scenario and the Indian Position*, The Road Ahead-Indian Journal of Computer Science and Technology Vol. 2 Issue 3 September 2011.

Telecommunications Regulations handbook.

Telecommunications Regulations-Competition-ICT Access in the Asia Pacific Region, Prepared by Hon David Butcher, ESCAP, United Nations-February 2010.

Vaz Natasha, Privacy and Telecommunication, April 2012.

Verma SK-*IP Protection of Software and Software Contracts in India: A Legal Quagmire!*, Journal of Intellectual Property Rights Vol. 17, July 2012. pp. 284–295.

Index

The numbers refer to paragraph numbers